T3-BPG-104

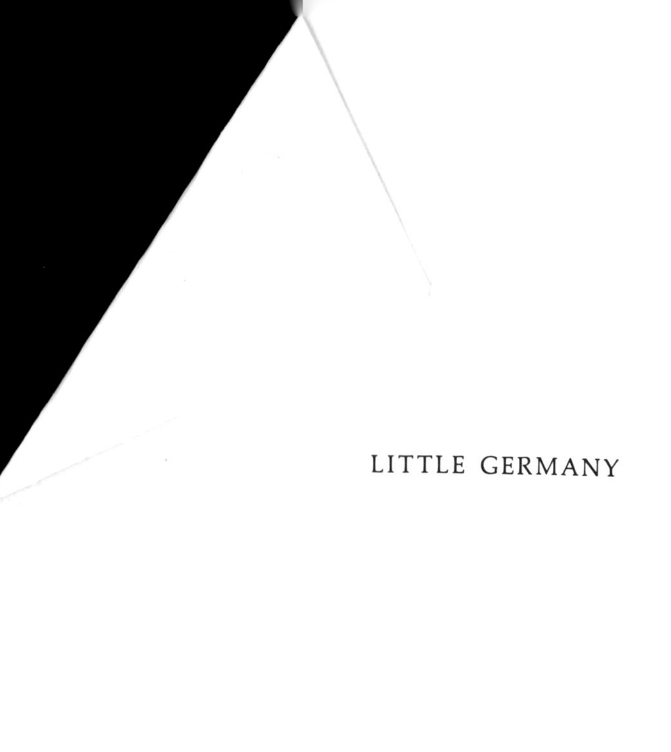

LITTLE GERMANY

LITTLE GERMANY

Ethnicity, Religion, and Class in New York City, 1845–80

STANLEY NADEL

UNIVERSITY OF ILLINOIS PRESS
Urbana and Chicago

Manufactured in the United States of America
C 5 4 3 2 1

This book is printed on acid-free paper.

Library of Congress Cataloging-in-Publication Data

Nadel, Stanley.
[Kleindeutschland. English]
Little Germany: ethnicity, religion, and class in New York City, 1845–80 / Stanley Nadel.
p. cm.
Translation of: Kleindeutschland.
Includes bibliographical references.
ISBN 0-252-01677-7 (alk. paper).
1. German Americans—New York (N.Y.)—History—19th century. 2. German Americans—New York (N.Y.)—Social conditions. 3. German Americans—New York (N.Y.)—Ethnicity. 4. German Americans—New York (N.Y.)—Religion. 5. New York (N.Y.)—Social conditions. 6. New York (N.Y.)—Ethnic relations. I. Title.
F128.9.G3N3313 1990
974.7'100431—dc20 89-20684
CIP

Contents

Acknowledgments

The debts I incurred in the process of writing this book are many. As any historian knows, our research is always dependent on archival and library staff members. So my first thanks go to the kind and helpful people who work at Columbia University's Butler Library; at the New York Public Library's Research Libraries, Annex, and Ottendorfer Branch; at the New York County Records Office; and at the New York Municipal Archives. Financial assistance to begin the process of turning a doctoral dissertation into this book came from the National Endowment for the Humanities in the form of an NEH Summer Stipend.

Research for this book began as a seminar paper for James P. Shenton and grew into a dissertation under his guidance and encouragement. It was Herbert Gutman who led me to begin the study in the 1840s rather the 1880s. I owe a special debt to Kenneth Jackson, who was the first to suggest that the dissertation might actually become a book, and who provided a critique which let me know how much still had to be done before that would come to pass. Since then, many others have read and commented on various versions of the manuscript as it developed from dissertation to book. Special thanks are due to David Gerber, Reinhard Doerries, Sean Wilentz, Bruce Levine, Kathleen Conzen, Bill Pencak, Walter Weitzmann, and Joan Vincent, and to a series of anonymous readers for the University of Illinois Press. Special thanks are also due to my former colleagues at the University of Illinois, particularly to Jim Barrett, Niels Jacobsen, and the late Tom Krueger. All of these colleagues made contributions toward whatever virtues this book possesses and helped me to avoid many errors. Even more errors in two languages were identified and corrected by my editor, Patricia Hollahan. Without her work, this would have been a much poorer book, and I thank her. Any errors and defects which I have still not corrected remain my responsibility.

A section of Chapter 7 was the basis for my article, "From the Barricades of Paris to the Sidewalks of New York: German Artisans and the European Roots of American Labor Radicalism." My thanks to Dan Leab and *Labor History* for permission to reprint that material here.

Finally, I owe some debts that can never be repaid. One to my parents for their continued support and encouragement over the years. Another to my children, Ché and Cory, for their faith and encouragement as their father persisted in his peculiar choice of a career, one which introduced considerable instability and uncertainty into their lives. To all of these and more, my thanks.

Introduction

Kleindeutschland, the German neighborhood on Manhattan's lower east side, was the first of the giant urban foreign-language settlements that came to typify American cities by the end of the nineteenth century. In a sense it was the prototypical immigrant community. For the first time in American history tens and hundreds of thousands of foreigners, people to whom the English language and American ways were virtually unknown, were congregated together as a gigantic alien enclave in the midst of the newly emerged American nation. Isolated by language and the increasing residential segregation of the developing metropolis, New York's Germans were the first group to face the problems of adaptation and innovation that have become characteristic shapers of the American immigrant experience ever since their time.

German New York was more than just a simple immigrant community. At a time when German-speaking peoples were living in many different states in Europe and the Americas, German New York was the third capital of the German-speaking world. Only Vienna and Berlin had larger German populations than New York City between 1855 and 1880.[1] When the German Empire was created in 1871, the single New York City neighborhood of Kleindeutschland, with about half the city's Germans, would have been the empire's fifth-largest city.[2] In American terms, the New York German metropolis would have been the fourth-largest city in the United States anytime between 1860 and 1880 (or, if Brooklyn had been incorporated into New York City in 1857 instead of 1897, the third largest after New York and Philadelphia). Kleindeutschland alone, in 1875, was larger than the combined populations (circa 1870) of Detroit and Milwaukee, or about equal to the population of Buffalo in 1880.[3]

German New York's influence extended far beyond the lower wards of Manhattan. Many of the formative organizations and personalities of the American labor movement were located in, or had their roots in, German New York. The Cigar Makers' International Union was one of the pioneers in developing the institutional techniques known collectively as American business unionism, and it did so under the leadership of a German immigrant to New York named Adolf Strasser at a time when the union's membership was mostly composed of Strasser's fellow German New Yorkers. Strasser's protégé, the founding president of the American Federation of Labor, was a Kleindeutschland-reared immigrant cigar maker named Samuel Gompers. Gompers was a key figure in building the federation and he helped to shape it in the mold of a business unionism that he himself saw as deriving directly from his experiences in German New York.[4] The early American Federation of Labor was bilingual (English and German were both recognized as official languages), and Gompers' leading critics in the late nineteenth-century AF of L were the German-American socialists. Like Gompers and so many of his friends, they too were products of the German experience in New York—for modern American socialism also had its roots in Kleindeutschland. German New York was the home of the First International in America and it was the first stronghold of socialism in American history (a history in which most strongholds of socialism and communism would be found in immigrant communities).[5]

As German New York was the first of the great foreign-language enclaves in America, it should come as no surprise to find that at least some of the later examples of the genre should have been directly influenced by German New York's model of adaptation and community formation. The problem is to distinguish the borrowing of ideas and institutional models from independent responses to similar conditions that took similar forms. The clearest case of borrowing is presented by the satellite Jewish community on Kleindeutschland's border that developed into the famous Jewish Lower East Side. As Ronald Sanders noted in his study of the Jewish community, "to a certain extent, this German community life provided a paradigm for the Jewish one that was to follow it."[6] Bohemian (Czech) immigrants also had an enclave on the fringes of Kleindeutschland, and it seems that the Bohemian immigrant culture that they created (and that spread to Bohemian settlements all across America) was, if anything, even more closely modeled on the German paradigm.[7]

This book is a study of the entire German-American community of New York City and its environs, from 1845 to 1880, including settlements in Williamsburg and Brooklyn across the East River, in Hoboken and other shore towns across the Hudson River, and in the northern suburbs from Yorkville and Harlem in Manhattan to the villages of Morrisania and Kingsbridge in Westchester County (until they became incorporated as New York City's Twenty-third Ward in 1874). The sense in which they formed a single community was necessarily somewhat limited; but New York's German-Americans were integrated by numerous overlapping affiliations and associations into a common ethnic metropolis. Within this metropolis, there were many smaller and more cohesive geographic and social German-American communities. These varied in size from a small cluster of houses in the village of Bloomingdale (now the city's Upper West Side) to the gigantic high-density conglomeration on Manhattan's East Side known as Kleindeutschland—which served as a focus for German-American activities throughout the greater New York area.

The concept of community, especially in a metropolitan context, is subject to numerous and inconsistent formulations. Where the concept is restricted to those whose interactions fit the classical sociological conception of *Gemeinschaft,* it may only apply to close family members in complex societies. On the other hand, Leo Schnore's "localized population which is interdependent on a daily basis, and which carries on a highly generalized series of activities in and through a set of institutions which provide on a day-to-day basis the full range of goods and services necessary for its continuity as a social and economic entity" can encompass all of a large metropolitan population, but loses all of the subjective components of the concept of community.[8] I would thus modify Schnore's definition to include the affective ties of community that are extended beyond simple primary groups on the basis of what are perceived to be "common" characteristics (such as common residence, common religion, common language, and common culture—all of which are liable to extremely subjective definitions as to what constitutes "common"). The outer limits of community in a subjective sense, the boundaries separating "us" from "them," can therefore vary from the family level to that of the ethnic group or nationality. Depending on the individual (or the situational context), the German-American resident of mid-nineteenth-century New York might have viewed him- or herself as a German or an American (nation), a Bavarian or a Mecklenburger (German region), a Berliner or a Frankfurter (German locality), a German-American (new ethnic group), a New Yorker (American locality), a Kleindeutschlander (neighborhood), or some combination of these. Community identity existed within these shifting boundaries and had varying levels of existence, with Kleindeutschland and German New York forming communities at different levels.

The more narrowly drawn community of Kleindeutschland was itself composed of many smaller geographic and social subcommunities. They were clustered together for mutual support and sometimes shared some (or many) of the same institutions and even some members, but they maintained a more or less distinct existence within the larger community. In New York City, the basic sociographic unit was the "block," a one-block-long stretch of roadway along with its associated buildings.[9] The New York neighborhood has typically been a series of contiguous communities of this sort that shared some generally recognized characteristics. In the case of Manhattan's lower east side, after the 1840s the overall defining characteristic was the Germanic origin of most of the area's residents. Thus it was known to outsiders as "Dutchtown" and to its residents as "Kleindeutschland."

"Kleindeutschland" is sometimes used in this study to stand for the entire German-American metropolis, particularly as a source of detailed demographic and social statistics. This is not to say that it was a statistically representative sample of the whole, but rather that its sheer size (it contained about half of New York's German-born population from 1845 to 1880)[10] led Kleindeutschland to overshadow and dominate the other German-American communities of the metropolis.[11] The heterogeneity of its subsumed subcommunities also helped to ensure that no element of the whole was entirely absent from Kleindeutschland. The text indicates where other German-American communities of the New York area differed substantially from Kleindeutschland (as in religious commitment or occupational distribution).

Nonresidential social parameters of community also divided the German-Americans of Kleindeutschland into subcommunities. German-American Catholics, Protestants, Freethinkers, and Jews were frequently divided into socially distinct communities even when they were integrated residentially. These and other such cleavages (along with less-than-total residential segregation from non-Germans) have led some analysts to conclude that there was no community at all among urban German-Americans.[12] This confuses complexity with chaos, however. Many of these divisions operated in a German-American context that served to reinforce the overall sense of German-Americanness or Germanness. The hostility between the German-American Freethinkers and Catholics, for example, had its roots in Germany and reinforced the German identity of both groups in a bond of mutual hatred that fostered a sort of segmentary solidarity.[13] One of the goals of this book is to begin to define some of these subcommunities and to elucidate the nature of their relationships (it will, however, be necessary to oversimplify some of the complexities of a situation where actual participant-observation would be required to discover subtle relationships that are now lost to the historian).[14]

The problem of community boundaries is intimately related to that of ethnic boundaries. By the 1850s, the German press of New York had begun to refer to "German-Americans" as well as to "Germans in America"—a new ethnic identity thus appears to have come into being.[15] This at a time when German ethnicity itself (at least in the related form of German nationalism) had not yet penetrated very far below the intellectually sophisticated strata of German-speaking Europe. Oscar Handlin concluded from this that the processes of emigration and resettlement had broken down the regional divisions of the Old World and dissolved them in the new ethnicity of German-America.[16] John Hawgood stressed the role of American nativism in the formation of this new ethnic identity, but also accepted the relative unity of the new formation.[17] In fact, the role of persisting local and regional loyalties within German-American communities has been essentially ignored.[18] Religious differences have attracted somewhat more attention, but their role in the formation and functioning of German-American communities and the forms of ethnicity that they generated has rarely been analyzed.[19]

Despite Oscar Handlin's suggestive comments about the origins of ethnicity, there has been a general tendency among historians (and others) to treat ethnicity as relying on primordial group characteristics (thus needing no explanation) that would eventually be submerged in the processes of assimilation. Even as the focus on assimilation was giving way to a perspective that allowed for the persistence of ethnic groups, as in Glazer and Moynihan's or Milton Gordon's works,[20] the historical and sociological approaches to ethnic groups continued to treat them as primordial and unitary phenomena.[21]

A new theoretical perspective has been highlighted by the work of the anthropologist Fredrik Barth.[22] Barth reinterpreted ethnic categories, describing them as "organizational vessels that may be given varying amounts and forms of content in different sociocultural groups," and in doing so he introduced a new focus on the subjective nature and flexible boundaries of ethnic groups.[23] This perspective was rapidly adopted by many anthropologists and some sociologists, though it has had little influence so far on historians.[24] Examining the political aspects of ethnicity, anthropologist Joan Vincent noted that ethnic groups can be radically redefined to expand or contract their boundaries to suit the needs of the moment. She thus stresses the notion of ethnicity as social process, the essence of which is lost by analyses that attempt to reify ethnicity into static entities.[25] Extending this line of argument even further, Ronald Cohen defined ethnicity as "a *series* of nesting dichotomizations of inclusiveness and exclusiveness." He posited a scale of ethnicity similar to a social distance scale, but one where "ethnicity is an historically derived lumping of sets of diacritics at varying distances outward from the person, so that each of these lumpings acts as a potential boundary or nameable grouping that can be identified with or referred to in ethnic terms, given the proper conditions."[26]

One of the more revolutionary implications of this new conception of ethnicity is that it does not require individuals, or even groups, to subscribe to either exclusive or indivisible ethnic identities. Context can determine the choice of an ethnic identity. The "German" in New York or St. Louis could be transformed into an "American" upon a return to Europe. Many German Protestants in America, finding that they had to deal with rabidly anti-Catholic Americans, preferred to stress their identity as Protestants and downplayed their Germanness—some even went so far as to create German sections of American nativist (antiforeign) societies. Some German immigrants found greater tolerance for Jews than for Germans in rural America, and they chose to identify themselves simply as Jews—while, at the same time, other German Jews felt that they had to create their own German synagogues rather than join those of their American coreligionists. The ability to choose between several possible ethnic identifications is often a distinct advantage in complex societies, and it appears that people constantly made (and make) such choices. Any theoretical concept of ethnicity that fails to allow for the possibility of making such choices can only impoverish our understanding of complex social realities.

Ethnic identifications are built upon those perceived cultural distinctions that many social scientists and historians have reified as "primordial" characteristics and that provided Cohen with his "historically derived lumping of sets of diacritics," but the perceived distinctions are insufficient in themselves to generate ethnic identities. Ethnic identities tend to be formed out of cultural differences in the context of structural oppositions—that is, situations in which members of socially marked groups find themselves in direct or indirect competition for scarce social goods such as economic resources, political power, desirable mates, or the favor of a deity. In fact, the United States has long been a society in which both economic resources and political power have been distributed on the basis of racial and cultural distinctions, a type of stratification that Michael Hechter termed a "cultural division of labor."[27] This is most apparent in the segmentation of the nineteenth-century American labor force along ethnic lines, where labor-force segmentation created structural oppositions between whites and nonwhites, Americans and immigrants, German immigrants and Irish immigrants.

In the context of the broader American society that made ethnic distinctions between speakers of the same language only when that language was English (that is, between English, Welsh, Scots, and Irish), New Yorkers from German-speaking lands were identified as, and perforce identified themselves as, Germans. This ascribed identity was inescapable, but it did not fully determine the self-identity of those subjected to it. In German New York, as in German-speaking central Europe, an identification as simply German was virtually meaningless in its generality. In essentially German contexts, subnational characteristics became paramount. Even in those contexts, however, German New Yorkers might have several potential or actual identifications among which to choose. In some contexts a religious identification—Catholic, Lutheran, Calvinist, Jew, or Freethinker—might seem most apposite (generally, of course, with an unstated geographic modifier such as German or Saxon preceding it). In other contexts, the Kleindeutschlanders' town or region of birth would be their most salient characteristic and the basis for their self-identification. In yet other contexts, spoken dialects would readily identify German speakers as members of one or another subnational group.[28]

Subnational characteristics, as paramount markers of identity in German New York, were natural bases for the formation of ethnic groups and their ethnic identity. These more-restrictive ethnic identities, as this work will make clear, developed institutional supports over the years and became increasingly concrete. At the same time, the tendency for people to opt for those sets of boundary markers that maximized the similarity of group members coexisted with a contrary tendency to opt for broader sets of boundary markers, ones that increased the utility of the group to its members by enlarging its size to significant proportions. The first tendency seems to have restricted ethnic formations to the small scale of *Heimat* (homeland, used to mean hometown), while the second tended to promote a pan-German ethnicity. The tension between the two produced intermediate ethnic formations along several different axes, and these contradictory tendencies were never resolved.

When it came to ethnicity, German New Yorkers did what most people have done—they formed their ethnicity out of the misty regions of their consciousness, and they did so on an ad hoc basis. Selecting from a broad range of historically developed options, they shaped their ethnicity in accordance with whichever set of rules seemed appropriate for the particular context. Then, having molded an image out of a mélange of culture, emotion, and ideology, they reified it into a seemingly timeless identity.

Presented with the complexity of German New York, with its fluid and multiple ethnicity, some readers may be tempted to abandon any notion that we are dealing with anything resembling a real social group bound by ties of organic solidarity. They might argue that diversity and complexity are one thing, while division and factionalism are quite another, and that religious and class hatreds are very different from the division of labor that Durkheim posited as the basis for organic solidarity. Kleindeutschland did indeed suffer from severe divisions based upon regional origin, religious differences, and an increasingly sharp class struggle. Nonetheless, I would argue that these divisions were not a barrier that prevented the development of an organically solidary community. In fact, they provided the mechanism for integrating such a large and diverse group of people into a community by drawing each of its members into a complex web of conflicting loyalties. A single individual would often be tied to very different groups of people by each of the different types of social division, resulting in a loyalty to the whole expressed by a combination of all of them—the German-American community of Kleindeutschland. As T. S. Eliot suggested:

> both class and region, by dividing the inhabitants of a country into two different kinds of groups, lead to a conflict favorable to creativeness and progress. And . . . these are only two of an indefinite number of conflicts and jealousies which should be profitable to society. Indeed, the more the better; so that everybody should be an ally of everyone else in some respects, and an opponent in several others and no one conflict, envy or fear will predominate. . . . If we consider these two divisions alone, of class and region, these ought to some extent to operate against each other: a man should have certain interests and sympathies in common with other men of the same local culture as against his own class elsewhere; and interests and sympathies in common with others of his class, irrespective of place.[29]

The crosscutting loyalties that were the basis of German New York's extreme complexity were thus, in the end, the basis for a form of organic solidarity and tentative unity that made Kleindeutschland, in Eliot's terms, the nation of "Little Germany" in New York.

The long tradition of research on German-Americans goes back before World War I, when German-Americans produced a large number of filiopietistic studies, culminating in A. B. Faust's monumental work, *The German Element in the United States.* They even had their own journal, the *Deutsch Amerikanische Geschichtsblätter.* But with the shock and demoralization that overcame German-America after its repression during the war, it stopped producing its own studies and was largely ignored by American historians. There was a revival of interest in German-America as part of the general flurry of interest in American immigration history around the 1940s,[30] but only Carl Wittke continued to devote serious scholarly interest to German-America through the 1950s.[31] Although Frederick Luebke has done some fine work on German-American politics in more recent years, as has Philip Gleason on the German-American Catholic hierarchy, they toiled in a nearly empty vineyard for many years.[32]

The rise of the new urban history, with its stress on communities and ethnic groups, has drawn a new generation of scholars to the study of

German-American communities. These scholars, often of non-German descent, have taken a less parochial interest in German-America—approaching it from the broader perspectives of social history.[33] German-American communities are now being studied for what they have to teach about more general processes of urbanization, community formation, and ethnogenesis (the creation of ethnic groups). Patterns of social mobility in German-American communities are now being explored in the context of the entire genre of social mobility studies that grew out of Stephan Thernstrom's work on Newburyport and Boston.[34] They are, thus, only part of a larger body of literature focusing on the relationship between ethnicity and mobility in America. When other works raised the issue of the relationship between class and community, this too became an important focus of the new community studies.[35] The leading example of the new German-American history, Kathleen Neils Conzen's *Immigrant Milwaukee*, is explicitly formulated in the context of urban history, so much so that German-Americans are not even mentioned in the title. The present work is more narrowly focused on the German-American community of New York, but it too is shaped by the broader concerns of the new urban history and is intended to be as much a reflection of the history of New York City as of the history of German-America.

Following the example of Fernand Braudel, I have developed this history of German New York on different levels.[36] One level is that of the social construction of Kleindeutschland, which took place largely in what Braudel called "social time," the slow development and change of basic social institutions, measured more often in generations than in years. On this level it is possible, even necessary, to examine separately the various spheres of social existence: urban geography, work, household and kinship, religion, and voluntary associations. Some of these aspects of social existence changed hardly at all in the mere thirty-five years covered by this study, others evolved relatively rapidly (as these things go) under the stress of adapting to new environments. In either case, they underlie and are essential to the understanding of the second level of historical development, that of *l'histoire événementielle* or the history of events. Whereas the history of social existence is often worked out through the daily repetition of essentially similar activities, the history of events is developed through the sequences of relatively unique incidents (or an analysis of the unique aspects of these incidents). While these sequences are parts of larger historical processes and are conditioned by the shifting social structures upon which they rest, they lend themselves to a different mode of exposition. Thus, the detached social-science mode of exposition appropriate to the examination of social structures gives way to a more-traditional historical narrative—one more appropriate for dealing with rapidly changing political developments. Each distinct level of historical development requires its own mode of exposition and neither can be reduced to the other without severely impoverishing the whole.

My overall goal is to present the immigrant community of Kleindeutschland as an organic whole, a community, without losing either its extreme complexity or its vitality. This has required more attention to the underlying community social structure than some partisans of narrative history might like, but to do less would miss aspects of Kleindeutschland's social life that were crucial to its inhabitants. I have tried to avoid letting the social complexity of German New York overwhelm the study and turn it into a catalogue of traits and institutions, but I have also struggled to avoid the opposite risk, that of oversimplification. Any attempt to reduce the terribly complex social reality of a substantial human community to the confines of a book must balance these two dangers and every possible choice will have its critics. In the end, I have selected the balance that seems to me to be most suitable, and I can only hope that it will please the reader as well.

A short note on my use of quantified data must be introduced here. In a number of chapters I have drawn a sample from the manuscript census lists (United States censuses for 1850, 1860, 1870, and 1880) for the four Manhattan wards that included Kleindeutschland. These wards included non-German districts as well as German ones (especially in the earlier years of Kleindeutschland's history), but the wards are the smallest census units to have kept the same boundaries from 1845 to 1880 (thus providing comparative statistics on their total population). It is also often impossible to identify the locations of the enumerations districts, so the only way to be certain of including the whole of Kleindeutschland is to take the entire wards.[37] Each sample was selected by taking the first household listed with a German-born resident, skipping x pages (x being calculated to provide a final sample of more than 385 households from each census—so as to achieve a minimum confidence interval of $+/-5$ percent at a confidence level of 95 percent or better)[38] and then taking the next such household to appear. This procedure gives some slightly added weight to German households in non-German areas (that is, it includes a larger proportion of such households than would be strictly warranted by their numbers in the four wards), but this actually helps to compensate for any distortion that may have been introduced by restricting the universe from which the sample was drawn to the largest and densest German concentration in New York.

In most cases I have presented numerical data in the form of percentages of either the whole sample or specified subsamples.

Basically my statistics are simply descriptive. In my occasional forays into cross-tabulation, I have used them to suggest inferences as to possible relationships that might exist between pairs of variables. Given the small size of some of the subsamples, I have generally forgone the temptation to use more sophisticated statistical procedures to give more quantitative precision to the relationships I have suggested. It is my feeling that any such precision would, under these circumstances, be of questionable reliability. In other words, I have treated quantified material in much the same manner as sources of impressionistic data and have tried to build my arguments on the convergence of different lines of evidence rather than on any alleged mathematical precision or statistical proof.

For the convenience of the reader, I have translated all quotations from German sources into English. I have tried to maintain the flavor of the original as well as I could, but I resisted the temptations of free translation and chose to stay as close to the original text as possible—even though that has sometimes compromised the elegance of the translation. Some German terms have been retained without translation. This is generally in cases where either there was no good English equivalent or where using it would have made my own writing more awkward. I should also point out that nineteenth-century German-Americans developed somewhat distinctive linguistic practices, sometimes using words, grammatical forms, and spellings that differed from proper contemporary German. Although my appropriation of their usage may sometimes offend linguistic purists, I have chosen to use the German of the people about whom this book is written rather than to "correct" them.

From the Old to the New World—German Emigrants for New York Embarking on a Hamburg Steamer. Collection of the Lower East Side Tenement Museum.

The first Steinway piano factory in New York, occupied from 1854 to 1860. The entire family and staff are assembled in front. From Theodore E. Steinway, *People and Pianos* (New York: Steinway & Sons, 1953).

East Third St. between Ave. A and Ave. B c. 1875. The German Catholic Church of the Most Holy Redeemer towers over the street. Courtesy of The New-York Historical Society, New York.

Temple Emanu-El uptown on Fifth Avenue in 1868. *Harper's Weekly*, 11/14/1868, photograph taken from John Grafton, *New York in the Nineteenth Century* (New York: Dover Publications, 1980).

A German Beer Hall on the Bowery. [London] *Graphic*, 2/10/1877, photograph taken from John Grafton, *New York in the Nineteenth Century* (New York: Dover Publications, 1980).

A German Band, 1879. From *Harper's Weekly*, 4/26/1879, photograph taken from John Grafton, *New York in the Nineteenth Century* (New York: Dover Publications, 1980).

Philipp Merkle in later years, from Deutscher Ordens der Harugari, *1847–1895, Funfzig Jubiläum* (New York: O. Neuberg, 1897).

Mainzer Carneval officers in regalia, from Mainzer Carneval-Verein in New York, *1859–1909, Einst und Jetzt* (New York, 1909–10).

Deutsch-Amerikanische Schützen-Gesellschaft Halle, 12 St. Marks Place. Photos by author.

The new Liederkranz Halle uptown, c. 1890. Note the sumptuous reception room and grand ballroom. Exterior view from Hermann Mosenthal, *Geschichte des Vereins Deutscher Liederkranz in New York* (New York: F. A. Ringler Co., 1897); interiors from Liederkranz Gesangverein, *History of the Liederkranz of the City of New York, 1847–1947, and of the Arion, New York* (New York: Liederkranz, 1948).

Kleindeutschland's two Turn-Verein halls, 1859 to 1870 on Orchard St. and 1871 to 1898 on Fourth St. From New York Turn-Verein, *Goldenes Jubiläum des Turner-Cadetten-Corps, 1864–1914* (New York, 1914). Courtesy of Sam Sanderoff.

Wilhelm Weitling. Reprinted by permission of Louisiana State University Press from *The Utopian Communist* by Carl Wittke.

"Kapital und Arbeit" (Capital and Labor), from *1883 New Yorker Pionier Illustriter Volks-kalender* (New York: New Yorker Volkszeitung, 1883).

The eight-hour-day parade of 1872, from *Frank Leslie's Illustrated Newspaper*, 6/29/1872.

CHAPTER ONE

Germany, German States, and Germans

Kleindeutschland had its roots in the social order of a politically fragmented German-speaking sector of Europe. Thirty-nine states and free cities made up the feeble German Confederation, a confederation that did not include the Germans of Switzerland and Alsace and that, in fact, technically excluded the Germans of East and West Prussia as well.[1] Each major state ruled over a diverse and poorly integrated population and many states, including some of the smaller ones, controlled territories that were separated from each other by the lands of other German princes. One leading historian of modern Germany concluded:

> the particular interest of Prussia and Bavaria, of Saxony and Württemberg and the rest, had written Germany off the political map of Europe. On the other hand, none of these states, not even Prussia, had succeeded in taking over, even within the limits of its own territorial boundaries, the loyalties which had formerly animated the Reich. Many were recent Napoleonic creations, but even those which had existed since 1648 had failed to establish identity of government and people, of state and folk, which gives endurance and stability to political society. They were still, at the end as at the beginning, the arbitrary product of accidental contingencies, superimposed on the population regardless of race, geography, or history; . . . they were unable to gather the life of the people round them, to make themselves the centres of popular life and activity, expressing the common interests of their inhabitants.[2]

True as this was, most of these states still contained some core territories that defined them historically and contained populations that identified themselves with the state. It was not that there were no Prussians or Bavarians who strongly identified as such. It was rather that Lutheran Prussia had a hard time incorporating the mostly Catholic Rhinelanders—who thought the Prussians were a lot of militaristic and uncouth foreigners: "then [c. 1850] and even much later the population of the Prussian Rhineland designated each officer and official simply as a 'Pruss.' The Rhinelanders did not yet feel themselves to be Prussians. If a young man had to become a soldier it was said, 'he has to be a Pruss.' There was even a curse word for it."[3] Catholic Bavaria had similar problems with its new subjects in Franconia (mostly Lutheran) and the Bavarian Palatinate (which included both Catholics and Calvinists). In fact, most of the German states faced similar problems in some part of their territory. These difficulties were based in part on religious differences, at least in these examples, but religion was only one source of competing loyalties. The German language was (and to a lesser extent still is) divided into dialects that were often only minimally intelligible to outsiders. These linguistic distinctions often formed the basis of German particularism, especially where these regional dialects were reinforced by strong regional cultures and/or religious lines. In other words, the failure of the German states to assimilate large numbers of their subjects did not mean that there were no strong particularist loyalties; they were just drawn more narrowly than (or they ran across the borders of) the German states.[4]

The Prussian state hammered most of the German Confederation into a new German empire in the years between 1866 and 1871 (excluding the Austrian Germans in the process), but it was an empire of princes and not a nation-state. A. J. P. Taylor pointed out that "the settlement of 1871, although it marked the end of the worst excesses of German particularism, . . . failed to eradicate particularist tendencies; rather these took on a new lease of life in a new constitutional form, securing a measure of genuine popular support hitherto unknown as the expression of the resistance of the people in the more liberal regions, in Westphalia and Baden and Bavaria, to the Prussian spirit which henceforward dominated the government of the Reich."[5]

After 1871, as before, it remained true that cultural, religious, and linguistic boundaries cut across those of states, customs unions, and empires, dividing German Europe into a multitude of small cultural and linguistic regions.[6] These regions, and not a mythical German nation, were the source of the German emigration that created German New York.

Studies of Euro-American migration also often begin with the assumption (at least implied) that emigration was the consequence of the breakdown of a rural order that had been stable since time immemorial. Europe's preindustrial population is thus portrayed as a peasantry long rooted to the soil of its birthplace, first by the bonds of serfdom and then by the ties of community, landownership, and inertia.[7] This image of Europe is not entirely imaginary, but Europe has also been swept over by continued movements of people and peoples at least since the German tribes overran the Roman Empire. Serfdom itself was often introduced to restrain an overly mobile labor force, though it was never entirely successful in practice.[8] From the late Middle Ages on, northern Germany underwent continued settlement as its low-lying wetlands were drained. A push to the east had begun even earlier as German lords extended their territories at the expense of the Slavic and Baltic peoples (Wends, Poles, Prussians, and others).[9] These lords often offered freedom from serfdom (a powerful inducement) to recruit German settlers for their new lands.[10] German settlers, with their more advanced agricultural techniques and manufacturing skills, continued to be recruited at times by non-German rulers to the east (the Russian czars were notable modern examples).[11]

While the flow of German peasants to the east and north slowed in the eighteenth and nineteenth centuries, German artisans continued to move across Europe in large numbers. During the *Wanderjahre* that followed their apprenticeship, the journeyman artisans traveled from town to town, perfecting their skills and searching for a place to settle. Entrance to a town guild could be both difficult and expensive, but it was impossible to settle or marry without guild membership.[12] A journeyman's life often led him to the developing centers of industry outside Germany. The Hounslow arms factory near London, for example, was established in the seventeenth century with imported German arms makers from Solingen,[13] and the nineteenth-century workshops of Paris were filled with German artisans and workers.[14]

The literate and mobile artisans were frequently the carriers of Jacobin and even more radical ideologies into both towns and countryside. In their colonies in the working-class districts of Paris, Lausanne, Geneva, and Zurich, German artisans established an underground republican subculture—one where socialist and communist ideas took root.[15] Republican artisans were also among the first Germans to be attracted to the new republic across the sea.[16] Skilled journeymen were, in any case, increasingly likely to emigrate in the nineteenth century because it became ever more difficult to achieve master's status in the stagnant German economies of 1815–50, and because they were faced with complete proletarianization in the industrialization boom that followed.[17]

The Emigration

As noted above, when the nineteenth-century emigration began Germany had not been a state for hundreds of years. The Congress of Vienna had reduced the multiplicity of independent German states to a mere thirty-nine, but many of these had hardly begun to win the loyalties of their new subjects (or indeed many of their old ones). Political disunity was compounded by a lack of economic and social integration that left Germany divided into distinct geophysical and social regions—a regionalism that was to persist into the twentieth century. The west and south were the most heavily populated, and they had been the centers of out-migration to other parts of Germany and Europe since the Middle Ages.

Peasant holdings there were small and the practice of partible inheritance tended to reduce the acreage below the minimum needed to sustain a household. This area was also the historic core of artisan production in Germany (indeed, with northern Italy, for all of western Europe).

By the nineteenth century, cottage industry was widespread in the south and west. In some areas, even factory work was welcomed as a means of maintaining households on inadequate plots of land. The lands along the Rhine had been forced to remove all guild restrictions on trade and production during the Napoleonic occupation and this sped the pace of economic development (at least while it was accompanied by free access to French markets). Giving a large section of the Rhineland to Prussia in the peace settlement of 1815 laid the basis for Prussian predominance in Germany—as well as providing most of the "Prussian"-born participants in the early waves of emigration to America).[18]

Saxony and Silesia, to the east, were the centers of nonguild artisan production, particularly in textiles. They first lost ground in world markets during the disorders of the Napoleonic period. When peace returned, they attempted to continue to compete on the basis of hand production. This competition with the newly mechanized British textile industry led to a steady degradation of the artisans' standard of living and culminated in the uprising of the Silesian handloom weavers in 1844 and a severe famine in 1847.[19]

The north and east were the colonized areas of great estates. As western Europe began to specialize in industry, this area came to specialize in the production of grain to feed it. This process was accompanied by a concentration of landholdings and the enserfment of the formerly free peasantry (sometimes referred to as the "second serfdom"). Here the population was indeed tied to the soil by bonds that were not to be broken until the second half of the nineteenth century.

After the end of the Napoleonic wars there was a burst of emigration, as the combination of trade crisis and agricultural disaster sent thousands from Baden and Württemberg onto the roads. While many returned home, about twenty thousand went on to the United States and another fifteen thousand went to Russia. It was noted at the time that artisans (who did not grow their own food) were especially vulnerable to famine and were therefore disproportionately numerous among the emigrants.[20]

In the succeeding years, there was a small but steady flow of migrants to the United States who built up a social network of contacts and information. Although many of these migrants lost touch with their homeland over the years, many did not, and it was these pioneers who were joined by kinsmen and friends in the hard times to come.

In the 1830s, the number of those leaving Germany increased. Emigration was eased by several factors. Bremen began to develop as a major tobacco-importing port and promoted the emigrant trade as a means of assuring a return cargo to America. At the same time, tolls were reduced or eliminated on the Rhine and steamboats were introduced. These innovations not only facilitated travel, they also promoted the importation of factory-made goods from abroad, thus increasing the economic pressure on the artisans of the Rhinelands.[21]

The peasantry of the Rhinelands was also feeling economic pressure. Population was rapidly rising in the countryside and prices were keeping pace (especially the price of land). Small farmers found it increasingly difficult to set their sons up with viable farms (or even to keep up mortgage payments on the land they already owned). Rather than see their sons go landless or turn to industry to supplement their incomes, many farmers sold out altogether and emigrated to the United States. There, they could establish themselves and all of their sons on land purchased with the proceeds from the sale of their holdings in Germany. Observers often remarked upon the frequency with which the emigrants of this period were substantial representatives of the lower middle classes, traveling with their entire families.[22]

The emigration of the 1830s spread from Baden and Württemberg to the Hesses, Hanover, Prussia, and Bavaria. Nonetheless, the Rhine was still the main highway out of Germany to the New World and most of those who took it were from lands near its banks (or those of its major tributaries). As late as 1857, over 85 percent of those emigrating from Bavaria were from the Rhine basin provinces of Franconia and the Palatinate, although these provinces had only a small portion of Bavaria's total population.[23] Similarly, Rhenish Prussia was the source of most of the "Prussian" emigration before the 1860s, and only later years saw substantial numbers of emigrants from the Prussia of Frederick the Great.[24]

The rising tide of people leaving Germany in the 1830s (about 125,000) dwarfed the earlier emigrations, but it was still small compared to the numbers of people moving from one part of Germany to another. From 1822 to 1844 Prussia had a net in-migration of just under 800,000 souls, while Saxony continued to grow from immigration up until the end of the 1840s.[25] The diversion of this river of internal migration from its traditional eastward course into a flood across the Atlantic made for a qualitative change in the emigration after 1843.

The transatlantic flood began in the 1840s, as the potato rot (first noticed in 1842) spread rapidly across Germany to reach crisis proportions in 1845–47. Grain prices rose 250 to 300 percent in two years and potato prices rose 425 percent in the same period.[26] Hunger riots were widespread. (The government of Hesse-Darmstadt responded to the rising threat of disorder by banning the return of artisans from "radical" Switzerland.)[27] With more and more steamboats plying the Rhine and new oceangoing steamships to ease the transatlantic passage, many people decided to abandon a Germany where their future was in peril. Farmers sold out and fled the potato rot while artisans purchased tickets to America with money that could no longer purchase food.

The revolutionary years of 1848–50 brought hope to many, and made travel too dangerous for many more, but they ended in failure for the republican cause and victory for the forces of reaction. This drove many liberal and radical intellectuals into exile, along with their peasant and artisan compatriots. The rapid rise of the exiles to prominence in the immigrant communities in the United States led to the mistaken labeling of all the immigrants of this period as "forty-eighters." The known activists of 1848–50 were only a small portion of the emigrants,[28] but many other emigrants had political motives too. Frederick Bultman, an apprentice locksmith in Hanover, was typical of many emigrants of those years. In 1852, when he was thirteen years old, he decided to emigrate to America. It was on the day he went to the tax collector's office to pay his father's taxes. He remembered the gilded royal coach he had seen and he suddenly realized that that display of royal wealth had been paid for by artisans like his father. On the spot he resolved to escape to America.[29] For Frederick and untold numbers of other emigrants, the United States was first and foremost the land of "kein König da," "no king there."[30]

The early 1850s had brought no economic relief. Bad harvest had followed bad harvest and the artisans bore the brunt of the crisis even more severely than before. In the state of Württemberg the bankruptcy rate among craftsmen rose from 1 in 250 in the 1840s to 1 in 76 in the 1850s—a tripling of the rate.[31] Thus, thousands of bankrupt and declassed master artisans joined their former employees in the move to America.

Despite the slight lull during the revolutionary years, the rising wave of emigration after 1843 carried nearly 1.5 million Germans to the United States before it broke over the rocks of depression and civil war in America (see fig. 1). The U.S. census report for 1860 gives us a good idea of the origins of this wave of immigrants. Two-thirds of the German-born residents of the United States were from the states of south and west Germany. Another 15 percent can be assigned to the Prussian Rhineland, making for a majority of over 80 percent (see map 1).[32]

The end of the Civil War in America (and the apparent widening of opportunity for landownership through the Homestead Act) took place at a time when Germany was strained by the tensions that preceded unification. Wars for supremacy in Germany and the threat of more general European wars were accompanied by increased conscription.

Draft dodgers fled across the seas to America.[33] At the same time, the movement to modernize the northern and eastern estates became widespread. German landlords on the great estates of the northeast discovered that they could increase their profits by replacing most of their resident labor force with seasonal migrants from further east. Harvest labor was imported from Poland on a large scale and the indigenous German labor force was largely cleared from the land over the next few decades. When the cash was available, they too went off to America.[34]

The second great wave of over one million emigrants from Germany to the United States (from 1865 to 1879) was quite different from its predecessor. Only one-quarter of its participants came from the states of the south and west that had provided more than two-thirds of the 1843 to 1860 wave.[35] Furthermore, only a small portion of the 53 percent of the second wave that came from Prussia were Rhinelanders. When the numbers from Prussia are combined with those from the other northern agrarian states of Hanover and the Mecklenburgs, they constitute a new and very different two-thirds majority (see map 1).[36]

Between 1880 and 1900, there was a third great wave of migration from Germany to the United States (nearly 1.8 million). It has been suggested that these migrants strongly resembled those of the second wave.[37] Unfortunately, the takers of the U.S. census ceased to record place of birth within Germany after 1880, and the new German Empire (despite its reputation for Prussian efficiency) did not keep any better records on emigrants. Thus little can be said for certain about the origins of these third-wave immigrants, who arrived after the period under consideration in this study.

Examining the origins of the migrants from Germany suggests that there was an internal structure to the migration that related their origin with their choice of destination. Just as they came from a sharply differentiated Germany, we must remember that they went to a heterogeneous America. Some groups were segregated on their arrival by their occupations and wealth; others were segregated by the time of their arrival and the changing needs of American industry; still others segregated themselves along the lines of religion and place of origin in Germany.

Most of the farmers who traveled with their families were bound for new farms in the United States. They tended to gravitate to the newly opened farmlands of the Midwest (particularly Missouri, Illinois, and Wisconsin, but they also settled in Michigan, Indiana, Iowa, and Nebraska). They often settled in communities organized around old-world relationships, like New Holstein, Iowa; Baden and New Bremen, Missouri; and Germantown and Herman, Wisconsin; but too little research has been done to be certain just how general this pattern was.[38] What is certain is

Map 1
The Sources of German Emigration in the Mid-Nineteenth Century

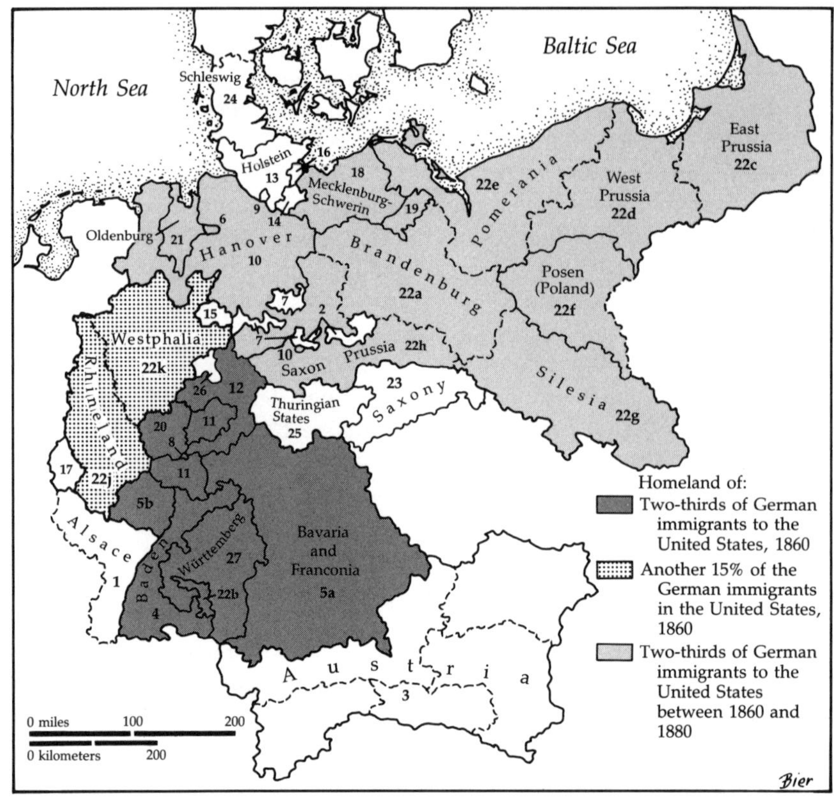

States of the German Confederation and Provinces of the German Empire

1 Alsace (French until 1871)*
2 Anhalt
3 Austria (German provinces)
4 Baden
5 Bavaria
  a Bavaria and Franconia
  b Bavarian Palatinate [Pfalz]
6 Bremen
7 Brunswick
8 Frankfurt
9 Hamburg
10 Hanover
11 Hesse-Darmstadt
12 Hesse-Kassel
13 Holstein
14 Lauenburg
15 Lippe-Detmold
16 Lübeck
17 Luxemburg
18 Mecklenburg-Schwerin
19 Mecklenburg-Strelitz
20 Nassau
21 Oldenburg
22 Prussia
  a Brandenburg
  b Hohenzollern
  c Prussia, East*
  d Prussia, West*
  e Pomerania
  f Posen [Poland]*
  g Silesia
  h Saxon Prussia
  j Rhineland
  k Westphalia
23 Saxony
24 Schleswig (Danish until 1865)*
25 Thuringian States
26 Waldeck
27 Württemberg

*Territories not part of the German Confederation but part of the Kingdom of Prussia and/or the German Empire.

Figure 1

German Migration to the United States
1830 to 1899

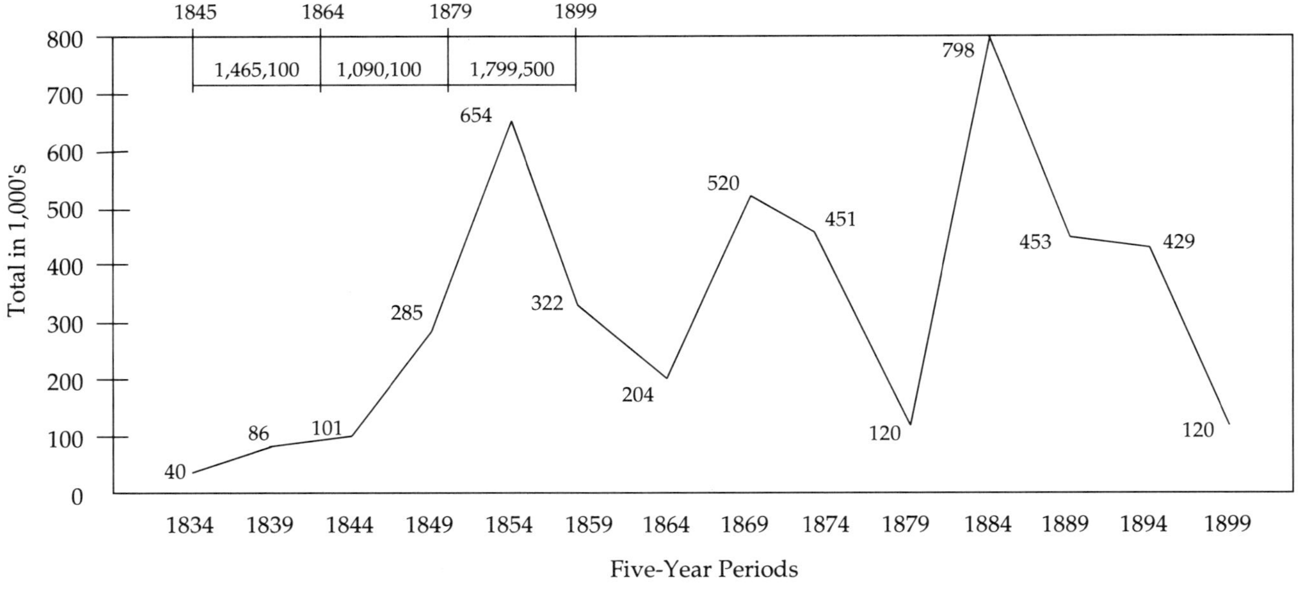

Source: Walter F. Wilcox, ed., *International Migrations, Statistics*

that the migration before 1880 was primarily from rural Germany to rural America and that the majority of the migrants settled on farms or in small towns.

Despite the basically rural nature of the migration, many of the immigrants from Germany went to the cities, where they constituted a significant portion of the population (see table 1). In 1860, when only 16 percent of Americans lived in places with a population of 8,000 or more, 36 percent of the German-born lived in cities of more than 25,000 people. Twenty years later German immigrants were even more urbanized, with 39 percent of them living in cities of over 35,000 people.[39] Back in Germany, even as late as 1900, the urban population (places of 20,000 or more) constituted less than 30 percent of the country's total population.[40] The German immigrant population of the United States was thus far more urbanized than the population of either Germany or the United States.[41]

Table 1
The German-born Population of Selected Cities, 1860–80

City	1860	1870	1880
New York	119,984 (15%)	153,940 (16%)	168,225 (14%)
Baltimore	32,613 (15)	35,491 (13)	34,337 (10)
Brooklyn	23,993 (9)	37,090 (9)	55,967 (10)
Buffalo	18,233 (22)	22,384 (19)	25,745 (17)
Chicago	22,230 (20)	53,020 (18)	76,561 (15)
Cincinnati	43,931 (27)	50,000 (23)	46,606 (18)
Milwaukee	15,981 (35)	23,173 (32)	32,433 (28)
Philadelphia	43,643 (7)	51,265 (8)	56,455 (7)
St. Louis	50,510 (31)	59,791 (19)	55,656 (16)

Sources: Eighth Census, *The Population of the U.S.*, pp. xxxi–xxxii, 609; Ninth Census, *Statistics of the Population*, pp. 385–89; Tenth Census, vol. 1, *Statistics of the Population of the United States*, pp. 520–23.

Nor were the Germans in America's cities simply similar conglomerations of people from all over Germany. Each city, rather, displayed a distinct mix. This indicates that there were not one but several German migrations. Let us consider the German-born populations of New York City, St. Louis, Chicago, Cincinnati, and Milwaukee. In 1860 only 31 percent of the Austrians living in those five cities lived in New York, while 46 percent lived in St. Louis. At the same time, 56 percent of the Württembergers lived in New York and only 15 percent in St. Louis. In 1870 we find that 55 percent of the Mecklenburgers were in Chicago and a further 37 percent were in Milwaukee, so that 92 percent of the Mecklenburgers lived in only two cities—cities that were then home for just 28 percent of the Germans of the five cities.[42]

Looking at this a little differently, in 1880 42 percent of the German-born population of the five cities lived in New York, but 59 percent of Württembergers and 66 percent of Hamburgers did so. At the same time, only 34 percent of the Prussian migrants to those cities had became residents of New York.[43] It is thus clear that there were many different German migrations from different parts of Germany. Each migration had its own settlement pattern in America's cities, or (as we shall see) even within each of its cities.

These different streams of migration followed channels established by early immigrants as they flowed into the labor pools of America. Social networks of information, contacts, and kinship guided each migrant's choice of a place to settle. People tended to settle in groups: national, regional, and local. On these bases, they chose one city over another, one neighborhood over another, one block or street or house over another. This is not intended to contradict the findings of the many studies of the relationship between employment and residence that demonstrate the primacy of the accessibility of work.[44] The availability of work, especially desirable work, was always a major consideration for immigrants. Nonetheless, it is necessary to recognize what some scholars have neglected, that within the constraints established by the labor market, immigrants frequently chose to live among kin, fellow townsmen, fellow provincials, or fellow nationals whenever possible. This preference, in turn, influenced the nature and structure of the settlements of German immigrants in the United States (as it did those of other immigrants).

This spatial dimension is frequently lacking in studies of immigrant communities, largely because more specific data on the origins of most immigrants is generally unavailable. This is why the German immigrants of the third quarter of the nineteenth century provide an unusual opportunity to examine the relationships between the origins and structure of their settlements.

The German-Americans of New York City were broadly representative of the German immigration as a whole, or at least its urban component. The early settlers were from the west and south, Rhineland Germany, and even as late as 1863 it was possible to report that "north-Germans are less frequently encountered than south-Germans. The leading contingents are from the Hesses, Baden, Württemberg and Rhenish Bavaria. One hears all dialects, but Berliner, Saxon and Westphalian are rare while Swabian and Upper-Rhenish modes of speech predominate."[45] In the later 1860s and 1870s there was an increasing tendency for immigrants to be from the Prussian lands and northern Germany (see fig. 2).

Careful examination of the census figures reveals that the New York settlers did not quite match the overall immigration from Germany. In all the years for which we have figures, Bavarians were overrepresented in New York (that is to say that the percentage of the German-born who came from Bavaria was higher in New York than in the United States as a whole). In fact they were increasingly overrepresented even as Bavarian immigration declined toward 1880.[46] Hessians were even more heavily overrepresented in the early years, but were underrepresented by 1880.[47] (There was an even sharper decline in other cities, so the emigration from the Hesses would appear to have become *more* rural in character as the years passed.)[48] Migrants from Prussian territories seem to have tended to pass through New York to settle further west, though their numbers were so great that even the relatively small proportion that remained in New York still constituted the largest of New York's German nationalities after 1870 (see fig. 2).[49] Hamburgers were also heavily overrepresented in New York, so much so that their increase in the decade from 1870 to 1880 was nearly equal to the entire immigration from Hamburg to the United States in that period.[50]

What stands out from all this is that New York's Germans were from those areas of Germany most likely to have been the sources of emigration for artisans, shopkeepers, and skilled workers. This continued to be the case even as the focus of the overall emigration shifted from west to east and from south to north in Germany. It was this urban and manufacturing background that made it easier for the Germans than for many other immigrants (particularly their Irish contemporaries) to adapt successfully to New York City's commercial and industrial economy.

We can also learn a lot about New York's German immigrants by examining the demographic structure of the German-born population.[51] The German migration to America has often been referred to as a family migration, one in which entire families moved together to the New World (including older parents traveling along with several grown or nearly grown children).[52] But, when we look at the demography of the New York immigrants, we get a very different picture. In 1850, 66 percent of the immigrants were in their twenties and thirties, while only 7 percent were under ten years old (a figure that was to drop steadily to 1.6 percent by 1880). At the same time, we find that 27 percent of Kleindeutschland was under ten years old when the American-born children of the immigrants are included in the statistics. Thus, even though there are many families with German-born children listed in the census, it is clear that they did not dominate the migration to New York City. Only a migration

Nativity of New York City's German Born

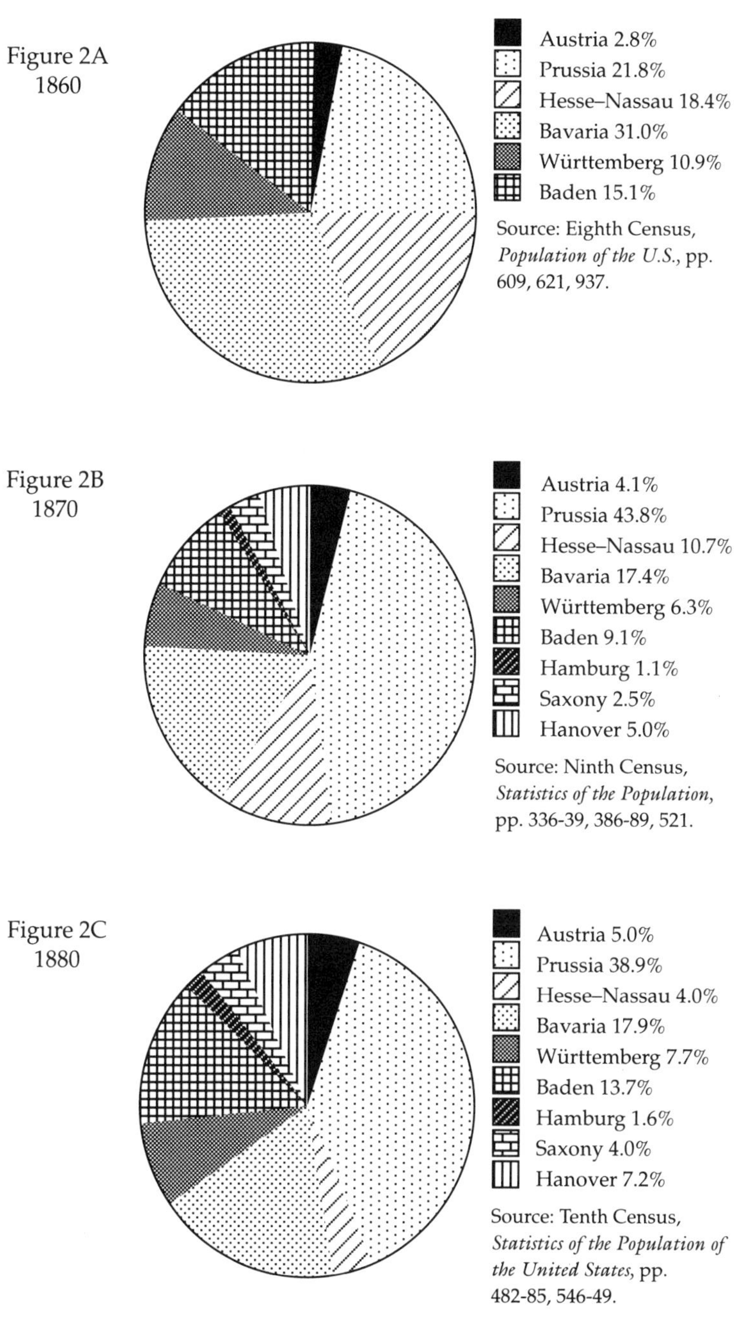

Figure 2A
1860
Austria 2.8%
Prussia 21.8%
Hesse–Nassau 18.4%
Bavaria 31.0%
Württemberg 10.9%
Baden 15.1%
Source: Eighth Census, *Population of the U.S.*, pp. 609, 621, 937.
Figure 2B
1870
Austria 4.1%
Prussia 43.8%
Hesse–Nassau 10.7%
Bavaria 17.4%
Württemberg 6.3%
Baden 9.1%
Hamburg 1.1%
Saxony 2.5%
Hanover 5.0%
Source: Ninth Census, *Statistics of the Population*, pp. 336-39, 386-89, 521.
Figure 2C
1880
Austria 5.0%
Prussia 38.9%
Hesse–Nassau 4.0%
Bavaria 17.9%
Württemberg 7.7%
Baden 13.7%
Hamburg 1.6%
Saxony 4.0%
Hanover 7.2%
Source: Tenth Census, *Statistics of the Population of the United States*, pp. 482-85, 546-49.

composed of unmarried individuals or young couples without children could have produced the demographic profile of Kleindeutschland.[53]

Another indicator of the character of the migration to the city is the sex ratio among twenty- to fifty-year-olds. If the migration were primarily of married couples (with or without children), a nearly equal ratio should appear in this age range. Instead, the ratio was 61:39 (male:female) in 1850, indicating a heavy predominance of single males. This was somewhat redressed over the next decade as wives, fiancées, girlfriends, and unattached single women came over to join the men. By 1860, the ratio was down to 52:48 (thus ending the first wave of migration on a fairly even note). The peak of the second wave, in 1870, found the ratio for all German-born New Yorkers back at 61:39. Therefore the predominance of single males must have been even greater in the second wave than it had been in the first, twenty years earlier. This time, however, there was no great following after them of German women, and the immigrant population remained heavily male a decade later (56:44). All in all, it turns out that we find a migration dominated by young males, which resembles the later "new immigration" from southern and eastern Europe (at least demographically) more closely than it does the traditional image of the distinctive German family migration.

The population pyramids for the German-born (see figs. 3–6) also underline the youth of the migrants. The aging of the original cohort of immigrants gradually lowered the proportion of the German-born in their twenties and thirties from 66 percent in 1850 to 42 percent in 1880. Despite this, the massive continuing influx of young immigrants kept the increase in the average age (of those born in Germany) over this thirty-year period down to eleven years (from twenty-eight years of age to thirty-nine).

These were the immigrants who went to New York. Now let us turn to the communities that they established there.

Figure 3

Ages of the German-born Population of Kleindeutschland in 1850

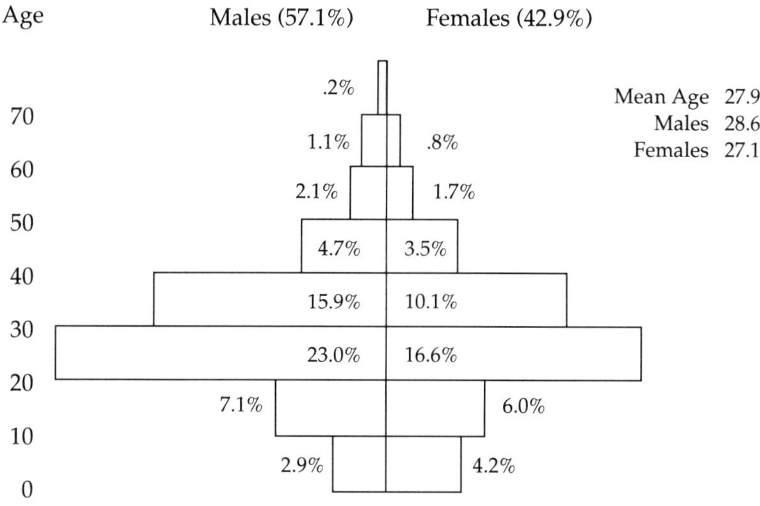

Source: Author's census samples

Figure 4

Ages of the German-born Population of Kleindeutschland in 1860

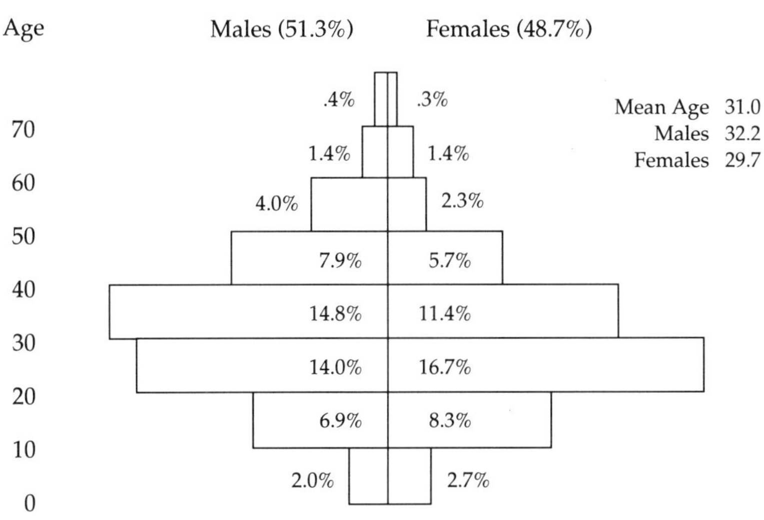

Source: Author's census samples

Figure 5

Ages of the German-born Population of Kleindeutschland in 1870

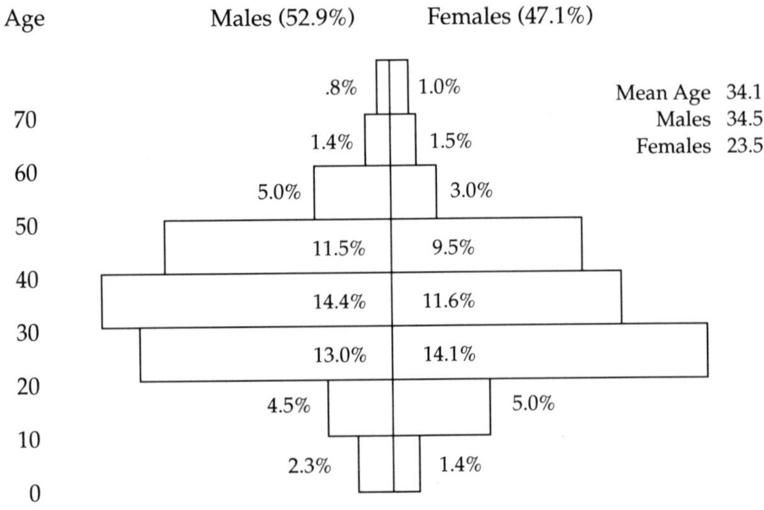

Source: Author's census samples

Figure 6

Ages of the German-born Population of Kleindeutschland in 1880

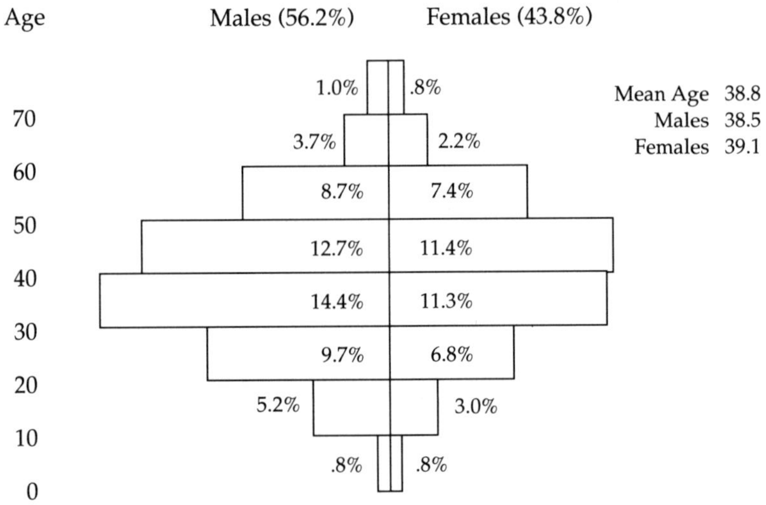

Age

Males (56.2%) Females (43.8%)

1.0% .8%

70

3.7% 2.2%

60

8.7% 7.4%

50

12.7% 11.4%

40

14.4% 11.3%

30

9.7% 6.8%

20

5.2% 3.0%

10

.8% .8%

0

Mean Age 38.8
Males 38.5
Females 39.1

Source: Author's census samples

CHAPTER TWO

German New York

The German communities of New York City were more than just social abstractions—distinguished from the rest of New York only by the use of a foreign language. They were also concrete geographic entities clearly segregated from the residential communities of English-speaking New Yorkers. Although some recent scholarship has indicated that immigrant ghettos were not characteristic of mid-nineteenth-century American cities,[1] the linguistically isolated Germans appear to have displayed a strong tendency toward self-segregation nearly everywhere they settled.[2] The commonly used "index of segregation" provides a rough measure of the relative segregation of New York's two major immigrant groups at mid-century (though it is a very rough measure indeed when applied to population units as large as New York City's wards).[3] Whereas the Irish had an average index of 17 between 1855 and 1875 (any index under 25 is generally taken to indicate little segregation), the Germans had an average index of over 29 in those same years.[4] In fact, if we correct the index to include the American-born children of German immigrants among the Germans (parents not being segregated from their children) the index for the Germans is raised to an average of nearly 35,[5] indicating a rather strong degree of segregation. Having thus demonstrated the separate existence of German New York, let us now examine it more closely.

Buildings and Blocks

Kleindeutschland, Deutschlandle, Dutchtown,[6] and Little Germany: these were the names of the main German-American neighborhood of mid-nineteenth-century New York. When the great emigration began in the early 1840s, it was already the largest residential center for the German-born population of the city. It grew steadily outward from a focus in the Eleventh Ward on Manhattan's East Side, and included most of the Tenth, Thirteenth, and Seventeenth wards as well (see map 2).[7]

This part of New York City later achieved fame as the Jewish Lower East Side. In 1845, however, it was a newly built-up area that was inhabited mainly by American-born workers and their families. The

Map 2
The Wards of Lower Manhattan, 1846–80,
with Kleindeutschland Marked

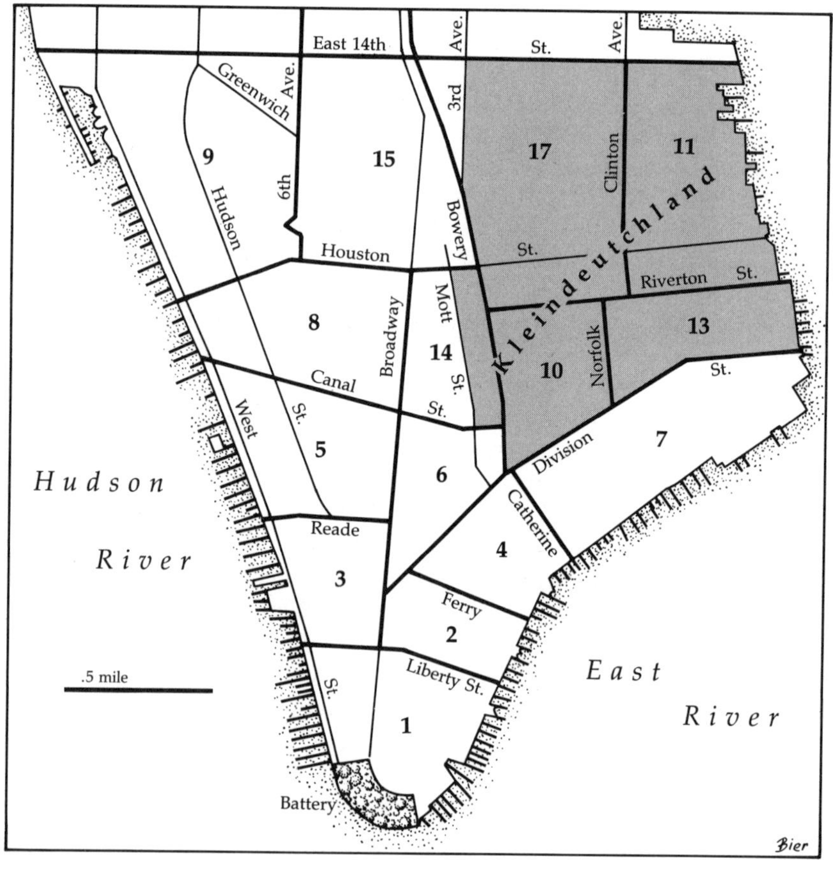

Adapted from William Perris, *Map of New York City and Vicinity*, 1858.

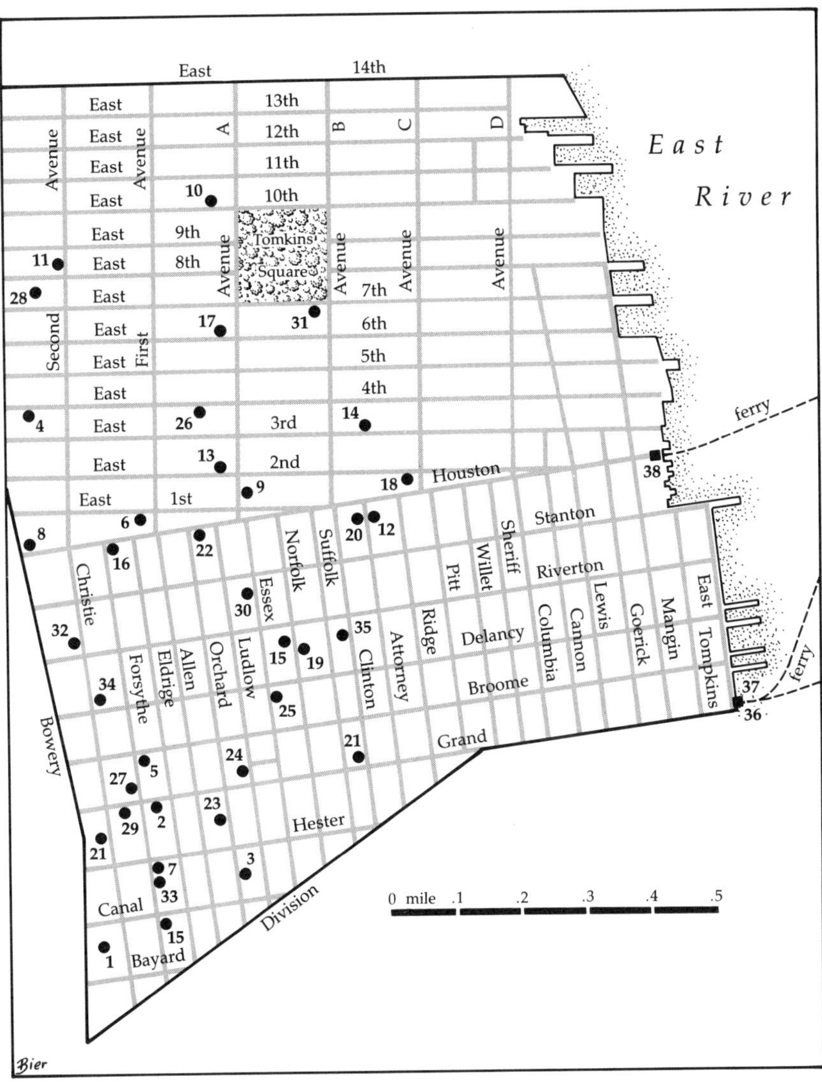

1. German theater district: Atlantic Gardens, Deutscher Volksgarten, Lindenmuller's Odeon, and der Stadttheater.
2. Sozialreformer Halle, 281 Grand St.
3. First Turner Halle, 27–33 Orchard St.
4. New (1871) Turnhalle, 66–68 E. Fourth St.
5. Tenth Ward Hotel, headquarters of the First International.
6. Justus Schwab's Saloon, 51 First St.
7. Erhard Richter's Lokal, 55–57 Forsyth St.
8. Steuben House (later Germania Assembly Rooms), 291–93 Bowery.
9. Concordia Hall, 30 Avenue A.
10. German Dispensary, 279 Tenth St.
11. Frei Leseverein/Ottendorfer Branch of the New York Public Library.
12. Samuel Gompers' first New York residence.
13. St. Nicholas Kirche (RC) on Second St.
14. Church of the Holy Redeemer (RC) on Third St.
15. German Reformed Church at 21 Forsyth St. (later at 149–53 Norfolk St.).
16. German Reformed Evangelical Mission, Houston and Forsyth.
17. St. Mark's Lutheran Church on Sixth St.
18. Deutsche Methodisten Kirche on Second St.
19. Anshe Chesed Synagogue on Norfolk St.
20. Rodeph Shalom Synagogue, 156 Attorney St. Later bought by Shaarey Rashmin Synagogue.

streets were either unpaved or paved with cobblestones, and they were lined with two-, three-, and four-story buildings made of wood, brick, and stone. Many of these had shops facing the street at ground level. Alleyways led into the interiors of the blocks, which were filled with the workshops and factories that accounted for 64 percent of the manufacturing establishments in the built-up portion of the city (and 57 percent of the manufacturing establishments in all of New York City).[8] The river districts of the Eleventh and Thirteenth wards contained some of the world's leading shipyards, birthplaces of many magnificent clipper ships (including the most famous American clipper, the *Flying Cloud*).[9] The Eleventh Ward was also the major slaughterhouse district, where more than half of the hogs slaughtered in the built-up portion of the city were killed.[10] Only the Seventeenth Ward still possessed tracts of open land, but these were to fill up during the next ten years, mostly with German immigrants.

By 1855, this now-distinctly-German district contained more than four times as many German immigrants as it had in 1845. It was almost completely built up and its center of gravity had shifted north and west.

The Thirteenth Ward had remained the least German (only about 33 percent) and had grown the least since 1845, that is, by only 18 percent. To the west, the Tenth Ward had grown by 26 percent and was now 45 percent German. In the northeast, the Eleventh Ward was still the most German (now 53 percent) and had nearly doubled its population. The Seventeenth Ward was the last to be built up and its population had increased by 120 percent. Still only 43 percent German in 1855, the Seventeenth Ward was to become the core of Kleindeutschland in later years.[11] The four wards of Kleindeutschland continued to become increasingly German and were over 64 percent German-American by 1875.[12]

There are both chronological and geographical dimensions to the diversity of Kleindeutschland. One of the best sources for exploring the geographical dimension is, however, limited to the formative period of the mid-1850s. The Perris fire insurance maps of the mid-1850s offer an unparalleled view into the materials, uses, and spatial relationships of the buildings that provided the physical structure of the neighborhood.

Each block was unique in detail, but generally resembled those around it. Few distinct boundaries are to be found, as district shades off into district. Commercial streets turn into industrial ones by imperceptible degrees and new districts emerge when enough distance has been traversed. We shall continue to use the political ward as our primary unit of reference, though it must be remembered that the wards were themselves large and diverse constructs. Figure 7 reproduces a pair of blocks from near the center of each of the four wards (as depicted by Perris). Examination of each of these blocks indicates the direction of diversity between the wards.

Figure 7

Kleindeutschland: Selected Blocks

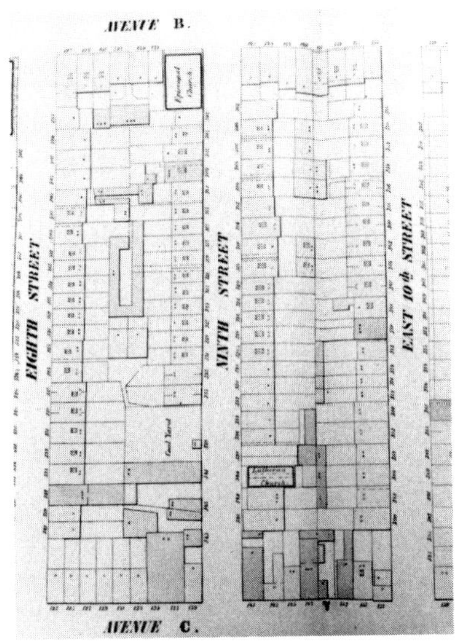

11th Ward

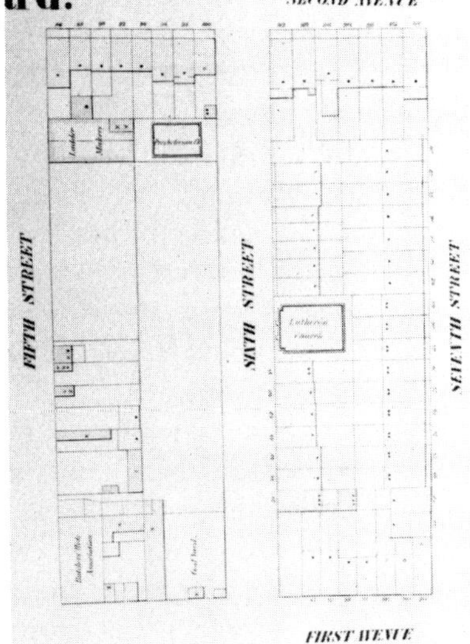

17th Ward

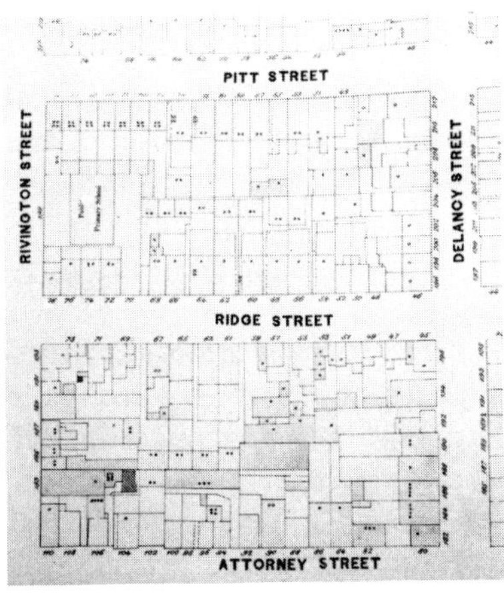

13th Ward

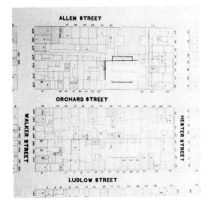

10th Ward

Source: William Perris, *Maps of the City of New York Surveyed under the Directions of Insurance Companies of Said City* (New York: Perris, 1853-56).

In the mid-1850s, the lower wards (Tenth and Thirteenth) still retained much of their early character. Frame structures frequently outnumbered masonry ones. Buildings tended to cover only a small portion of their lots and often shared the lot with more than one other structure. Each block was therefore a jumble of buildings and a maze of alleyways, with its industrial workshops generally tucked away on internal courtyards.

On the west, the Tenth Ward displayed a more commercial character. Our sample blocks show only fifteen industrial structures in the Tenth, as contrasted with forty on those in the Thirteenth. A German visitor to New York wrote of "the Bowery, Chatham Street and Grand Street (which last we called the grand street with the small houses), where the richest materials are used to make up clothes, carpets and furniture."[13] Grand Street was a major shopping center, with many dry-goods shops and even department stores.[14] The wards' industrial workshops tended to be small artisan operations with only a few employees. Most of these were involved in the manufacture of furniture or clothing.[15]

In 1856, a fire burned down a section of Forsyth Street in the southwest corner of the Tenth Ward. Damage reports on the nine buildings that were burned give a further view into the structures outlined on the Perris maps. Five of the nine were residential and contained three or more families each. Another was a frame structure that contained a cigar store and a shoemaker's workshop. All of these were adjacent to the three-building complex of workshops where the fire began. In addition to the incendiary sawmill, the complex contained two textile businesses, two mirror-frame makers' shops and a mirror maker's. All these workshops were located in the less industrial section of Kleindeutschland.[16]

Moving east, toward and across the Thirteenth Ward, more and heavier industry appeared. Artisans' workshops gave way to small and not-so-small factories. Some of these produced the same products as the artisans' workshops, and furniture factories predominated. Other factories operated on a larger scale, up to a fire brick manufactory with forty employees and a capitalization of $27,000.[17]

These factories were still intermixed with housing in ever more crowded conditions. The Tenement House Committee of the New York State Legislature said, in 1856, that the Tenth Ward was characterized by "dirty conditions without ventilation and without room sufficient for civilized existence." In the Thirteenth Ward, they found a building called Manhattan Place, which had 96 rooms, 146 families, and 577 persons—averaging six people to a room.[18]

The upper wards were northward extensions of the lower, formed on a new and more regular pattern. The jumble of internal alleyways and buildings faded away, with newer and larger brick and stone buildings occupying most of their lots. The Eleventh Ward carried the industrial character of the Thirteenth northwards along the river. Large-scale operations, like Jones' Brewery, coal yards, and timber yards found room for expansion there, along with the shipyards. Most of the slaughterhouses of the preceding decade remained in the ward as well. Thirteen-year-old Samuel Gompers arrived in the Eleventh Ward a few years later, and he remembered the ambience:

> Father began making cigars at home, and I helped him. The house was just opposite a slaughterhouse. All day long we could see the animals being driven into the slaughter pens and could hear the turmoil and the cries of the animals. The neighborhood was filled with the penetrating, sickening odor. The suffering of the animals and the nauseating odor made it physically impossible for me to eat meat for many months after we had moved to another neighborhood.
>
> Back of our house was a brewery which was in continuous operation, and this necessitated the practice of living-in for the workers. Conditions were dreadful in the breweries of those days and I became familiar with them from our back door.[19]

Gompers' recollections make it clear that the orderly patterns depicted by the Perris maps for the northern wards still allowed for very unpleasant conditions. In fact, the aforementioned Tenement House Committee report refers to the Folsom Houses in the Eleventh Ward as being so bad that "it is astounding that everyone doesn't die of pestilence."[20]

The Seventeenth Ward provided a striking contrast, being the newest, least industrial, and best residential portion of Kleindeutschland. The Perris maps show a high proportion of first-class brick and stone houses. Tompkins Square (known to the Germans as the Weisse Garten) provided a large open public space in the eastern portion of the ward, and the broad reaches of First and Second avenues opened grand boulevards through the western portion. Along Second Avenue and many of the side streets, the houses were set back from the sidewalk, lending an air of graciousness that further distinguished the Seventeenth from the other wards. This atmosphere of comfort was certainly a factor in the persistence of German settlement in the Seventeenth Ward long after the rest of Kleindeutschland had been abandoned to the settlers of the "new immigration" in the later years of the century.

The tenement houses of Kleindeutschland, especially those north of Houston Street, were large structures designed to get the greatest possible use out of each lot. They were generally five or six stories tall and built with bricks. A double-lot structure, fifty feet wide and seventy feet deep, held forty-eight apartments and accommodated at least that many families. Each floor had eight apartments with four facing the street and four facing the rear:

> These apartments are certainly small, but are therefore the more elegant [efficient]. A parlor with two windows and, attached thereto, a windowless bedroom, in which there is room for a double bed—and nothing else! Closet, kitchen, cellar, woodshed or the like is unknown; not even a corridor or pantry is to be found. Overall—how large is the parlor with the two windows? Ten feet long and ten feet wide, seldom more! Such a residence naturally doesn't cost much . . . on the top floor (front or rear) only about four dollars or less (per month) . . . [this leaves no room for children and if one needs more room] it is necessary to rent in a house with ten or twelve families. There it costs eight or nine dollars for a pleasant apartment with three windows and two bedrooms. One of these has its own entrance which provides a little additional light. Truly a magnificent dwelling, and for an honest man good enough! Princely accommodations (that is princely for a New York German worker) might be had for ten or twelve thalers a month. For such a sum one gets two living rooms (one of which is naturally used for a kitchen) and two roomy bedrooms—and, for a final luxury, place for coal and wood.[21]

Tenement-house design did not come under the effective influence of social reformers until 1879. At that time they were able to legislate improvements that were incorporated in the vastly superior "dumbbell" design (a new style of tenement that later became notorious as the pestilential "old law tenement"). A narrow air shaft and a common water closet on each floor constituted major improvements over the prelaw tenements. Later denunciations of this improved version suggest just how bad their predecessors were.[22]

By the 1870s, Kleindeutschland had reached its final physical form (as Kleindeutschland). Only 6.5 percent of its residential buildings were still made of wood (and three-quarters of these were in the lower wards that were being abandoned by the Germans).[23] The cobblestone streets were filled with the clatter of streetcars and the rumble of wagons, while the language of the shops and factories was German. The first of America's great foreign-language enclaves was at its peak, glorying in its status as the capital of German-America:

> At the beginning of the '70s, after a decade of continuously rising immigration, Kleindeutschland (the German city in the ever-growing Cosmopolis) was in fullest bloom. Kleindeutschland, called Dutchtown by the Irish, consisted of 400 blocks formed by some six avenues and nearly forty streets. Tompkins Square formed pretty much the center. Avenue B, occasionally called the German Broadway, was the commercial artery. Each basement was a workshop, every first floor was a store, and the partially roofed sidewalks were markets for goods of all sorts. Avenue A was the street for beer halls, oyster saloons and groceries. The Bowery was the western border (anything further west was totally foreign), but it was also the amusement and loafing district. There all the artistic treats, from classical drama to puppet comedies, were for sale.[24]

The People of German New York

The people of Kleindeutschland were no more uniform in their German origins than were the blocks they inhabited. There was no rigid segregation of populations, but the presence of strikingly different proportions from each of the major German states in each of the wards suggests that each "nationality" had separate concentrations of settlement in which they formed the dominant element. This seemed so natural to the Germans that it was rarely remarked upon by contemporaries. One German journalist did note that "the Brandenburgers and Plattdeutschen seem as little inclined to be among the Süddeutschen as among the Irish and Americans whom the Germans have thrust from their quarter."[25] That this was based on positive regional sentiments is indicated by Ernst Steiger's recollection of his first New York residence: "on the first evening I was taken into the family circle with great gusto because I was 'a Saxon.' "[26] There were times when negative feelings also ran strong, "the Plattdeutsche is against the High German, the Swabian against the Bavarian, the Würtenberger [*sic*] against the Prussian."[27]

The regional neighborhoods of Kleindeutschland were sometimes quite small. In high-density Manhattan, where each block contained hundreds of families, small colonies of several dozen families from the same locality are hard to pick out from their neighbors—though they can be found in profusion if the effort is made. Even larger settlements of several thousand families could interpenetrate and they become obscured in aggregate statistics. The issue is further complicated by the high degree of residential mobility in a city where the first of May was celebrated as "moving day."[28] Despite these difficulties, it is clear that Kleindeutschland was largely composed of regional settlements (see table 2).

In 1860, Germans born in Prussian territories comprised only one-fifth of the German-born population of New York. However, they concentrated in the Tenth Ward to such an extent that they constituted fully one-third of its German-born population. Increasing immigration from Prussia raised their numbers until they reached a third or more of Kleindeutschland's German-born by 1880, but by then they comprised nearly one-half of the German-born population of the Tenth Ward, thus giving the entire ward a decidedly Prussian cast.[29]

The Bavarians (including Rhinelanders from territories subject to the king of Bavaria) were the largest German "nationality" in the Kleindeutschland of 1860. They had large settlements in all the German wards except the Prussian-dominated Tenth. As time went on, they withdrew to the northern wards (Eleventh and Seventeenth). At all times, however, the most distinctive characteristic of their settlement pattern remained that they would be found wherever the Prussians were fewest.

Table 2
Index of Relative Concentration for Immigrants from Selected German States in Kleindeutschland's Wards, 1860–80*

German State	Year	Number from State in Sample	Index: 10th Ward SW	17th Ward NW	11th Ward NE	13th Ward SE
Austria	1860	21	0	90	220	0
	1870	33	176	67	155	21
	1880	37	202	38	115	85
Baden	1860	93	104	81	121	99
	1870	122	48	140	84	64
	1880	63	111	80	90	151
Bavaria	1860	187	59	118	104	117
	1870	178	74	110	121	76
	1880	134	52	139	103	71
Hanover	1860	31	71	42	198	73
	1870	44	131	64	105	159
	1880	49	50	103	50	245
Hesse-Nassau	1860	99	85	119	52	231
	1870	124	67	111	141	57
	1880	86	63	124	119	58
Prussia	1860	130	152	90	54	62
	1870	311	125	92	69	130
	1880	275	135	68	116	96
Württemberg	1860	74	119	94	108	46
	1870	94	88	74	147	137
	1880	52	28	157	109	49

*Only those German states with significant numbers of immigrants appearing in the author's census samples are shown in this table. 100 means that the proportion of immigrants from these states among the Germans of the quarter equals their proportion among all the Germans of Kleindeutschland. From author's samples of manuscript censuses (U.S. censuses for 1860, 1870, and 1880).

Germans from Hesse-Nassau shared predominance in the Thirteenth Ward in 1860 with the Bavarians. As there were only half as many Hessians as Bavarians in Kleindeutschland, this means that they were very heavily concentrated in the ward. They too moved northward during the next decade and were mostly to be found along the border between the Eleventh and Seventeenth wards by the mid-1870s.

Badeners and Württembergers seem to have been fairly evenly spread throughout the four wards in the earlier years, with no major concentrations evident. In the late 1860s, they moved north to the upper wards, with the Württembergers finally settling in the Seventeenth. The Badeners doubled back against the general northward flow and settled in the Thirteenth Ward by 1880.

The Hanoverians never formed a major segment of the population of Kleindeutschland, rising from 4.5 percent in 1860 to 6.4 percent in 1880, but they displayed a very strong tendency toward self-segregation. They began to settle in the lower Eleventh Ward and then spread south across the border of the Thirteenth. By 1880, the Thirteenth Ward had developed into their major settlement area, containing a veritable "Little Hanover," and they comprised the largest single German "nationality" in the ward after the Prussians.

It should again be stressed that the classification by German state of birth is really too broad. It fails to distinguish, for example, between "Prussians" from the Prussian-ruled Rhinelands and those from Prussia itself or those from Prussian Poland. It can therefore be assumed that these extended categories obscure the details of the actual patterns of settlement. Despite this, they are far more useful than the categories ordinarily used—north Germans and south Germans—which are so crude as to have had little or no significance either for settlement patterns or for patterns of social interaction.[30] German particularism did not end with the voyage across the Atlantic or with the choice of an American city, and this must be kept in mind when analyzing German settlements in America (as we shall see when we examine the organization of social life in German New York).

The many German-Americans of New York living outside of Kleindeutschland must not be forgotten. Some lived in relative isolation as shopkeepers in non-German neighborhoods. In 1850, James Fenimore Cooper noted the prevalence of Germans among New York's small shopkeepers: "the Germans are driving the Irish from the field. Even the groceries are passing into the hands of the Germans and beer is supplanting whiskey."[31]

In 1852, young Frederick Bultman arrived at his cousin's grocery in the notorious Five Points district (mostly native and Irish) and found

> a small little shack, one story high and very dilapidated. The front being used as a grocery store, then came a bar. In front of this bar was an open space perhaps 12–13 feet square with a large cast iron drum stove in the entry with guard and footrest around it. Here were seated a noisy crowd of the toughest, hardest looking men I had ever seen. We walked into this room and came to another door which led into the living rooms? I question this because it really was only one room, one corner of it was partitioned off for a kitchen. In the other corner on the same side stood the bed. The rest of it was dining room, sitting room, etc., etc., all in one. Between the bar and the living rooms was a little space about four feet by eight feet without window. It was used as a sort of store room or general utility corner. About four feet from the floor was a second story as it were. A cleat on each side

of the wall supported some boards on which was the bedding and this constituted my room. The volume of business on the grocery end of the store was rather small but the other end of it was equal to a little gold mine. The The patronage of the bar room was made up one might say of bums, beggars (professionals), pickpockets, gamblers, yeggmen[32] and all the other classes of criminals. They would plan and relate their exploits around the big stove apparently without fear.[33]

Also near the Five Points was a collection of German-run and largely German-occupied boardinghouses. One of these, on Centre Street, was run by Hermann Hocking of Bavaria and his wife with the help of a pair of German servants. In 1855, it housed twenty-one men, including fourteen Germans, three Irishmen, two Dutchmen, one Frenchman (possibly Alsatian), and one Hungarian.[34] The life of a German boardinghouse was described as "a practical life, half family and half hotel, a little from each (though not always the best). . . . The arrangement of a boardinghouse is very simple. A housekeeping room that also served as the dining room for the boarders; a kitchen with a range capable of handling a cauldron large enough to cook for thirty; bedrooms, as many as possible and as many beds in each room as possible; a chair, washcloth and towel for each man; perhaps a chamber pot for every two men and a table for every three; one mirror and dresser for all who share a room. That's the entire arrangement."[35]

There were also other German neighborhoods in greater New York which were more than just collections of boardinghouses. Some were smaller versions of Kleindeutschland, though rather less diverse. This was particularly true of such major settlements as those in Williamsburg and Hoboken. Others showed a distinct regional and sectarian character, like the southwest German Catholic neighborhoods of Brooklyn's Eighteenth Ward.[36] These latter might be analogous to the more localistic subdistricts within Kleindeutschland.

In the 1870s the Steinway Piano Company began to develop a company town at Long Island City for its predominantly German work force.[37] This town displayed the same sort of occupational specialization as the less formal settlements found around many German breweries. An occupational specialization of another kind existed on "Dutch Hill," a squatter settlement on the promontory at Fortieth Street and First Avenue (overlooking Turtle Bay and the present location of the United Nations). This area was notorious for its poverty and rundown shacks:

Some are of the primitive block form, with a hole in the roof for a chimney; others are arched, others with a sharp Gothic gable. Occasionally something entirely new in architectural style will meet you in the shape of a rectangular box with diamond lattice work, which, on nearer approach,

> you discover to be a railroad car banked in, and made into a house. . . . Each house has a retinue of goats and pigs. . . . All the inhabitants of these buildings are squatters—they have found a plot of ground and have built their log cabin on it, to remain until the rightful owner turns them away. When they move they sell their house to some newcomer for $5 or $10. They are all Irish and German laborers; many of them working in the quarries nearby, and others, especially the German women, living on the sale of the rags and bones which they and their children gather all the day long through the streets of the City.[38]

All of these settlements and settlers combined to make up the metropolis of German New York. It is hard to estimate how many people were part of this metropolis, but the question can be made more manageable by focusing on those who lived within the bounds of New York City itself (Manhattan Island in those years).

The usual procedure used to find the size of an ethnic community based upon nationality is to refer to the census tabulations. This is indeed what Ira Rosenwaike did to develop the standard tables on "Irish and German Ethnic Groups by Nativity" for his population history of New York City,[39] and the census gives us a German population as presented in the first part of table 3. The inadequacy of these figures is brought home, however, when it is noted that even the most heavily German and Irish districts are presented as having American-born majorities. The distortion arises from the inclusion of the American-born children of the immigrants with the older-stock Americans, rather than with their parents. This causes a massive undercalculation of the size of immigrant communities before 1880 and a correspondingly severe understatement of the predominance of the immigrant population in many of America's cities during this period.

To find the true size of the German-American community in New York City (or of any other immigrant community in the United States in this period) it is necessary to return to the manuscript censuses and calculate the ratio between those born in Germany and those born elsewhere who are nonetheless part of the community. This procedure leads to the estimated German-American population shown in table 3, which is from 48 percent to 120 percent higher than that indicated by the census tabulations.

The corrected figures show the development of a great German-American metropolitan center. The German-American community grew tenfold within thirty years and by 1875 encompassed one-third of New York City's population. By 1880, it had reached the size of the entire city of New York in 1845.[40] The German New York metropolis, with over half a million people, was thus a third German capital, larger than any German city other than Berlin or Vienna.[41]

Immigration and natural increase both played their parts in the growth of Kleindeutschland. Only immigration could account for the changes in

Table 3
New York's German-born and German-American Population, 1850–80

Year	German-born Population of New York City (% of New York City total)	Estimated German-American Population of New York City (% of New York City total)	Estimated German-American Population of Metropolitan New York
1850	56,140 (11%)	83,099 (17%)	—
1860	119,997 (15)	200,394 (25)	257,162
1870	153,938 (16)	282,476 (30)	382,236
1880	168,225 (14)	370,095 (31)*	549,142

*The 1880 U.S. census gives a count of New Yorkers of German stock (which does not include Austrians or other German speakers and their children) of 360,960—a comparable figure.

Sources: *Seventh Census of the United States, 1850*, pp. lii, 39; Eighth Census, *Population of the U.S.*, pp. xxxi–xxxii, 316; Ninth Census, *Statistics of Population*, pp. 365–95; Tenth Census, *Statistics of the Population of the United States*, pp. 520–23, 538–41. The estimates for the German-American population of New York City are corrections based on samples drawn from the census manuscripts for 1850, 1860, 1870, and 1880. The estimated German-American population of metropolitan New York shows similarly corrected figures for New York City, Brooklyn (1880-Kings County) and Hudson County, N.J.

origin of the German-born population in this period of rapid growth. By 1880, however, the American-born children of the immigrants came to outnumber their German-born parents and siblings by 201,870 to 168,225, demonstrating a very high rate of natural increase.

The shifting balance between immigration and natural increase may be seen graphically in the accompanying age pyramids (figs. 8–11). In 1850, the age structure of Kleindeutschland was very heavily weighted toward the young adults who made up the bulk of immigrants. The high fertility of these young adults rapidly expanded the base of the age structure, so that children under ten years old made up the largest cohort by 1860.[42] The preponderance of those in their twenties among female immigrants (even through 1870)[43] assured that the teenage cohort remained disproportionately small. By 1880, natural increase had completely eclipsed immigration as the primary source of community growth. At that point the age pyramid took on a "normal" shape for a rapidly growing population.

Residential Persistence and Community

Some studies show that the settlers of the German communities of the American Midwest often arrived there after several years in New York (in a process known as step-migration).[44] It is difficult to estimate just how

Figure 8

The Total Population of Kleindeutschland in 1850

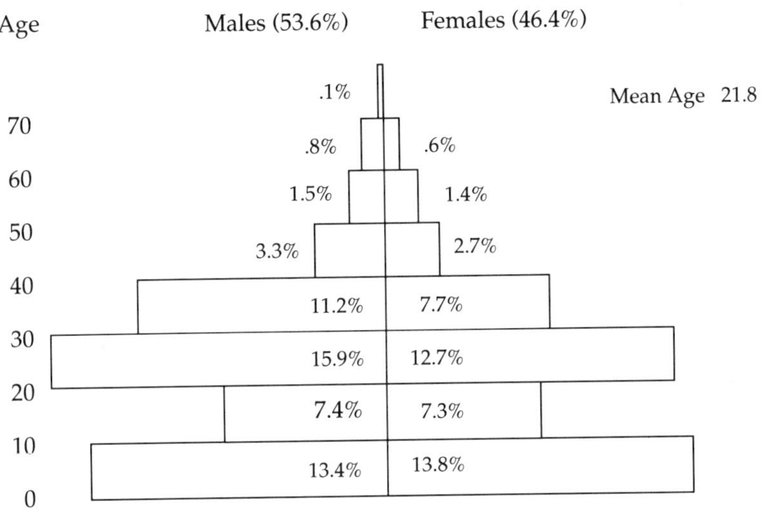

Source: Author's census samples

Figure 9

The Population of Kleindeutschland in 1860

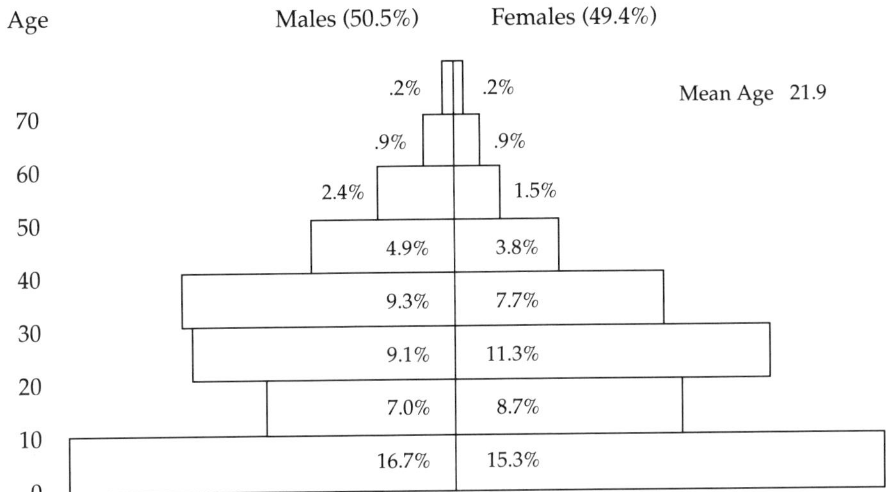

Source: Author's census samples

Figure 10

The Population of Kleindeutschland in 1870

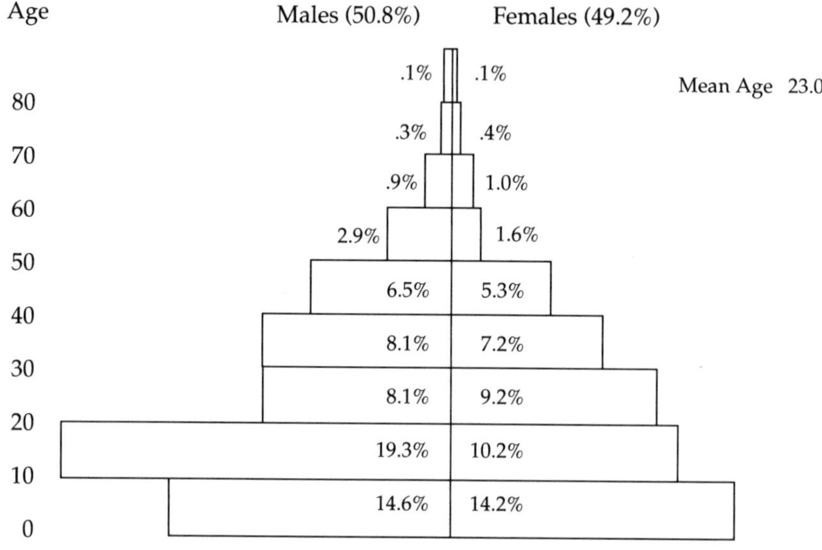

Source: Author's census samples

Figure 11

The Population of Kleindeutschland in 1880

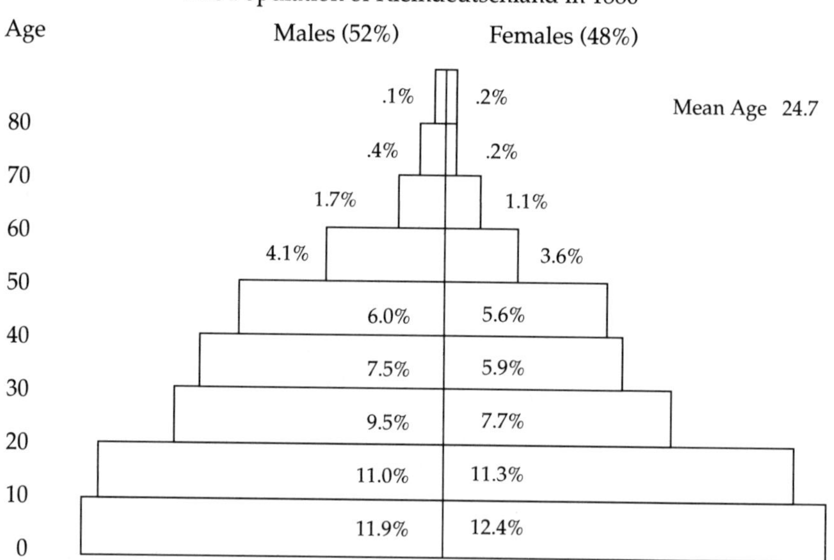

Source: Author's census samples

significant this practice was, but the steady increases in the size of the over-forty age cohorts in German New York indicate a strong core of residential persistence.

The interpretation of persistence is a somewhat subjective matter, however. When Thernstrom was considering nineteenth-century Newburyport, he criticized the view of "community as a self-contained entity with a stable population core" as an "illusion" and a "myth."[45] If this logic is extended to a far more fluid immigrant settlement like Kleindeutschland, it raises the question of whether a community may be considered to have existed there at all. Thernstrom and others have tested persistence by taking a sample of the population and seeing how many members remained ten, twenty, and thirty years later. This method is appropriate for studying the geographic mobility of individuals, but it tells us much less than we need to know about the stability of a community. When community dynamics are the object of our study, it becomes necessary to analyze the resident population in terms of how long its members have been present. This will tell us if there is in fact any stable core.

Tracing sample members back through city directories is a laborious and uncertain process, especially when dealing with a very large and often incompletely recorded immigrant community like Kleindeutschland. The manuscript census provides another source of information about the persistence of at least part of the population. Those families with children born in New York (admittedly a more stable element of the population) can be assigned a minimum period of residence in the city—one equal to the age of the oldest New-York-born child.[46]

In 1850, 82 percent of Kleindeutschland's residents lived with their families, and 37 percent of these families had children who were born in New York (see table 4). The average minimum length of residence for the families with children born in New York was 6.3 years, with about 25 percent of these families having lived there for ten years or more, and 3.5 percent for twenty years or more. This was a new population without many old-timers, but, with an average stay of over six years, it was not entirely green either.

A decade later, families with children born in New York were much more representative of all of the city's German population. They accounted for 64 percent of all families by 1860. The massive influx of newcomers, which enlarged the population nearly 2.5 times in that decade, kept the average minimum length of residence down to 6.7 years (though about 25 percent had lived in the city ten or more years). The old-timers, with twenty or more years of residence, were thus reduced to only 2.5 percent. In effect, the more stable core of population was of hardly any greater residential persistence than that of 1850, but it now comprised nearly 60 percent of the residents of the quarter.

The decade of the 1860s saw the Civil War and economic disruption, followed by renewed immigration. By 1870, the more stable core of Kleindeutschland's residents had expanded to encompass 69 percent of the community's families and they had an average minimum tenure of 11.6 years. In addition, the long-term residents (those of twenty or more years) had now become a significant sector of the population—11.8 percent.

The final decade of our study, ending in 1880, was one of increasing population stability. The economic crash of 1873 reduced immigration to a trickle for the next seven years. Second-generation German-Americans were now forming families in Kleindeutschland, and by 1880 the majority of Kleindeutschlanders had been born in New York. The core families now made up 80 percent of the total and their average minimum length of residence was an impressive 16.8 years. By this time, nearly one out of every six families had lived there for twenty-five years or more.

Literary evidence confirms that Kleindeutschland was not merely a statistical but also a self-conscious community. One author's metaphor for the German quarter was "unser Haus," our house. There, new immigrants were carefully inspected for respectability by all the residents of the block as they moved in. If they were "gut in Zeug," "well turned out," the neighbors soon dropped by to welcome them to the street (and to see if they shared common ties in the old country). It was a highly sociable community and one resident concluded that: "Our quarter is justly called 'little Germany'; it is an island of true German small-towners in a metropolitan sea of houses."[47]

Thus the community of Kleindeutschland grew from a thin cluster of new immigrants in the 1840s into a large and stable ethnic enclave. The people of Kleindeutschland were neither Thernstrom's transient poor nor Handlin's uprooted peasants, for they had set down roots in their new land.

Table 4
Residential Persistence of
Kleindeutschland's Families, 1850–80

Year	Residents Living in Families	Number of Families in Sample	Families with N.Y.-born Children	Average Minimum Residence in Years	Families Living 20-yrs or more in N.Y.C.*
1850	82%	318	37%	6.3	3.5%
1860	91	411	64	6.7	2.5
1870	90	439	69	11.6	11.8
1880	91	504	80	16.8	34.0

*Of families with New-York-born children or second-generation German-American adults.
Source: author's census samples.

CHAPTER THREE

Marriage, Family, and Household

Kinship and the Immigrant

Kinship is the oldest and most basic social mechanism for ordering human existence. Even in complex societies organized around a sophisticated division of labor and complicated by class and ethnic formations, the primary attachment of most individuals is to a group of close relatives.[1] The Germans of Kleindeutschland followed this pattern by forming their community around these primary relationships.

Of course, many individuals emigrated alone to America and had no kin there to receive them. Some of these emigrants may have deliberately broken off the ties to their families of origin by crossing the ocean. All but the most isolated individuals, however, remained enmeshed in the complex of economic, social, and psychological needs that are most often met by family and kin. If they lacked kin in America, such immigrants were forced to rely upon the ties of friendship and common origin (or even to depend upon the operations of the marketplace) to meet these needs. They lived in boardinghouses or lodged with their employers; sometimes they boarded with the family of a friend or coworker. They were "joiners" who filled the ranks of voluntary associations and they were the mainstay of the multitudes of beer halls and wine cellars of Kleindeutschland.

Most immigrants found this familyless condition unsatisfactory. The pseudofamily of the boardinghouse was no substitute for the real thing and networks of friends were rarely as reliable as those of kin. The social contacts of associations and saloons were major sources of satisfaction to those with or without families, but they were rarely sufficient. Psychological stability, long-term satisfaction, and cultural expectations all demanded the reestablishment of family and kin. Most unattached immigrants soon remedied their condition. They encouraged family members and kin to join them from Germany when they could (often sending a prepaid ticket along with their letters to facilitate the process). With or without old family ties, they married and established new families in New York.[2]

Some men waited until they were economically secure, and then used family networks in the old country to find brides "uncontaminated" by the freer atmosphere of the metropolis. Others sought a wife among the young women who attended the numerous dances and festivals, or even among the beer hall serving-girls of dubious reputation (that is, "dubious" to the sort of straitlaced Victorian observers who provide most of the reports on these places). Some ambitious young men looked for widows with businesses that needed tending. Women had fewer options, but the rigors of a single woman's life in New York provided a great incentive toward marriage, whether of love or convenience.

Endogamy[3]

Selecting a spouse was a far from random matter, even from the point of view of a disinterested observer. Who married whom reveals a good deal about the values of those who immigrated to Kleindeutschland. First of all, they married their "own kind." In 1850, German-born men heavily outnumbered German-born women. Yet, only 8.1 percent of the Germans whose oldest child had been born in New York (and therefore of those who were most likely to have married in America) were married to native-born Americans or others of non-German origin (Irish, English, and Scots). This figure slipped to 7.8 percent in 1860, and then (in what has been portrayed as the period of heaviest migration of singles)[4] dropped to 4.4 percent in 1870 and 2.5 percent in 1880. Thus we find a picture of increasing endogamy with no sign of assimilation into the wider population through marriage. Only a severe shortage of suitable candidates within their ranks drove some German immigrants to seek spouses elsewhere.[5] Lest it be thought that our sample might be biased by the inclusion of some couples who married in Germany, but had no children before emigrating to the United States, the 1880 census data provide a check. The 1880 census recorded the parents' place of birth, which allows us to calculate the degree of outmarriage for those children of the German immigrants who were born and raised in New York. Only 5 percent of these were married to non-German Americans.[6] These 92 to 97.5 percent endogamy rates for Kleindeutschland are very high, but a study of intermarriage in Detroit in the 1890s found the Germans to be among the most endogamous groups in the city, with 78.4 percent of their marriages within the group.[7]

That Germans married Germans is not too surprising. Even the second generation's clear preference for German-American marriage partners fits comfortably within our expectations and parallels the known behavior of other immigrant groups in the United States. A closer examination of the figures, however, leads us to some more-striking conclusions. The ultimate social test of one's kind is "would you marry one?" Put to this test, the Germans of Kleindeutschland turn out to have had a much narrower conception of "their own kind" than we might have supposed. In addition to a probable tendency to marry within their faith, they displayed a strong tendency toward a regional or subnational endogamy, one that closely parallels the patterns of social interaction observed by anthropologists among modern urban migrants in Africa and Latin America.[8] While only a few studies have looked for similar patterns among American immigrants, they have been noted among Jews, Italians, Slovaks, and Rumanians in the twentieth century and among some Irish in the nineteenth century.[9]

In 1860, the largest "nationality" in Kleindeutschland was the Bavarians. Seventy-two percent of married Bavarians were married to other Bavarians.[10] If we add those married to spouses from other states in the southwest part of Germany (that is, Baden, Württemberg, and the adjacent Hesses), the endogamy rate is raised to 90 percent. By 1880, Bavarians constituted a much smaller portion of the pool of possible marriage partners in Kleindeutschland and only 55 percent of them were married to other Bavarians. Regional endogamy was still strong, however, and 80 percent were married to spouses born in Bavaria or adjacent states. Second-generation Bavarian-Americans also practiced this regional endogamy. In 1880, 43 percent were married to Bavarians or their descendants and 85 percent to German-Americans from within the region.[11]

The Prussians reversed the Bavarians' pattern of decreasing endogamy as they replaced the Bavarians as the leading "nationality."[12] In 1860, they constituted less than 20 percent of the population, but they were married to other Prussians 65 percent of the time. Marriages to spouses born in the other northern states (which broke up the geographic continuity of Prussia) raises this endogamy rate to 76 percent. Twenty years later, in 1880, they were the largest "nationality" in Kleindeutschland. The proportion of Prussians married to other Prussians increased to 77 percent and their rate of regional endogamy went up to 86 percent. Their children appear to have intensified this pattern, having an endogamy rate of 92 percent (though this may somewhat overstate the case as the sample of second-generation marriages is small).[13]

The Germans from the smaller states (or those less well represented in Kleindeutschland's population) were less able to attain the high levels of state endogamy set by the Bavarians and the Prussians.[14] Their rates of inmarriage ranged downward, from the Württembergers' 64 percent in 1880 to the Hanoverians' low of 22 percent in 1860 (still a high rate when we remember that Hanoverians were only 4.5 percent of New York's German population that year). Despite their lesser exclusivity, they still displayed a strong marriage preference for Germans from their home region. While the Badeners demonstrated an unusually low rate of endogamy for a major "nationality" in 1880 (only 24 percent),[15] their regional endogamy rate was much higher—76 percent were married to spouses from Baden or an adjacent territory.

This pattern of high regional endogamy is repeated by each of the "nationalities" that made up Kleindeutschland's population.[16] Religious compatibility was one of the factors contributing to regional endogamy, but the lack of intermarriage between Catholic Bavarians and Catholic Austrians (for example) suggests that this is not a sufficient explanation. Linguistic compatibility may have been at least as important in the selection of a spouse, given the relative lack of mutual intelligibility between nineteenth-century German dialects.[17] After all, a couple might want to be able to relax at home and use their native speech (though this would not have been a factor in the continuing endogamy of the English-speaking American-born generation). What we can say for certain is that the social boundaries were marked, and that they were rarely crossed by matrimony.

Kleindeutschlanders were not the only German-Americans to practice such provincial and regional endogamy. Similar practices seem to have been common in Philadelphia and Pittsburgh at the time. The Pittsburgh case is most instructive, because the endogamous patterns showed up strongly within congregations, where virtually all marriages were within the faith. This, then, eliminates the possibility that the Kleindeutschland figures might have been produced by a convergence of religious and regional endogamous patterns, in which regional endogamy was only an artifact of an underlying religious endogamy.[18]

These patterns of state and regional endogamy, combined with the indications of residential concentration by nativity (presented in Chapter 2, above), provide evidence for a pervasive informal social separation between Germans of different "nationalities" in Kleindeutschland. For the Germans of New York, family and kin (and, very likely, friendships as well)[19] were organized on a regional basis, one that had its roots in the settlement patterns of the ancient "tribal" divisions of the German barbarians and in the continued persistence of a highly developed German particularism into the modern era. The result was a sort of subnational ethnicity that was at least as compelling for many Kleindeutschlanders as the broader German ethnicity ascribed to them by nationalist ideologues. Indeed, the new nationalism of the nineteenth century, which culminated in the German Empire of 1871,[20] does not seem to have greatly affected social organization on the level of family formation and kinship.

Family Structure

The reconstitution of family form and structure from single-census data leaves much to be desired. It gives a view of each family at only one point in time and rarely captures the entire picture. Some children are not yet born and others are already gone from the home, or even dead. Some information, like age at marriage, is simply not to be had. Despite these problems, however, the census data do provide access to the family life of the community and can be used to reconstruct some of its outlines.

While we do not know the average age at marriage in Kleindeutschland, we do know that the average age at which women had their first child was 23.9 years (fluctuating irregularly between a high of 24.2 and a low of 23.3). It would therefore seem likely that women were married by age twenty-three or younger.[21] Men averaged 28.1 years at the birth of their first child, so they were probably married by the age of twenty-seven.[22]

Husbands were older than their wives in 84 percent of Kleindeutschland's families, by, on the average, just over five years (5.1 to 5.6 years). There was no pattern of regular change in this figure and it seems to have been independent of any demographic changes that took place. This was not the case for the 16 percent of families in which the wife was older than her husband. The proportion of such families remained the same (while the number and proportion of older women in Kleindeutschland's population rose) but the age difference between wife and husband slowly increased from 2.8 years in 1860 to 3.7 years in 1880. The rise was probably the result of an increase in the numbers of widows who had remarried and who had married younger men (the proverbial clerk or journeyman who married the boss's widow).[23]

The changing age structure of Kleindeutschland is reflected in the development of its families. From 1850 to 1880, the average age of family heads rose from 35.5 to 42.8. The families of the later years were generally older and had more children (see table 5), rising from an average of 2.66 children to 3.16 children. That this change is the result of the census having caught families at a later stage in their developmental cycle, rather than a change in fertility, is indicated by the lack of any corresponding changes in the figures for women's ages at the birth of either their first or their last child.[24] These rapidly growing families were a major source of Kleindeutschland's growth, especially in periods when immigration slackened. Indeed, in each census year after 1850, the average number of children for Kleindeutschland's families was greater than the United States average, and considerably greater than the average for families in the Northeast.

Most of the factors in family formation seem to be German-national in

Table 5
Age of Family Head and Number of Children per Family, 1850–80

Year	Average Age of Head of Family in Kleindeutschland	Average Number of Children per Family in Kleindeutschland	Average Number of Children per Family in U.S.*	Average Number of Children per Family in N.E. U.S.*
1850	35.5	2.66	2.76	2.40
1860	37.5	2.72	2.67	2.36
1870	40.5	2.95	2.34	2.13
1880	42.8	3.16	2.70	2.38

Sources: For U.S. and northeastern U.S. figures, see Rudy Ray Seward, *The American Family,* pp. 93, 133. Kleindeutschland figures from author's census samples.

character, insofar as variations in numbers of children and age of mothers at first and last births fluctuate around the "national" average (that is the "national" average for Germans in New York) without regard to state or region of origin. There is, however, one exception to this. Women from Baden and Württemberg (adjacent states in the region known as Swabia) had the same number of children as their compatriots but they had them later in their life cycle, having their first child when they were about a year older than women from other parts of Germany and their last child when they were two to three years older than other women in Kleindeutschland.[25] This could be a manifestation of religious influence, as Catholic areas in Germany are reported to have been associated with later marriage.[26] The Bavarians, who were also (most likely) Catholics from southwest Germany, had their children as young as other Kleindeutschlanders, however, so we are more likely to be dealing with a Swabian regional characteristic than a religious one.

The association between early/late first births and early/late last births does suggest one interesting conclusion: despite the rapid rate of natural increase, which suggests unrestricted procreation, the people of Kleindeutschland appear to have been practicing some form of family limitation. This conclusion is reinforced by the low average age of mothers at the birth of their last child—only thirty-six years.[27] Coitus interruptus and abstinence were the most likely methods of birth control used, though abortifacients were widely advertised in the German press (under the guise of pills to "regulate the monthly cycle") and even infanticide was not unknown.[28]

Patterns of family formation and childbearing within Kleindeutschland were affected more by occupational and economic factors than by the mother's place of origin in Germany.[29] Men without skills or property married later and had children later than other men. Their wives were also older when their children were born, but, as this was the case for last children as well as first, their completed families were of average size for the community. Skilled workers and artisans (and their wives) began their families at about the average age for Kleindeutschland, but continued having children a little longer and had more of them. White-collar workers also had their first child at about the average age, but they typically married younger women who then started having children at an early age. Few white-collar workers remained in that category long enough to complete their families, and it appears likely that most of them joined the ranks of the propertied.[30] Those who owned property were more likely to have married late, but like white-collar workers they married younger women. The wives of property-owners were, in keeping with their youth in starting families, younger than any other group of women at the birth of their last child.[31] Despite the early completion of their families, the wives of property owners still managed to have more children (or at least more surviving children) than any other women in Kleindeutschland. Finally, professionals married late but had about the average number of children. The economic logic of many of these variations is obvious, but the Kleindeutschlanders' success at adapting their family size to their circumstances reinforces the notion that they were carrying out effective family planning.

The consistent occupational and class differences in family development cut across most of the regional boundaries that frequently divided Kleindeutschland into separate communities. They contributed, instead, to the formation of ethnic norms that distinguished Kleindeutschland as a whole from non-German communities in New York City. Within these broad cultural norms, the timing and spacing of childbirth was a matter of relatively rational response to economic factors. This notion of ethnic norms as predominant is reinforced by Olivier Zunz's study of Detroit, which indicates a stronger correlation between ethnicity and fertility than between occupational status and fertility.[32]

The families of Kleindeutschland took many forms, but most took the form that is generally the most common—the nuclear family.[33] Over 66 percent of all families consisted of a husband and wife and their children. Another 15 percent were couples without children, so nuclear families accounted for over 80 percent of all of Kleindeutschland's families. Women without spouses headed about 7 percent of the families, which was well under the United States averages in this period (10 to 11 percent)[34] and only a fraction of the 18 percent of Irish families in New York's Sixth Ward that were headed by women.[35]

It is generally taken for granted that immigrants, having a relatively small older population and fewer kinship links in the United States than natives, were less likely than native-born Americans to form extended families. Seward's demographic history of the American family shows this to have been the case for the United States as a whole,[36] but German New York (at least) appears to have been an exception. While the percentages for extended families in the nation ran from 2.4 to 3.4 percent from 1850 to 1870 and then jumped to 7.3 percent in 1880, the Kleindeutschland figures varied between 6.5 percent and 13.9 percent (see table 6).[37] These relatively high figures are consistent with Zunz's finding for 1880 Detroit, that 10.4 percent of all German families were extended.[38] Lest this be thought to be a peculiarly German trait, we note that the percentage of extended families among the Irish of the Sixth Ward was 11 percent in 1855.[39]

Table 6
Extended Families as a Percentage of All Families, 1850–80

Location	1850	1860	1870	1880
United States	2.4	2.7	3.4	7.3
Northeastern U.S.	3.4	3.8	4.2	8.8
Kleindeutschland	13.9	6.5	9.0	8.3

Sources: For U.S. and northeastern U.S. figures, Seward, *American Family*, pp. 86, 130. Kleindeutschland figures are from author's census samples.

These census-based figures may also significantly understate the numbers of extended families in German New York. Extended families that were not in desperate circumstances would not have crowded into one of Kleindeutschland's small tenement apartments. They would, rather, have occupied two or more adjacent apartments where they would have been counted by the census as separate households and families. For example, in 1883 the tailor Konrad Carl lived in a three-room apartment on the fifth floor of a Christie Street tenement with his wife and three children (a simple nuclear family to any census taker or to any researcher relying on census records). What didn't show in the census return was that the adjacent three-room apartment had been occupied by his married daughter and her family ever since her marriage a few years before. Carl himself considered this arrangement to be an extended family household.[40] Then there was the Gompers clan, which lived at 85 Columbia Street in 1880. It dwarfed Carl's little extended family. Numbering twenty-five individuals, nine adults and sixteen children, the clan occupied four adjacent apartments comprising one entire floor of the tenement. The Gompers clan was not a true extended family because Samuel Gompers, his father, his father's brother, and his father's brother-in-law each maintained a distinct nuclear household with separate finances. Nonetheless, the adjacent apartments, separated by stairs from their neighbors and with their doors often left open on the common hallway, made for a physical and social proximity that would have amounted to a pretty close approximation of the real thing.[41] Unfortunately, we have no way of estimating how common these patterns might have been, but they may well have been fairly typical by the late 1860s.

Even the understated census-based figures, however, force us to reconsider one of the major myths of the social sciences. Thomas Jefferson was far from the first political theorist to characterize cities as dens of social disruption and degeneration, whose debased plebeians were contrasted with the virtuous yeomanry of the countryside. In the course of the nineteenth century this primal myth was incorporated into the developing social sciences by analysts like Henry George—who called the urban masses "the new barbarians" and compared them to those who extinguished Roman civilization, warning "Go through the squalid quarters of great cities, and you may see, even now, their gathering hordes! How shall learning perish? Men will cease to read and books will kindle fires and be turned into cartridges!"

This tradition of analysis, though in rather less apocalyptic terms, continued to be developed in the works of such seminal figures as Louis Wirth in sociology, Robert Redfield in anthropology, and Oscar Handlin in history.[42] They portrayed rural migrants as abandoning the extended family along with other rural virtues, in response to the disrupting influences of urban life. Later revisionist considerations of the problem have questioned the notion that the extended family was a widespread practice before urbanization and have presented the predominance of the nuclear family as a form of continuity, but they have not challenged the premise that the extended family is somehow a desirable manifestation of virtue. Contrary to both the stereotype and the revisionist formulation, however, we have found that urban life promoted the extended family among immigrants. The adoption of this form of family was not the selection of a desirable option but rather a response to the shock of a transition that called upon all the resources the kinship network could muster. The consolidation of residence was one way of easing the strain upon immigrant families. Even after the initial period of adjustment to America's cities, the extended family continued to provide essential unemployment and retirement benefits for many immigrants— who were, after all, among the more vulnerable members of an American society that provided little in the way of such benefits.

Contrary to our received wisdom, the high proportion of extended families among urban immigrants will help to explain the fact that extended families were far more common in the northeastern states (where immigrants from Ireland and Germany provided the bulk of the urban population) than in the rest of the country. Thus, the still-prevalent notion that immigrant families were the "least likely to be extended" will have to be reversed on the basis of the evidence developed here.[43]

There were, however, state and regional variations in the distribution of different types of family structure in Kleindeutschland (see table 7).

Badeners did not form extended families and had an unusually heavy concentration in two-generation nuclear families. Bavarians were also more likely than other Germans to live in two-generation nuclear families, but in their case it was because there were fewer childless couples and Bavarians were as likely as the members of most other groups to be found in extended families. Hanoverians reversed the Badeners' pattern, forming extended families at half-again the average rate (and thereby reducing the proportion of two-generation nuclear families). The roots of these patterns are obscure. Did Badeners leave their aged parents to fend for themselves—or did they support them in independent households? Was there a causal relationship between the Hanoverians' preference for living in extended families and their high degree of residential segregation from other Germans? These questions, raised by our analysis of the data, deal with areas that were important to the people we are studying. Unfortunately,

Table 7
Variation in Kleindeutschlanders' Family Structure by German State of Origin, 1860–80

German State	Number of Families in Sample	Percentage in Two-Generation Nuclear Families	Percentage in One-Generation Nuclear Families	Percentage in Extended Families	Percentage with Coresident Siblings
Baden	97	80.4	17.5	1.0	1.0
Bavaria	187	79.7	9.1	8.6	2.7
Hanover	41	70.1	14.6	12.2	2.4
Hesse-Nassau	126	75.4	14.3	8.7	1.6
Prussia	209	74.9	15.1	9.7	0.4
Württemberg	85	74.1	17.6	7.1	1.2

Source: Author's census samples.

we cannot answer them with the sources available to us, but we can at least note their significance.

Family structure, like the patterns of family formation and childbearing, varied with occupation as much as with origin (see table 8). Although one-fifth to one-half of unskilled workers lived apart from their relatives (the great variation in this proportion suggests the high mobility of this sector of the work force), the rest of the unskilled were more likely than other Kleindeutschland families to have no children and to live in single-generation nuclear families. They were also, however, more likely than any other group of workers to live in extended families, nearly twice as likely as the artisans and skilled workers who were economically more secure.[44]

Nearly two-thirds of semiskilled and service workers lived in nonfamily settings. This was because most of those who fit this category were live-in servants. Sisters in service together also account for the higher than usual proportion of coresident sibling families among these workers. Those who did live with their families were the least likely of all to live in extended families.

Table 8
Variations in Family Structure
by Occupational Category in Kleindeutschland, 1850–80

Occupational Category	Number of Families in Sample	Percentage in Two-Generation Nuclear Families	Percentage in One-Generation Nuclear Families	Percentage in Extended Families	Percentage with Coresident Siblings
Unskilled	38	68.4	21.0	10.5	0.0
Semiskilled and Service	86	72.0	19.8	3.5	4.7
Artisans and Skilled	597	75.9	17.1	5.7	1.3
White-Collar Workers	37	67.6	16.2	8.1	8.1
Proprietors	307	73.0	13.7	12.4	1.0
Professionals	55	76.4	9.1	12.7	1.8

Source: Author's census samples.

White-collar workers were predominantly store clerks and, like servants, often young and single. Half to two-thirds lived in nonfamily settings, frequently with their employer and his family. The common practice of younger brothers clerking for their older siblings resulted in white-collar workers being found in sibling coresidences nearly six times more frequently than other Kleindeutschlanders.

Artisans and skilled workers displayed the strongest preference for the nuclear family of any group in Kleindeutschland. They were free from the pressures of employers that kept servants from forming their own households, older and more independent than clerks, and free from the more severe economic constraints that impelled the unskilled to rely on extended family households. At the same time, they were unable to afford the more expansive living quarters that appear to have enabled wealthier Kleindeutschlanders to welcome nonnuclear relations into their households without discomfort. Thus only 5.7 percent of Kleindeutschland's artisans and skilled workers lived in extended families.

At the upper end of the social scale, the property-owning bourgeoisie[45] of Kleindeutschland formed extended families at a rate of 12.4 percent. The bourgeois preference for extended families is most noticeable in 1870, when a good breakdown by property holdings is available. That year, two-thirds of the proprietors living in extended families had holdings worth $10,000 or more. Of all wealthy families, 31.25 percent were extended, compared with only 3.9 percent of those of proprietors with holdings worth under $1,000.

The only occupational category that showed a greater proportion of extended families than the bourgeoisie as a whole was the professionals, though their rate did not begin to approach that of the wealthy. A correlation between wealth or class and the extended forms of the family is commonly found in western industrial societies,[46] but it generally takes the form of a linear relation where the greater the wealth, the higher the incidence of extended families. The pattern of Kleindeutschland, where the poorest also had a higher incidence of extended families, calls for a more sophisticated explanation of the relationship between class and family structure than is usually suggested.

The Household

Like the census takers of 1850–70, modern Americans are prone to confuse the concepts of family and household.[47] In our discussions so far, we have been dealing only with related members of the household, i.e., family members, and have ignored non-kin. Non-kin were not, however, of negligible importance, either in absolute numbers or in their significance to family economies and social relations. In 1850, nearly half of all family-based households included nonfamily members (see table 9).[48] The rapid falling-off of this figure, to less than half of this rate by

1870–80, suggests that recent immigrants were often the ones most likely to bring nonfamily members into their households. This may have resulted from a greater need for the stabilizing effect of the income from boarders in the family economy of new arrivals. This hypothesis is reinforced when we note that the percentage of families with boarders (as opposed to employees) dropped even more drastically, from 30.3 percent to 11.1 percent. The similarity of the 1870 and 1880 figures, however, indicates that the proportion of families taking in boarders did not continue to decline even though the proportion of recently arrived immigrants did so through the later years of our study.

Table 9
Percentage of Households with Nonfamily Members
in Kleindeutschland, 1850–80

Year	Percentage with Nonfamily Residents	Percentage with Boarders/ Lodgers	Percentage with Employees Resident
1850	42.0	30.3	11.9
1860	27.0	16.5	10.5
1870	19.6	11.7	7.9
1880	19.6	11.1	8.5

Source: Author's census samples.

As with family structure, we find that immigrants from different parts of Germany varied in their willingness to accept nonfamily members into their households (see table 10). Saxons and Württembergers were the most resistant to mixed-kin households while Prussians and Hanoverians were most open to them. Again, as with family structure, the roots of these patterns are obscure. The large differences between the "nationalities" do suggest that some cultural differences were having a significant effect on these households, even if we cannot explain their nature, and this again reinforces the general sense we have developed that subnational ethnicity was a major factor in the daily life of Kleindeutschland.

Occupational variations are of the sort that would be expected. Poor families shared their quarters to make ends meet while those who were somewhat better off took in boarders to get ahead. More successful families had servants to help out with the work of caring for boarders, or dispensed with the boarders and just had servants. The majority were able to dispense with boarders but could not afford servants.

This is a pattern that seems obvious because it is conditioned by factors that we tend to see as "natural" and "objective," though they are

Table 10
Variation in Household Structure by
German State of Origin in Kleindeutschland, 1850–80

German State	Number of Households in Sample	Percentage with Non-kin	Percentage with Boarders	Percentage with Resident Employees
Baden	95	22.1	9.5	12.6
Bavaria	182	18.1	13.7	4.4
Hanover	40	22.5	17.5	5.0
Hesse-Nassau	120	20.8	12.5	8.3
Prussia	252	25.8	15.9	9.9
Saxony	35	11.4	2.9	8.6
Württemberg	80	13.8	7.5	6.3
All Germans	804	22.1	13.1	9.0

Source: Author's census samples.

really no more so than the cultural values that have underlain the other patterns of family and household structure we have examined. The effective definition of what a family can "afford" at any given income level is clearly something that can change with the cultural expectations and values of different sectors of the population; for example, immigrants from some parts of Germany may have been more willing to give up some privacy (by taking in boarders) to maintain the level of respectability symbolized by having servants, while immigrants from other parts of Germany may have valued privacy as a greater symbol of respectability (or as a greater value in its own right).

Conclusions

We have found that Kleindeutschland was not a homogeneous mass of randomly differentiated families and households, but rather an ethnically based community with a distinct social structure. Kinship and residence organized the community along two axes, one economic and the other cultural. In such matters as variations in numbers of children and the age at which families were begun, the economic principle predominates, while in the selection of marriage partners and neighborhoods cultural (subnational or regional) affinity appears to have carried more weight. One could attempt to quantify the relative importance of economic and cultural factors in each case, but it is probably more meaningful to regard Kleindeutschland's social organization as a complex web of interlocking and mutually dependent relationships. These combined to determine the patterns of formation, size, and structure of Kleindeutschland's families and households. At the same time that "nationality" and class divided the population into small and fairly homogeneous groups (like Bavarian shopkeepers or Hessian artisans), the population was integrated by the crosscutting and overlapping of affiliations. For example, a Bavarian shopkeeper was both a Bavarian and a shopkeeper; it was the combination of these two identities that helped to locate him and his family in the social world of Kleindeutschland. Thus the very principles that provide the rationale for the community's internal differentiation can also be seen to have provided the mechanism for integration. The large and heterogeneous population of Germans in New York were members of a new and growing community—Little Germany.

CHAPTER FOUR

Making a Living

German immigrants to New York City were drawn into a rapidly expanding commercial and industrial metropolis. By the 1840s it had long been the premier city of North America and its importance in the American and world economies continued to grow through the rest of the century. This economic expansion made New York attractive to the multitudes of German immigrants, but it was also the multitudes of German (and Irish) immigrants who made the expansion possible.[1]

The immigrants did not merely enter the economy as isolated individuals—they colonized it. At first the Germans dominated a few trades; then many trades, entire industries, and even whole sectors of the economy became German in character. This chapter will examine the ethnic division of the New York economy, focusing on the emerging German sectors, and then look at the development of many of the most important German occupations. We shall see how the economy of Kleindeutschland evolved and became the basis for a German-American class structure, in which German factory workers and shopkeepers were flanked by a German criminal underclass and by German captains of industry.

Germans in New York's Economy

The earliest year for which we have an ethnic breakdown of New York's occupational structure is 1855. That is a full decade after this study begins, but it is just after the peak of the first major wave of immigration from Germany and it provides an excellent base against which to compare data on changes in the occupational structures of New York City and Kleindeutschland.[2]

Some occupations were already German preserves, with Germans accounting for more than half of their practitioners. While many of these were small, specialized trades like furriers and brewers (with fewer than three hundred practitioners each in 1855), other German-dominated trades had thousands of members. There were nearly seven thousand German tailors, thirty-seven hundred German shoemakers, and twenty-seven hundred German furniture makers who dominated their trades in

1855. German bakers and tobacco workers were not far behind in numbers and thoroughly dominated their sectors of the economy (see table 11).[3]

Table 11
Numbers of German-born Workers in Selected Trades in New York City, 1855–80, and the Percent of Each Trade, German-born.

Trade	1855	1870	1880
All Occupations	45,764 (22%)	78,410 (22%)	96,657 (18%)
Tailors[a]	6,709 (53)	7,536 (41)	8,381 (42)
Boot and Shoemakers	3,721 (55)	3,350 (48)	1,220 (42)
Cabinetmakers and Upholsterers	2,153 (61)	3,103 (61)	2,833 (51)
Bakers	1,987 (54)	2,111 (55)	2,721 (54)
Tobacconists	1,227 (61)	2,812 (51)	3,555 (27)
Butchers	n. a.	2,391 (49)	3,102 (42)
Brewers and Distillers	190 (53)	482 (70)	1,243 (74)
Carpenters	1,664 (22)	2,889 (28)	2,597 (25)
Laborers	1,870 (9)	3,335 (12)	2,955 (8)
Domestic Servants	4,493 (14)	5,406 (11)	6,614 (12)

Note: These figures are for German-*born* only, thus they do not reflect the actual totals for Kleindeutschland either in absolute numbers or percentages. This is especially true in the later years when nearly 25 percent of Kleindeutschland's labor force was American-born.

[a]This category includes seamstresses in 1870; the 1880 figure is an estimate intended to continue to exclude the milliners and dressmakers previously listed separately.

Sources: For 1855 figures, Ernst, *Immigrant Life in New York City*, pp. 214–17; for 1870, *Ninth Census of the United States*, p. 793; for 1880, *Compendium of the Tenth Census*, p. 892.

There were other occupations in 1855 where the Germans were the largest ethnic group even though they were not a majority (or not yet a majority). This was the case in some occupations that employed large numbers of Germans, like food dealers (3,045 Germans), peddlers (941 Germans), and musical-instrument makers (324 Germans). Although they did not dominate all the skilled trades by any means, most of the occupations that they did dominate were skilled trades[4] or related to the distribution of food and dry goods. Altogether, there were 45,764 gainfully occupied Germans listed in the 1855 (New York state) census of New York City and at least 58 percent were in occupations that the Germans dominated. Most of those Germans who worked outside these trades were either in domestic service, general labor, or carpentry (see table 11).

Over the next twenty-five years the Germans and the Irish continued to divide an expanding immigrant sector of the economy (one that included most of the productive labor in the city) along much the same lines that had developed by 1855.[5] In 1880, half of the Germans were engaged in manufacturing while half of the Irish were in general labor or service. They thus established a long-lived ethnic division of the New York labor market, one that continued long after the Germans and the Irish had had their places taken by later immigrants from eastern and southern Europe.[6]

The mid-nineteenth-century ethnic division of labor between the Germans and the Irish was common to both of the major eastern manufacturing centers, New York and Philadelphia. Farther west unskilled German laborers were more common. The midwestern cities contained fewer Irish laborers competing for unskilled jobs and they attracted large numbers of Germans from rural districts, immigrants who went to these cities hoping to work there only long enough to save toward the ownership of midwestern farms. Indeed, while Germans provided their proportionate share of unskilled laborers in the midsize manufacturing centers of Baltimore, Chicago, Cincinnati, and St. Louis, they provided far more than their share of unskilled workers in less-industrialized cities from Syracuse to Milwaukee.

On the other hand, even in cities with large numbers of unskilled German workers, substantial numbers of skilled Germans tended to dominate the same trades (especially clothing, shoe, and furniture making).[7] In other words, skilled German-American artisans and workers either migrated to and stayed in the major manufacturing centers where there was employment for their skills or they settled in smaller centers to the extent that there was employment available in their trades. At the same time, unskilled German-Americans tended to seek employment in cities where the Irish didn't already dominate the unskilled labor markets—that is, by moving west of the heavily Irish coastal cities.

Kleindeutschland's Economy

While the Germans staked out certain sectors of the economy early in their immigration, they rapidly diversified into other areas.[8] In 1850, tailors, shoemakers, bakers, and furniture makers accounted for 46 percent of the working population of Kleindeutschland, while grocers and peddlers accounted for 56 percent of all businessmen.[9] Some diversification would have developed simply because the population of the German community grew faster than the German trades, but some trades appear to have been deemed increasingly undesirable and were actively avoided by new immigrants. Most trades grew in terms of numbers of Germans employed, even if their relative importance to the work force of Kleindeutschland declined. For example, the proportion of the German work force that toiled in the notorious cellar bakeries of New York dropped by more than half from 1850 to 1860, but there was still a small increase in the numbers of German bakers (see Table 11).[10]

Skilled shoemakers (the second-largest category of workers in 1850 Kleindeutschland) found it increasingly difficult to compete with the shoe factories of New England and their proportion of the Kleindeutschland labor force declined 56 percent in the 1850s. In this trade, there was an absolute decline in numbers as well as a decline relative to the entire German-American work force. Thus, a 15 percent drop in numbers translated into a 75 percent decline in relative importance by 1880.[11]

Tailors far outnumbered the members of any other German trade in every year between 1850 and 1880 (as they did in most urban German-American settlements in those years). In fact, the growth of the tailoring trade considerably outstripped that of Kleindeutschland in the 1850s, even though working conditions had begun to decline as early as the 1840s (as we shall see below). When the ready-to-wear clothing industry began its rapid expansion during and after the Civil War, most of the skilled tailors failed to reap the benefits because a large proportion of the new production was given over to less-skilled workers. Though some tailors made the transition to the highly skilled and well-paid position of cutter, many others were forced to rely on work that required much less skill and to work for wages comparable to those of newly recruited semi-skilled needleworkers.[12] Their numbers continued to rise, but their share of the Kleindeutschland work force dropped 60 percent by 1880.[13]

The large relative declines of baking, shoemaking, and tailoring were not, in general, matched by a massive expansion of other single trades. Only cigar making became a major employer of Germans on a scale comparable to these declining German trades. Most of the new jobs were spread out among dozens of smaller trades that grew between 1850 and 1880. Printers, for example, increased from 0.2 percent of the work force to 2.0 percent, while dressmakers (a nonexistent trade in 1850) amounted to 3.2 percent of Kleindeutschland's work force by 1880.[14]

While the German crafts diversified in New York, the business sector of the German community grew at a rate that surpassed that of the overall population of Kleindeutschland. Thus it expanded from 17 percent of the work force in 1850 to 21 percent in 1870. After that German New York's business sector continued to grow, but its growth was no longer reflected in Kleindeutschland because a large proportion of the business and professional elite began to abandon the quarter for more fashionable neighborhoods uptown.

In the 1840s and 1850s most German businesses were low-capital shops, especially groceries, or the even lower capital enterprises of Kleindeutschland's many peddlers. These remained entry-level businesses in later years, but they were overshadowed after the mid-1850s by the emergence of larger and better-capitalized operations. Groceries dropped from 38 percent of all German businesses in 1850 to 15 percent in 1860, while peddlers declined from 18 percent to 10.6 percent in the same decade. Some grocers became full-scale wine and liquor dealers or saloonkeepers, while successful peddlers became dry-goods and clothing shopkeepers. At the same time that many artisans were being reduced to sweated workers, others were becoming the manufacturers who sweated them in the production of many other products. By 1870, nearly 25 percent of the businessmen of Kleindeutschland were recorded as owning property valued at $10,000 or more.

Second-generation Kleindeutschlanders were even less likely than their parents to occupy unskilled or semiskilled positions. On the other hand, they were nearly twice as likely to be doing skilled work in the tobacco industry (though that provided an uncertain future, as it too was beginning to decline to the status of a sweated trade). They were also twice as likely to be found in the rising machine trades (machinists and printers). The big difference, however, lay in the fact that almost 25 percent of second-generation Kleindeutschlanders were white-collar workers (while another 12.3 percent were in business or the professions).[15] Unlike the members of some other nineteenth-century immigrant groups (like the Irish and the southern Italians), they were thus moving rapidly into "American" sectors of the economy.[16] In moving into these white-collar occupations in such large numbers, Kleindeutschlanders were not necessarily typical of contemporary second-generation German-Americans elsewhere. Philadelphia's second-generation German-Americans are reported to have followed a similar pattern (though to a lesser extent), but this pattern is not found in cities where the proportion of unskilled laborers was high among first-generation German immigrants.[17]

The long-term trend of the economy in the middle of the century was toward constant expansion, but it was subject to regular boom and bust cycles—punctuated by the major crashes of 1857 and 1873. There were also economic crises and opportunities associated with the Civil War. These fluctuations were compounded by the tens of thousands of new German immigrants who entered New York's economy between each of our census year profiles (not to mention the thousands who left). The result was a great deal of fluidity in the labor market and little continuity from one census to the next. Despite the discontinuities, the labor force of Kleindeutschland turns out to have been consistently organized on subethnic lines.

The Plattdeutsch grocer, for example, was a popular stereotype before the Civil War and, indeed, 75 percent of the grocers in our 1860 sample turn out to have been born in Hanover.[18] It is typical of Kleindeutschland's occupational fluidity, though, that there were no Hanover-born grocers in our 1870 sample (a change confirmed by the fading out of the Plattdeutsch-grocer stereotype).[19] In 1860, one-quarter of all German-born shoemakers were Hessians (then 15 percent of the labor force); in 1870, one-third were Badeners (again 15 percent); and in 1880, one-quarter were Württembergers (only 7 percent of the labor force that year). While there was never a consistent mix of "nationalities" among the German shoemakers, with a different one predominating in each census year, most of them came from the states of southwest Germany that had a large surplus of such artisans.

The rapidly expanding clerical sector was exceptionally consistent in drawing an ever-larger portion of its workers from the same region of Germany. In 1860, when 8 percent of Kleindeutschland's working population came from the cities of Bremen and Hamburg or their Hanoverian hinterlands, 22 percent of German-born clerical workers came from that region. A decade later, when they still amounted to only 8 percent of the population, these "nationalities" accounted for 31 percent of the clerical workers; and by 1880, they accounted for 60 percent of all German-born clerical workers (at which time they had reached 10 percent of the German-born work force). Tailors, on the other hand, tended to remain consistently representative of the entire population of Kleindeutschland until the late 1870s, when the trade developed into a Prussian preserve.[20] Regardless of the consistency (or lack thereof) in the origins of the members of the different trades over the years, there remains a strong statistical relationship in every census year between a person's occupation and his state of birth in Germany.[21]

These changing patterns of occupational specialization within the German community were the outcome of the local and regional bases of personal association and kinship, which acted as major forces in the recruitment of employees and the distribution of credit. Frederick Bultman's cousin (see Chapter 2) helped establish this pattern when he brought Frederick over from Hanover, trained him in his grocery, and offered to set him up as an independent grocer.[22] Frederick, who had originally been trained as a locksmith, did his share by choosing instead to learn the machinist's trade and apprenticing himself to a Hanover-born machinist for three years. It was the accumulation of such chains of association that formed the patterns of occupational specialization found in Kleindeutschland.

Kleindeutschland at Work

Any work that focuses on an ethnic community runs the risk of romanticizing ethnic solidarity and ignoring class divisions. The preceding section on the subethnic concentrations in various occupations may suggest a romantic picture of solidarity; a *gemütlich* ethnic community, where all worked together for the good of all. In fact these ties of ethnic and subethnic loyalties often masked the most brutal conditions of exploitation. They did get people jobs, but their operation did not benefit everybody equally. Further examination of some of Kleindeutschland's leading occupations will make this clear.

By some accounts the German tailor in New York City was a jolly fellow: "The tailor is the luckiest man in all America. The first thing he does upon arrival is to marry. Then he sets up shop, goes to a clothing merchant and gets precut cloth to sew. His wife's assistance is essential in this work, but they get along well. Sundays they are off to the concert-saloon, where he drinks beer and she drinks punch."[23] Angela Heck, a tailor's wife and helper, was very pleased with her new way of life. She wrote home that her husband had been hired right off the boat, the pay was good, and the worst food eaten in New York was better than the best at home. In her enthusiasm, she said to tell her friends in the vineyards "they should burn their baskets and get themselves a tailor, even if he's just a windbag."[24] The reality was considerably less rosy, however, as the author of the first account then suggests: "Then the children arrive and interfere with production by taking the wife away from her work. The tailor tries to get work doing custom tailoring to order, real tailoring, but he fails and must return to piecework."[25] Here we have the reality of the degraded trade. The tailor was not an independent craftsman, nor was he a journeyman craftsman doing skilled work for a master of his trade. He was unable to do "real tailoring," and had to work on the putting-out system doing semiskilled work ("gets precut cloth to sew") for a clothing merchant—perhaps a former master tailor but more likely a jumped-up dry-goods merchant (or even a former peddler). The artisan's workshop, with a traditional *Vorleser* to read aloud to the other workers, had been largely displaced by the clothing merchant and the putting-out system. This system dominated clothing production in New York by the 1850s and brought the tenement sweatshop into existence. There, the typical tailor and his family worked a sixteen-hour day, seven days a week. For this the tailor got about $7.00 a week, $10.00 if his wife was also working.[26]

The already degraded tailoring trade was transformed further with the invention of the sewing machine. In the 1860s, the clothing merchants forced the tailors to buy sewing machines to standardize the stitching on garments, each of which was now being produced by several different tailors in the increasing division of labor that accompanied the putting-out system. At first this had a beneficial effect for the tailors, as productivity rose faster than piecework rates fell, bringing a family wage up to a peak of $20–$25 a week in the early 1870s. Even better for the tailors, the noise made by the sewing machines in the small tenement apartments forced the end of late-night work and shortened the tailors' working day. After the panic of 1873, however, piecework rates fell rapidly and the shorter workday proved a liability. An intensive speeding-up of the pace of work was required to try to keep income from falling too low, and even so the tailors' family wage dropped back down to $8–$9 a week by the early 1880s. At the end of this cycle, productivity had tripled while wages were down to about where they had started—and the tailors now had to work harder and had to carry the additional burden of having to provide their own sewing machine (or pay their employer rent for the use of one).[27] Under these increasingly poor conditions, tailoring gradually ceased being a German trade. "Polaks," Polish Jews from Prussian Poland (often counted in the census as Prussians or Germans) and the Austrian and Russian empires, had generally displaced the Germans and were the dominant element in the trade by the early 1880s.[28]

Wilhelm Weitling, a famous utopian socialist organizer and theorist, managed to do relatively well as a tailor in New York. He did so, however, only by exploiting the labor of his wife and his sister-in-law as well as his own (not to mention that of the servant girl they had to hire at $5.00 a month so that the women could both be free to work).[29] In 1866, his able sister-in-law organized the family into a business producing high quality fancy white vests and, for a short time, they achieved a joint income of $100.00 a month. Impressive as this was, it did not last. By the winter of 1870 the Weitlings' income had dropped to less than $20.00 a month and they were threatened with starvation. Even with three working adults, a tailoring family was always in a precarious position at best, doing well only through severe self-exploitation, and more often subject to the exploitation of clothing merchants—who were no less ruthless when the person they so used was a *Landsmann*.[30]

Some tailors survived the initial transformation of the clothing trade with their skills relatively intact, by becoming a new elite of the trade—the cutters who cut the cloth that lesser tailors would sew. Like the tailors, the cutters suffered from regular slow seasons when production practically ceased, but a highly skilled cutter might be kept employed on short time in the slow season so that he would be available when work picked up again. Beyond the increase in job security, cutters also got much better wages, about double the tailors' rate. It was reported that in the boom days of the early 1870s a large number of cutters managed to become property owners on their accumulated savings, while others went into business for themselves (it only took about $500 to set up a shop at that time). Then, after 1874, the machine revolution hit the cutters too. Instead of a skilled cutter marking every other piece of cloth and cutting two at a time, a skilled marker (still called a cutter) marked every tenth piece of cloth to be cut ten at a time by a semiskilled machine operator. By using prepared patterns, six markers and one operator were said to do the work of a thousand old-style cutters, and wages were down to $15 a week. Nor could cutters easily become independent contractors anymore. By the early 1880s it reportedly took $50,000 rather than $500 to set up as a clothing manufacturer.[31]

Tailors and cutters alike, along with other German artisans, had a particularly difficult time adapting to the "American" pace of work. Even as early as the 1840s, labor shortages and the breakdown of traditional work patterns in American workshops had led to a much faster and harder work rhythm than immigrants were used to. The New York *Tribune* noted early on: "There is not perhaps a more industrious class in our city than the Germans. They rise early and retire late, and although when arriving on our shores they do not *drive business,* as is a distinguishing characteristic of our mechanics; yet after some time among us a decided improvement in this respect can be plainly observed."[32] Charles Steinway agreed that Americans worked harder. Shortly after he arrived in New York he wrote his brother, "I cannot advise you to come here if you are able . . . to make a living in Germany. . . . People here have to work harder than abroad."[33] Steinway and other German immigrants did make the adjustment, but it was a hard one and sometimes, as in the tailoring trade, it was an adjustment that had to be repeated as the years passed and the pace of work grew ever faster.

Bakers toiled for even longer hours in their cellars than the tailors did in their sweatshops and "were in many respects in a state of absolute slavery, having not only to work late in the hot bakehouses of the city, but afterwards to carry heavy loads of bread at an early hour of the morning, until many of them had become stooped and round-shouldered from the practice."[34] The *Sun* reported in 1863 that "there is scarcely a trade in existence whose members are worked as hard as this, the hours being usually sixteen, and in many instances twenty-four for a day's work."[35] Five years later, bakers were still working the same long hours for $10.00–$20.00 a week.[36] In 1872, when nearly one hundred thousand workers in New York City struck for the eight-hour day, the bakers went out for a twelve-hour day—and lost.[37]

Again the employers who fought to maintain the workers' long hours were their *Landsleute.*

Skilled German shoemakers also found their way into New York's dank cellars. As early as 1845 the *Tribune* reported that:

> There is no class of mechanics in New York who average so great an amount of work for so little money as the journeymen shoemakers. . . . We have been in more than fifty cellars in different parts of the city, each inhabited by a shoemaker and his family. The floor is made of rough plank laid loosely down, the ceiling is not quite so high as a tall man. The walls are dark and damp, and a wide desolate fireplace yawns in the centre, to the right of the entrance. There is no outlet back and of course no yard privileges of any kind [i.e., water or toilet facilities]. . . . In this apartment often live the man with his workbench, his wife and five or six children of all ages . . . and perhaps a palsied grandfather or grandmother and often both. In one corner is a squalid bed, and the room elsewhere is occupied by the workbench, a cradle made from a dry-goods box, two or three broken and seatless chairs, a stewpan and a kettle.[38]

Before the Civil War, most New York shoemakers were still artisans, doing handwork in small shops. They were reduced to poverty by competition from the putting-out system and the unmechanized factories that had established a foothold in New York and dominated the national shoe market from New England.[39] The key inventions that were to revolutionize the shoe industry were not made until 1857 and 1862, and the average New York shoemaking shop still had only 9.1 workers in 1860. Ten years later the shoemakers of New York worked in factories averaging more than twenty-six employees each.[40] Not only had the industrial revolution in the shoe industry arrived, it drove wages down from the $7–$8 per week of 1853 to $6–$7 per week in 1865—and this despite a period of severe inflation.[41] A few German shoemakers were able to take advantage of changing conditions in the trade and become manufacturers, while others were driven down into the ranks of factory workers by their *Landsleute.*

Breweries were small operations in the 1850s and 1860s. A brewmaster and five to ten workers worked together fourteen to eighteen hours a day. The long hours and grinding work kept the men on the verge of physical collapse and it was often the sharp prod of the boss's fist that kept them going. Room and board were provided by the brewer, though often the room was a hop sack on the brewery floor and the board little more than "all the beer you can drink." In the larger breweries, foremen exercised the boss's prerogative of beating the men and the room and board were provided by saloons that dealt with the brewery. For this the men were generally paid $20–$25 a month. By the late 1870s, the breweries were bigger, but the working conditions and pay were no better. Conditions may even have deteriorated as the brewers became big businessmen and stopped working alongside their men.[42]

The German cigar makers often worked at home before the Civil War. They worked on a putting-out system—getting their materials from a "manufacturer" who paid them for their finished cigars. Although it seems to be the same system under which the tailors were reduced to sweated labor, it is reported that the cigar makers were not so exploited.[43] After the war, cigar manufacturing became a factory trade and was almost completely dominated by Germans.[44] Samuel Gompers remembered these factories well:

> Any kind of an old loft served as a cigar shop. If there were enough windows, we had sufficient light for our work; if not, it was apparently no concern of the management. . . . Cigar shops were always dusty from the tobacco stems and powdered leaves. Benches and work tables were not designed to enable the workmen to adjust bodies and arms comfortably to work surface. Each workman supplied his own cutting board of lignum vitae and knife blade.
>
> The tobacco leaf was prepared by strippers who drew the leaves from the heavy stem and put them in pads of about fifty. The leaves had to be handled carefully to prevent tearing. The craftsmanship of the cigarmaker was shown in his ability to utilize wrappers to the best advantage to shave off the unusable to a hair-breadth, to roll so as to cover holes in the leaf and to use both hands so as to make a perfectly shaped and rolled product. These things a good cigarmaker learned to do more or less mechanically, which left us free to think, talk, listen, or sing. I loved the freedom of that work. . . . I was eager to learn from discussion and reading or to pour out my feeling in song. Often we chose someone to read to us who made a particularly good reader, and in payment the rest of us gave him sufficient of our cigars so he was not the loser. The reading was always followed by discussion. . . . The fellowship that grew between congenial shopmates was something that lasted a lifetime.[45]

The cigar factories employed up to seven hundred workers each, but the workers' sense of fellowship helped them to maintain a great deal of collective control over the conditions and pace of their work (not to mention their ability to resist wage cuts—a skilled worker like Samuel Gompers made about $18.00 a week). These conditions were only partially undercut by the introduction of non-German, tenement-house production in the 1870s. The Germans continued to be the main producers of fine quality cigars. It was these relatively good conditions that helped make cigar making the most popular of the skilled trades for second-generation Kleindeutschlanders in 1880.

In some ways the cabinetmakers' trade retained the most artisanal character of all the German trades. Highly skilled German furniture makers, many with experience in the fashionable workshops of Paris, were attracted to New York's rapidly expanding furniture industry. At first they sought employment in the large furniture factories of Duncan Phyfe, Charles Baudouine, Alexander Roux, and Rochfort and Scarren (all still engaging in hand production) but, after they had a chance to learn about the American market, they often set up shop on their own. They established typical artisans' workshops with one to five employees and they specialized in single products like veneered box sofas or French bedsteads or chairs. Ernst Hagen recalled: "Others made bureaus, but would not make the glass frames for them, which was a branch by itself. . . . The work was all done by hand, but the scroll sawing, of course was done at the nearest sawmill. The employers (boss Cabinet makers) having no machinery at all, the moldings were bought at the molding mill and the turning done at [a] turning mill. The hardware, locks, hinges, bolts, and etc. was mostly imported from Germany. The journeymen cabinet makers had [to] supply their own tools and work benches."[46] These traditional artisan workshops maintained German-style apprenticeship practices, with apprentices serving from age fourteen or fifteen to twenty-one and "it was the custom in the German Factories to board and lodge in the [employer's] house."[47]

For all the lingering appearance that these were traditional artisan workshops, however, most were firmly tied to national markets. They either sold their products at wholesale auctions or they provided them directly to large mercantile houses, mostly for export to the South and West. A small proportion were able to maintain high standards, producing for the luxury market and paying their journeymen $8–$15 a week. Most were what were called "slaughter shops," which produced poor-quality furniture and paid only $6–$8 a week.[48] When the furniture factories of western cities like Cincinnati and Grand Rapids mechanized their operations in the 1870s "all the smaller cabinet makers were simply wiped out . . . and even the larger establishments [had] a hard time in competing."[49] Indeed, after 1880 New York's furniture industry became only a memory as far as mass markets were concerned and this leading German trade faded into insignificance.

Piano makers were also highly skilled and favored workers. They remained so even though the German piano makers went through an industrial revolution in the 1850s. Albert Weber began the Weber Piano Company in 1851 with two employees, and Steinway and Sons started in 1853 with ten workers.[50] Handwork rapidly gave way to the division of labor and the introduction of machinery, however, and Steinway and

Sons built a new factory for 350 workers in 1860. There, the crude work was done by heavy machines, like the seven-horsepower planer that ran at 1,200 rpm and planed a surface 16-feet long by 42-inches wide.

> A second machine, of three horsepower, planed boards 16 feet in length and 34 inches in width, making 32 revolutions a minute, representing the labor of 28 workmen. It would require the extent of a goodly-sized volume to describe the 102 different planing, sawing, jointing, drilling, mortising, turning and other machines used in this factory, and to elucidate their various objects. . . . No workman is permitted to work at more than one branch of the business; thus from the very fact that every workman is continually making only one and the same article, he achieves an absolute perfection of his work . . . in this great and strictly adhered to division of labor, the article, until it is finally completed, passed through the hands of a number of different workmen, none of whom receives it from the previous workman unless it is perfectly faultless in every respect.[51]

Soon after the Steinways developed their "new system" of piano manufacture it was adopted by others. By the 1870s Kleindeutschland's piano makers were making pianos this way, not only for the Steinways but also for nearby competitors (like Sohmer and Co. and the Decker Bros., each only a block away from Steinway Hall, and the large Haines Brothers factory six blocks away on Twenty-first Street).[52] Even unskilled laborers made $11.00 a week in the piano factories of the late 1860s and skilled workers made $14.00–$20.00 a week.[53] Steady work at these rates made the piano makers an elite among German workers, but the manufacturers were few and well organized, so labor relations frequently turned into contests of strength that pitted German workers against German bosses.

Most other artisan and factory occupations that the Germans of New York engaged in (and there were hundreds) fell between the extremes that we have depicted. Relations between German workers and their *Landsleute* employers ranged from mutual affection and respect to brutal exploitation and hatred, sometimes within the same industry. One of the distinctive features of the German immigrants was that, like the older-stock Americans but unlike most of their Irish fellow immigrants, many of them were able to become employers in artisan trades and then to participate in their industrialization. This gave German New York a fully developed class structure by 1880. While class antagonisms attenuated the sense of community solidarity, the inclusiveness of the German world, with all its oppositions, served to reinforce the Kleindeutschlanders' ethnic identity as German-Americans.

Women's Work

Women workers were consistently underenumerated by census takers and this was as true of Kleindeutschland as it was of the rest of the country. We have seen in Chapter 3 that nearly 33 percent of all German households took in boarders in 1850 and that over 10 percent still did so in 1880. This women's work was often essential to the household's survival, but it was ignored in the census tabulations of gainful employment as long as the women concerned were not heads of households (and sometimes even when they were). Then there were women who did part-time needlework at home, but whose work was not recorded by the census takers. There were also many women who worked full- or part-time in shops owned by their husbands or fathers, but since they got no formal wage, they too were left out of the census calculations. In all, these women may have raised the proportion of women participating in the labor force of Kleindeutschland from the 17–20 percent range recorded by the census takers to something closer to 35–40 percent.

Formal employment, as recognized by the census takers, was clearly the domain of young and single women. Thirty-three to 46 percent of working German women (depending on the year) were under twenty years old and 75 to 80 percent were under thirty. Only before the Civil War was there a widespread occupation for German women who were over thirty. In 1860, 54 percent of Kleindeutschland's tailoresses had passed their thirtieth birthday, but the days of mature women tailors passed with the spread of the sewing machine and factory production of clothing. By 1870, 80 percent of the tailoresses were, like their sisters in the other needle trades, under thirty. Older women who had to support themselves seem to have had virtually no choice but to take in laundry, and the ranks of the German washerwomen were dominated by women over forty (60–75 percent).[54]

Work in the needle trades was a good way for unmarried girls and women without children to supplement the family income, if only a little extra was required. The pay for this work was dismal, as the *Tribune* reported in 1853: "Though some thousands of females in different callings—milliners, dressmakers, shop-assistants—make between $3.50–$6.00 a week which could be considered a living wage, there are hundreds of women tailoresses and seamstresses who have an average yearly income, if fully employed, of only $91.00."[55] The census manuscripts indicate that most of the German women engaged in these trades were indeed supplementary wage earners. This stands in sharp contrast to the Irish women who dominated the women's needle trades in those years, as many of the Irish women were on their own. For those German women forced, like their Irish sisters in the trade, to subsist on these starvation wages, prostitution was sometimes the only means of survival. In 1864 the *Tribune* asked its readers, if they were to have a sister in that position, "where would you look for that sister in twelve months?" (though we may note that a census of the city's prostitutes found that only 18 percent had worked in the needle trades before taking up their trade).[56]

While prostitution was not all that frequent a recourse for impoverished needlewomen, the condition of women who depended on sewing for a living was indeed very precarious. The extreme poverty of these women is exemplified by two German sisters who migrated to New York in 1852. Cecelia and Wanda Stein were both unmarried when they arrived in Kleindeutschland with Wanda's young illegitimate child. The two women took up embroidery for a living, but it wasn't much of a living. Even with the two sisters putting in long hours at their craft, life was very hard and they sometimes had to borrow money from friends to survive. After two years in New York, they confided to a friend that "if things grew much worse," they would send the boy to his father and take poison. In the fall of 1855 things grew worse. Their employer went out of business and the two sisters were unable to find work. Soon the rent was due and the larder was empty. They had already borrowed all that they could, their money was almost gone, and they were unwilling to become prostitutes. On September 4 they reached the end of their rope. They got their landlady to give them another day to pay the rent and used their last few pennies to buy some flowers. Setting out the flowers to cheer up the bare room, they got into their one bed with six-year-old Edward. Settled in bed, each of the three took a drink from a bottle of prussic acid—and their troubles were soon over.[57]

For women workers, the major alternative to sewing was employment in domestic service. In service, subsistence was assured and there was generally an additional payment of one or two dollars a week.[58] All that was required in return was a little "light" housework for fifteen or sixteen hours a day, six-and-a-half or seven days a week. Furthermore, much of the work was done in dark and poorly ventilated kitchens under the exacting eye of the mistress of the household.[59] Better-paying jobs with American families required a knowledge of English and often meant isolation from the German community. Despite these drawbacks, two out of every five of Kleindeutschland's wage-earning women were in service in 1860. As other options became available, however, the percentage of German women in service dropped to 19 percent in 1870 and 17 percent in 1880.[60]

Service and factory work were not easily compatible with maintaining a household, particularly if children were involved. Homework was more compatible, but the return was minimal (as housework cut into production and reduced already low wages to around a dollar a week). A boarder, on the other hand, required only a marginal (though substantial) extension of housework and brought in $1.50 to $3.00 a week (most of which was pure income).[61] The worker's wife, who could earn no more than $3.00 a week sewing (and probably less), could thus double the family income by taking in three of her husband's coworkers as boarders. If they didn't have children (or had an extra room or two for some other reason), she might be able to take care of up to ten boarders and raise the family income to levels enjoyed by shopkeepers and other small businessmen. Even one boarder, however, might make the difference between getting by and starving when the primary wage earner was subject to seasonal unemployment (as most were).

There were real disadvantages to taking in boarders, though. There was, first of all, the additional work for the wife (which only increased as she got older and had more children). Then, the increased crowding and loss of privacy adversely affected the entire family. There was also the danger to the family posed by introducing male boarders into the home (the young wife's affair with a handsome young boarder was a stock theme in the theaters of the day—and in the suicide reports). As the residents of Kleindeutschland prospered they indicated an increasing unwillingness to tolerate the disadvantage of having boarders. By 1880, nearly 90 percent of Kleindeutschland's families were able and willing to forgo this source of income. What stands out most clearly is that the married women of Kleindeutschland not only preferred to avoid work outside the home (as did most other American women of the time—regardless of ethnicity), but that they succeeded in doing so while also demonstrating that they preferred to work only for their families even when at home.[62]

There was an alternative mode of employment for young women that does not appear in the census reports: German serving girls were a conspicuous portion of Kleindeutschland's female labor force. Eighteen- to twenty-year-old girls in colorful uniforms and short skirts (or low-cut gowns) worked as waitresses in the large, respectable beer halls and higher-class dance halls.[63] Former servants and seamstresses found a brighter social life and better pay in the beer halls than they had known in hot kitchens or dim factories and sweatshops. Marriage often followed this change of occupation, as it brought them into far more contact with men than did other forms of employment. Some young women took advantage of the potential for easy money present in such situations and began to engage in occasional prostitution (the police considered all the serving girls prostitutes, though they reported that "the girls employed to dance do not consider themselves prostitutes").[64] This association was somewhat traditional; the German term for serving girls, *Dirne*, means both 'girl' and 'prostitute'.

Those most inclined toward easy money soon moved on to the "basements with friendly service," the cellar saloons. There, about two thousand German women provided the "friendly service."[65] A German journalist described them as classic bar girls, each with "a low-cut dress, a ring on every finger and an obscenity on her lips."[66] They were paid by the drink and frequently supplemented their income by prostitution. By age thirty, their career was ended and our sources lead us to presume that they then faced only the gutter after ten years of alcoholism and degradation.[67] In fact, it is quite as likely that many of these women simply married and turned to more prosaic occupations.

Child Labor

Child labor (that is, the employment of children under sixteen) has generally been recognized as having been both important and widespread in mid-nineteenth-century America, but remarkably little analysis of child labor before the last decades of the century is available. This is particularly true of New York City, where the concern of contemporary reformers was to get the children off the streets and into, not out of, the factories: "Children over twelve years of age thus become a benefit instead of a burden to their parents, while they are trained in habits of industry, and instructed in some useful art for future life. It may not here be in place to consider the merits or demerits of the English 'Factory System' of employment of children . . . , but it appears clear in regard to thousands of children in this city, that they had better be thus employed, than as now suffered to run to ruin in the streets."[68] Thousands of children were already in the factories or had found other employment. The *Times* estimated that the 1854–55 depression had left some ten thousand children unemployed in New York City.[69] By the early 1860s, the Newsboys' Lodging House was taking in an average of four to five thousand working boys a year[70] and they were surely outnumbered by working boys and girls who lived with their parents.

Such questions as who these children were and what were their ages and nationalities were of little interest to their contemporaries (except when it was a question of selecting some particularly heart-rending examples to generate public support for reform charities)—and seem to have attracted nearly as little attention from historians. It is nonetheless possible to retrieve some of these data from the manuscript censuses of 1860–80, even though they do not take note of anywhere near all of the children who earned money one way or another. At the very least, they can provide us with some solid minimum figures for those years.

According to the manuscript census, few children of ten or eleven (or younger) appear to have worked in Kleindeutschland, and most children of that age were recorded as being in school. Those who were working were most likely to have been errand boys or girls in domestic service. It is likely that more girls than were recorded as having done so helped their mothers or sisters with their sewing and more boys picked up spending money through part-time work, but that nobody thought to mention these to the census taker.

Table 12
Child Labor Patterns in Kleindeutschland
by Age and Sex, 1860–80

	Age	1860	1870	1880
Boys				
	12	7.7% (13)	0.0% (19)	4.0% (25)
	13	7.7 (13)	36.8 (19)	24.0 (25)
	14	30.8 (12)	47.4 (19)	58.3 (25)
	15	69.2 (13)	57.9 (18)	66.7 (24)
Girls				
	12	0.0% (16)	0.0% (21)	11.5% (26)
	13	0.0 (16)	19.4 (21)	12.0 (25)
	14	12.5 (16)	20.0 (20)	25.0 (24)
	15	12.5 (16)	25.0 (20)	25.0 (24)

Note: Figures in parentheses are base Ns for adjacent percentages.
Source: Author's census samples.

Twelve- to fifteen-year-old workers show up much more frequently in Kleindeutschland's census returns and we can see how the patterns of child labor developed in this community (for the changing proportions of each age group that worked, see table 12). Twelve- and thirteen-year-old boys were sometimes employed, though only thirteen-year-olds were employed in significant numbers. About one-third worked as apprentices in skilled trades or did unskilled jobs in workshops (like stripping leaves for cigar makers or fetching and cleaning in bakeries), but most were employed to run errands or work in stores as clerks and check boys. These proportions were nearly reversed among fourteen- and fifteen-year-old boys, who were more likely to work at learning trades (60 percent) than in stores or businesses (40 percent).[71] This was the traditional age for boys to start their apprenticeship in Germany and a majority of boys of this age in Kleindeutschland were recorded as having jobs.

In examining turn-of-the-century Detroit, Olivier Zunz found that there too German-American boys typically left school and began work at age fourteen.[72] Stressing the importance of teenagers' earnings to the family economy and contrasting this immigrant pattern with an American tendency to keep teenage boys in school for another two years, Zunz treats this as child labor. Given, however, that real child labor (that is, the employment of children, not teenagers) was a significant option in mid-nineteenth-century New York and was passed up by German parents, it seems wise to distinguish between the two. Despite the great importance of teenagers' earnings for improving household living standards, sending fourteen-year-olds out to work was not a Dickensian exploitation of child labor. It was rather a combination of continuing their education and a simple beginning of their adult careers in accordance with German tradition.

Kleindeutschland's girls were generally much less likely to work for wages than were boys of the same age. The kinds of jobs girls did make it probable that many of those who did work did so at home. Over two-thirds of the employed girls (twelve to fifteen years old) worked in the sewing trades and most of these were in branches that allowed for homework rather than those that required them to go out to factories.[73] Another one-fifth worked in domestic service (frequently under the worst conditions, because of their youth and lack of skills), while one-sixth worked in stores as shop assistants. The vast majority of Kleindeutschland's girls were neither employed nor in school (they left school at a younger age than their brothers). It seems likely that they were home learning the many skills that were considered essential for their hoped-for future roles as German-American *Hausfrauen*.

There was another kind of working child who was not picked up by the census, the street urchin. Ragpickers, coal pickers, match peddlers, and beggars did not usually report their occupations to the census takers, even if their activity was essential to the family's survival. They often turned to the Children's Aid Society for help, though, so we can get some idea of their activities from the society's records.[74]

In the depression of 1854–55, more than thirteen hundred children were brought to the attention of the Children's Aid Society and one-eighth of them came from the German community. This was less than half of the Germans' proportion of the city's children, so we can infer that Germans were underrepresented among the city's more desperate children.[75] Many were from families that had recently arrived in New York, like four-year-old Katarina K., who was found picking coal for her widowed mother—nine months from Germany. Eleven-year-old Karl G. was a real economic asset to his family, who sent him out to beg every day (and beat him on his return if he had not brought home enough money). Still, many more German children were brought in by desperate parents who could not provide for them than came to the society's attention because of parental abuse. Only about 10 percent of the German children that the society saw were reported engaged in scavenging activities, so we must conclude that these occupations were marginal to the experiences of Kleindeutschland's children.

New York's German Businesses

New York City was, above all, a rapidly expanding commercial metropolis and many Germans made places for themselves in its commerce. As much as one-quarter of Kleindeutschland's working population owned some sort of business at any one time and some German-American businessmen were successful enough to join the commercial elite of the city. Most, however, remained petty entrepreneurs and shopkeepers, though increasingly prosperous ones.

Peddling was the bottom level of business activity, and was often resorted to because of lack of skills rather than a taste for entrepreneurship. Many peddlers were German Jews who simply transferred their traditional role in the German economy to the United States.[76] A small stake from a sympathetic *Landsmann* (with a reduced rate of interest for relatives and coreligionists), and Kleindeutschland had a new businessman. Still, many peddlers failed in this enterprise and turned to the factories for easier work and more certain reward. Others were successful and opened stores on the profits made from peddling.[77] So many Germans made the transition from dry-goods peddler to clothing merchant that they took over most of New York's dry-goods market by the end of the 1850s.[78]

The German dry-goods dealers were in an excellent position to take advantage of the growing popularity of ready-made clothing. They already owned stocks of cloth, so they were able to become petty manufacturers, via the putting-out system, without any significant further investment. Some specialized in cheap clothing for the southern market (it was estimated that this trade employed thousands of tailors in New York City by the 1850s), while others produced almost as cheap clothing for the New York City poor. The market for ready-made clothing boomed when uniforms were needed for the Civil War, and the Germans, who had begun manufacturing clothing in the 1840s and 1850s, came to dominate the production of ready-made clothing for the rest of the nation (a position that they maintained through the end of the century).[79]

Grocers always outnumbered peddlers, sometimes by two to one, and they were the other low-ranking businessmen of Kleindeutschland. Their small shops with smaller stocks often depended on liquor sales for their profits, but they could be "little gold mines."[80] A successful grocer used his profits to set up relatives and former clerks in their own groceries and then used their profits to move into a more established business, perhaps a beer hall or a formal liquor store. This process was so common that the stereotypical Plattdeutsch grocers of the 1850s and early 1860s had almost disappeared by 1870, to be replaced by more recent immigrants from other parts of Germany.

While Kleindeutschland's grocers and cellar saloonkeepers sold whiskey, gin, or schnapps, the better saloon and beer hall keepers purveyed wine, lager beer, and Continental civilization. The *Bierwirth,* or innkeeper, was often a declassed professional—a lawyer or civil servant who was unable to transfer his profession to the new land.[81] Given a little capital, he could parlay his social status and skills into a successful business, one that helped him to regain an important and influential place in his community. By providing employment for musicians and a stage for amateur theater and choral groups he could improve his business and be a patron of the arts (like Joseph Dolger, who hosted the Beethoven Männerchor in his saloon on Third Street). If, like Eugen Lievre and Justus Schwab, he was politically radical, he could open his doors to trade union and socialist meetings, thus furthering his ideals and establishing a large and loyal clientele.[82] If his politics were more moderate, Tammany Hall always had a place for a popular saloonkeeper. Even piety could be turned to account, as the prominent Catholic saloonkeeper who opened a saloon across the street from the German Catholic cathedral demonstrated by attracting considerable business from churchgoers.[83] The saloonkeepers were thus key figures in many sectors of the German community, and the one political issue that could be counted on to unite the Germans was opposition to Sunday closing laws, which threatened not only German-American culture but particularly the livelihood of the German-American saloonkeepers.

Kleindeutschland's Professionals

German New York had had a small professional class even before Kleindeutschland began to take form in the 1840s, but it expanded rapidly in the 1840s and 1850s. Unlike the many lawyers who were forced to turn to saloonkeeping and other business pursuits, doctors, pharmacists, opticians, ministers, journalists, and teachers were able to continue at their old professions in America. Indeed, German physicians were so numerous in New York that it was estimated in the mid-1850s that one-third of the city's doctors were German born and trained.[84] Many of these German doctors (including Joseph Goldmark, Abraham Jacobi, Ernst Krackowitzer, Wilhelm Löwe aus Calbe, John Menninger, and Friedrich Roessler) were well-known political refugees, as were a fair portion of the other German professionals who found their way to New York.

In the 1850s these professionally trained and articulate men formed an elite in Kleindeutschland. They took the lead in numerous voluntary associations of all sorts, social, political, and charitable. Between their leadership of the voluntary associations and their near-monopoly of the press, they dominated public discourse. Public issues were issues that concerned them, and issues that did not tended to be invisible. Their hegemony was short-lived, however, as a German-American upper class rose up to challenge their predominance in the 1860s.

Going Up

Before the Civil War there was no real economic elite in Kleindeutschland. The businessmen who would later claim social and political hegemony over the German-American community were still only part of the middle classes and were devoted to making their fortunes. Their influence in the community was minimal, as was demonstrated in the case of the two Gustavs. In 1860 the New York *World* contrasted the protemperance merchant Gustav Schwab—the "good Gustav"—with the saloonkeeper Gustav Lindenmuller—the "bad Gustav"—as part of a temperance campaign. It is clear from the responding editorial in the New Yorker *Staats-Zeitung,* Kleindeutschland's establishment daily, that the saloonkeeper's standing in the community was much higher than that of the rising merchant.[85]

In the 1840s and 1850s, the brewers of lager beer were the social equals of the ordinary saloonkeepers. As late as 1860, each of New York's forty-six breweries had, on average, fewer than a dozen workers and produced only about $36,000 worth of beer a year.[86] Even then, economic and technical changes in the industry had begun to transform the brewers from poor, near-peasant "frogs" into "Brewer Princes" (like George Ehret, Jacob Ruppert, and Henry Claussen). Production grew fivefold by 1880 and the German-American brewers of New York left their humble beginnings far behind.[87] A popular tale of the time told of the saloonkeeper's wife from Avenue A who went to visit her old friend "Lieschen," the brewer's wife, at her new home on Fifth Avenue. "Lieschen" refused to see her old drinking companion from the days before she had "risen in life."[88]

The brewer princes, like the saloonkeepers, promoted German culture and German beer—sometimes separately and sometimes as the same thing. They supported and funded many of the musical and scientific associations of Kleindeutschland, along with important institutions like the German Hospital (now Lenox Hill Hospital).[89] They made the fortunes of their relatives (like August Strassburg, who became America's leading trader in hops after he married Jacob Ruppert's sister), and they kept leading German-American architects (like Adam Weber and Marc Eidlitz) employed building their breweries, mansions, and philanthropic institutions.[90] The brewers became one of the key elements in the developing German-American elite of New York (though their crude social origins sometimes kept them from being fully accepted by the more genteel elements of New York German society until a more sophisticated second-generation reached maturity).

Unlike German-American communities in other North American cities (though similar in this regard to the German settlement in Buenos Aires), more of Kleindeutschland's elite German-American businesses were developed out of the trade with Germany than from any other sector of the economy. New York City was the major port of entry for European goods into North America and attracted the interest of German exporters. One-third of the men selected for inclusion in a memorial to the German elite of New York had their fortunes based on this trade.[91] Indeed, most of them had begun their American careers as New York agents for German trading houses. Although they often remained dependent on their German connections even in later years, their status approximated that of junior partners of the major German firms.

August Belmont (Schönberg), the American representative for the House of Rothschild banking interests, retained little contact with his fellow German-Americans, but he had arrived in New York before there were many German-American businessmen (in 1837) and his commercial dealings were with older-stock Americans.[92] Other German merchants were less cosmopolitan. In 1850, Heinrich Kunhardt and his brother came to New York and opened shop as the agents of the Hamburg-Amerika steamship line. Needless to say, their fortunes rose rapidly along with those of the famous shipping company. Gustav Schwab (the "good Gustav") started in Bremen as a clerk for the commission merchant firm of H. H. Meier. When he came to New York, in 1844, it was to work for the related firm of Oelrichs and Company. Although he left Oelrichs to start his own firm, he retained a close connection with the firm by marrying Oelrichs's daughter. When, in 1859, Oelrichs and Company became the American agent for the North German Lloyd steamship line of Bremen (partly owned by Schwab's old sponsor, H. H. Meier), Gustav Schwab returned to Oelrichs as a partner—to handle that account. Schwab became a director of many American companies and was a leader of the major philanthropic organization, the German Society of New York.[93]

Other men with less magnificent trade connections in Germany also parlayed their contacts into substantial fortunes and membership in the economic elite of Kleindeutschland. They imported textiles, wines, watches, or pharmaceuticals from Germany and they exported American leather and other goods. What all these merchants had in common was their close connection with the mercantile classes in Germany, for they were often much closer socially to their German counterparts than to the masses of German-American working people in New York. Ronald Newton has equated their Buenos Aires counterparts with the residents of extraterritorial trading quarters in the classical cities of the Mediterranean and the Orient, and this equation would not be inappropriate for the German mercantile element in New York. Unlike the German businessmen of Buenos Aires, however, they were far too small a segment of the German immigrant population to dominate it socially.[94]

It was these merchants and importers who formed the core of one of Kleindeutschland's first major business operations. Hugo Wesendonck, scion of a wealthy German textile family and political refugee after 1848, used his family fortune and his own political renown to organize the Germania Life Insurance Company in 1860. He used his connections with the textile business to recruit a number of wealthy dry-goods importers and his connections with the 1848 Frankfurt parliament to recruit some well-known forty-eighters (including the aforementioned Dr. Wilhelm Löwe aus Calbe, leader of the liberals at the Frankfurt parliament of 1848 and the last president of the German National Assembly). They broadened their base by bringing in Max Schaefer, the brewer prince; Oswald Ottendorfer, the *Staats-Zeitung* editor (and another forty-eighter); Joseph Seligman, a Jewish ex-peddler who had become the leading German banker in New York (after August Belmont); and C. Godfrey Gunther, wealthy son of German immigrants who was active in politics and would soon be elected mayor. Thus, a coalition of all the wealthiest sectors of the business and social elite of 1860 Kleindeutschland was assembled around the core of merchants to launch a national insurance company for German immigrants.[95]

A third major element in the German elite of New York was made up of former artisans and petty manufacturers. Men like Henry Steinway (Heinrich Steinweg) and his sons took advantage of new machines and combined them with old skills to transform small workshops into large factories.[96] Conrad Poppenhusen, a former textile manufacturer from Hamburg, made a modest fortune manufacturing items like combs from whalebone. He judiciously loaned some of the money to Charles Goodyear, a struggling inventor, and gained control of the patent for the vulcanization of rubber. He then founded the American Hard Rubber Company and became one of America's great industrialists.[97] Poppenhusen and the Steinways were the most successful of the German manufacturers, but they were joined by many of their compatriots who had developed successful businesses and made themselves modest fortunes.[98]

The social origins of the manufacturers spanned the gap between those of the beer barons and those of the merchants. They were thus able to connect disparate groups into a more cohesive social elite. The members of this elite began to sever their physical links with Kleindeutschland in the 1860s and 1870s, as they began to move uptown to more fashionable quarters. They retained, however, a self-conscious German identity and claimed for themselves the leadership of all of New York's German-Americans.

The elite was not a closed social group, however. Some leading members of the professional class, which was being displaced as the dominant group in German New York, were drawn into the new elite. Not only journalists *cum* publishers like Ottendorfer and the Lexow cousins but upper-crust political exiles like Dr. Löwe aus Calbe and prominent architects like Eidlitz and Weber were admitted to their social circles. Nor was the elite completely restricted to entrepreneurs and leading professionals. On occasion it even admitted some of the sons of more or less ordinary immigrant workers. The eldest son of the communist tailor Wilhelm Weitling began his career at the age of fourteen as an office boy for Conrad Poppenhusen. He ended it as vice president and chairman of the American Hard Rubber Company (and president of a bank as well). A younger Weitling son became the export manager for a company that sold steel structures to Brazil, and Weitling's daughter was a teacher in the New York City schools.[99] This family was unusually successful (though unevenly so as only the eldest son really moved into the elite), but the pattern of workers' children entering potentially upwardly mobile white-collar occupations was, as we have seen, a common one.

The developing German-American elite remained distinct from the native elite of New York, though it sometimes lost its children to the natives. Business ties to Germany or dependence on the German-American market were often the ties that bound the second and third generations to a German identity. If these were weak or lacking, the second or third generation often merged with the broader Knickerbocker-Yorker-Yankee elite of the city.[100] The brewers and German-language publishers were the least likely members of the elite to cut their ties to the German community, as they depended on those ties for their profits, but they were joined by others who had no such economic incentives. The strong ethnic group solidarity that had developed in the early years when the elite was part of the fabric of Kleindeutschland was maintained by numerous social institutions and tended to promote the continued existence of a distinct German-American elite in New York until it dissolved under the intense anti-German pressures of World War I.

Criminal Classes

Like most major nineteenth-century cities (and many modern ones) New York had a large and active criminal underclass. Native-born and immigrant New Yorkers participated in illegal economic activities in great numbers, but they did not always participate equally in every sort of criminal endeavor. It was an era when thousands of American and Irish-American toughs and criminals were organized into the notorious fighting gangs of New York (the Dead Rabbits, the Pug Uglies, the Bowery Boys, the Whyos, and the Gas House Gang),[101] but they had few German counterparts. Some Germans, like "Dutch Jake" Haeffer in the 1840s, joined these gangs.[102] In the 1860s and 1870s "Dutch Heinrichs" headed one of the most vicious groups of criminals in the city, the Hell's Kitchen Gang, but few of his followers shared his origins.[103] Indeed, German gangsters appear to have been sufficiently unusual for several to have been given the same nickname—"Dutch."

Kleindeutschland did have its own gang for about a dozen years after the Civil War, but the "Dutch Mob" (led by "Sheeny" Mike Kurtz, Little Freddy, and Johnny Irving) never made it into the leading ranks of New York's underworld. In the end, it was easily dispersed by a police terror campaign in 1877.[104] The German immigrant community thus stood in marked contrast to its Irish contemporaries and later Jewish and Italian immigrant communities in failing to produce a significant violent underclass.[105] On the whole, German New York's artisans and skilled workers were able to create a stable enough environment for their families to protect their community from the widespread juvenile delinquency and criminality that desperate poverty generated in other immigrant communities. Which is not to say that there was no criminal element, only that it took other forms.

Newly arriving German immigrants provided a lucrative source of plunder for the German criminals of the type known as "runners." They met the immigrants as they disembarked and stole their baggage, or led them to "ein gutes Gasthaus" that specialized in separating German immigrants from their cash. They posed as "ticket agents" and sold the new arrivals tickets for their passage west—at exorbitant prices. Some made this trade even more profitable by selling counterfeit tickets.[106] The runners' trade was severely curtailed after 1855, when the immigrant reception center opened at Castle Garden and they lost their access to new arrivals,[107] but swindling greenhorns continued to be a prosperous trade for some as long as there were greenhorns to swindle.

Skilled German engravers and printers sometimes capitalized upon the fact that New York was a bigger market for banknotes than for German books. The multitudes of different notes circulating as currency tempted them into counterfeiting on a grand scale. Carl Ullrich was arrested in 1856 with plates for printing forged notes from the Bank of England, Prussian and Saxon banks, and the Rockville Bank of Connecticut—he was only nineteen years old, but his plates were said to be very good.[108] The German counterfeiters were rarely arrested, but their activities were attested to by frequent notices of forged German banknotes published in the New Yorker *Staats-Zeitung*.[109]

Another skilled criminal activity was robbing bank safes—and the Germans always specialized in the skilled trades. The most famous of the German bank burglars was Max or Mark Shinburn, a Prussian with pretensions to gentility. He robbed banks from Baltimore to Vermont during the 1860s and 1870s, but his base was in Kleindeutschland. After a satisfying career he retired to Europe, where he was reputed to have bought himself the title of Baron Shindell of Monaco.[110]

There was, however, one criminal activity in which a number of German-Americans excelled. Kleindeutschland provided New York with most of its leading fences from 1850 to the 1880s. The fences of the 1850s, like Moses "Joe" Ehrich and "Old Unger" of Eldridge Street, were shopkeepers who did a thriving trade in stolen goods. Their operations were limited and they had to compete with many other fences, both German and Yankee.[111]

One of their competitors was Fredrika "Marm" Mandelbaum, who began her career peddling her loot from door to door. By 1862 she was using a haberdashery shop at 79 Clinton Street as a front and was reputed to have become a veritable female Moriarity of organized crime in New York. Not only did she dispose of stolen goods, she also selected the teams of thieves who acquired them and told the teams where and when to steal (she ran an intelligence network of dishonest servants to get this crucial information). At one point she reputedly established an academy of crime on Grand Street, which offered courses in everything from picking pockets to cracking safes (it is reported that she closed the academy after the son of a high police official was discovered among the students). Her organization was not disciplined enough to hold out against the reform drive of the early 1880s, however, and she was forced to abandon New York for a safer haven in 1884.[112]

Most of the German women thieves were, like Pauline Sholken, young women who took jobs as servants in order to rob their employers.[113] Some, like the notorious "Black Lena" Kleinschmidt, moved on to more profitable operations like blackmail. "Black Lena" did well enough to build herself a mansion over in Hackensack, and joined New Jersey society as the supposed widow of a South American mining engineer.[114]

Despite the notoriety of the Mandelbaums and Kleinschmidts, the most common form of criminal activity for German women was prostitution. It is hard to say how many German women were involved in this trade. Contemporary estimates of the total number of prostitutes in the city at any one time vary widely. In 1866, a bishop denounced the wicked city and claimed that it held 20,000 prostitutes. The police responded that there were only 3,300.[115] Both figures are suspect and William Sanger's prostitution census of 1858 estimated that the city then had about 6,000 prostitutes. The proportion who came from the German community is also subject to sharply differing estimates. A police census in 1856 reported that 90 percent of the city's prostitutes were foreign born and that about 40 percent were German, but a report from Blackwell's Island (where arrested prostitutes were imprisoned) only two years later stated that half the prostitutes were American-born and only one-eighth were from Germany—essentially the same proportion reported by Sanger that year.[116] In any case, it is certain that hundreds, or even thousands, of Kleindeutschland's girls and women were engaged in prostitution at any one time and that they were greatly outnumbered by their Irish and American sisters in the trade.

Most of the German prostitutes worked in small-scale and relatively respectable brothels. Three or four young women would pay half their earnings (for room and board) to a couple who ran the establishment, the man tending bar in front and the wife doing the cooking and cleaning. Sanger's description of these establishments (some of which would appear to have been Griesinger's "basements with friendly service" but which were described very differently by Sanger) sounds most domestic:

> There is a public bar room opening directly from the street. . . . the room is very clean; a common sofa, one or two setees, and a number of chairs are ranged round the walls; there is a small table with some German newspapers upon it; a piano, upon which the proprietor or his bar-keeper at intervals performs a national melody; and a few prints or engravings complete its furniture. Two or three girls are in different parts of the room engaged in knitting or sewing; for German girls, whether virtuous or

> prostitute, seem to have a horror of idleness, and even in such a place as this are seldom seen without their work. . . . He [the visitor] is surprised at the entire absence of all those noisey elements generally considered inseparable from a low-class house of prostitution.[117]

Behind the barroom was a series of small bedrooms where the women took customers who wanted more than a drink and conversation. Whether the young women were independent entrepreneurs working out of a convenient locale or actually employees working under the control of the couple who ran the establishment is unclear. It may, in fact, have varied from one house to another.

Conclusions

The mature economy of Kleindeutschland included an occupational range that went from street urchins to magnates and included most of the occupations in between. While it was weighted toward the middle elements —the skilled workers, artisans, and shopkeepers—there was plenty of scope for class formation, and fully fledged class antagonisms developed between the German workers and their German employers.[118] As we shall see, this antagonism gave rise to the increasingly class-conscious German-American trade union movement of New York that impressed Samuel Gompers as being so "virile and resourceful,"[119] and that was the backbone of American socialist organizations from the Arbeiterbund (Workers' League) of the 1850s to the Socialist Labor party of the 1880s and 1890s.[120]

The developing class conflicts further complicated an already complex social situation in German New York. New business elites sought to take their "rightful" place at the head of community institutions and were resisted by older elites, while workers sought to develop their own autonomous institutions. The result was often a series of parallel organizations and institutions, as several alternative subcultures struggled for hegemony over the German-American community.

CHAPTER FIVE

Religion

The American ethnic community has typically been homogeneous in religion. Irish, Polish, or Italian generally meant Roman Catholic (although each practiced the religion in a distinctive national style); Scottish, Welsh, or Scandinavian usually meant Protestant (though it might be of a Presbyterian, Methodist, or Lutheran variety); and Greek meant Eastern Orthodox. Kleindeutschland too reflected the religious condition of its homeland, but the German states were far from homogeneous in religion. Neither Protestantism nor Catholicism had been able to establish itself as the sole religion of the German nation, despite the decades of wars and massacres that devastated Germany in the seventeenth century. After the Thirty Years War, each German state established the religion of its ruling house, but this sometimes left large portions of the population disaffected and alienated from the state religion. This problem was exacerbated by the major consolidation of the German states by the Congress of Vienna after the Napoleonic wars. Mostly Protestant Franconia was swallowed by Catholic Bavaria, while both Catholic and Calvinist territories in the Rhinelands were incorporated into Lutheran Prussia. Then, to complicate the picture further, virtually all of these territories had Jewish ghettos and/or communities of emancipated Jews.[1] This religious turmoil often weakened all religious ties in many parts of Germany and hastened the spread of secularization in the nineteenth century.

Thus Kleindeutschland developed into a social patchwork. Religious communities that placed religion before nationality (as in the motto of the *Katholische Volkszeitung*, "First Catholic, then German")[2] were mixed with secular communities where religion was of secondary, or even minimal, importance.

What especially distinguished German New York from many other immigrant communities in America was the overwhelming predominance of its secular subcommunities over its religious ones. In 1860, the New Yorker *Staats-Zeitung* reported the estimate that about half of New York's Germans were completely unaffiliated with any religion.[3] On another occasion, the *Staats-Zeitung* suggested that fewer than one out of five German immigrants were regular churchgoers.[4] Because Kleindeutschland's *Kirchendeutschen* (church Germans) were not the dominant element in German New York, they are not being given a central role in the overall analysis of German New York. Nonetheless, the issue of religion and Kleindeutschland's religious subcommunities must still be considered if we are to have any real understanding of German New York.

Catholics

The largest of the religious communities of Kleindeutschland was Roman Catholic. The early emigration from Germany was largely from Catholic regions in the south and west and the immigrants brought their Catholicism with them to the New World. It was a Catholicism forged in the religious struggles of Germany and it frequently displayed the fervor of its Counter-Reformation origins. For Catholic activists, the Protestant "heresy" was as important and alive an issue in the nineteenth century as it had been in the time of Martin Luther.[5] With non-Catholic Germans cherishing equally bitter memories of past and current outrages, the line separating devout Catholics from non-Catholic Kleindeutschland was sharply drawn.

It is difficult, however, to determine the size of the German Catholic community. Contemporary estimates from the 1860s vary from 28,000 to 49,000, while Jay Dolan has estimated that the number may have been as high as 70,000. Dolan, however, includes in his estimate thousands of nominal Catholics who hadn't received sacraments in "twenty, thirty or forty years." As even the lower estimates include all those confirmed in the church, regardless of later beliefs and practices, it is more reasonable to speak of a Catholic community that encompassed perhaps one-third of Kleindeutschland's population (a figure comparable to estimates for other German-American communities in the mid-nineteenth century).[6]

While some of Kleindeutschland's Catholics may have been "First Catholic, then German," they were German enough to insist upon worshipping in German churches. They petitioned for a priest "who is capable of undertaking the Spiritual Care of our souls in the German language" as early as 1808.[7] The slogan "language saves faith" would be heard for a century.[8] New York and Kleindeutschland got their first German Catholic church in 1833, with the arrival of a wealthy Austrian priest named Johann Stephen Raffeiner. He used his own money to lease a church in the Thirteenth Ward and laid the basis for the formation of the St. Nicholas Kirche on Second Street. It was characteristic of the relationship between the German Catholics and the non-German hierarchy that the national parish for Germans was not formally accepted by the diocese until nine years later.[9] The German churches remained conspicuously separate from the diocese through the years and finally participated in a German-American challenge to the authority of the Irish-American hierarchy in the late 1880s.[10]

New York's bishops tolerated the independent Germans, with "their narrow national feeling," and did little either to interfere with them or to advance Catholicism among German New Yorkers. In the words of one New York Irish churchman in 1865, "our ordinary authorities almost ignore their [the Germans'] existence." New German churches were established by their congregations, who would first build a church and then ask the bishop for a priest. Bishop Hughes did foster the growth of the German churches to the extent of appointing Johann Raffeiner as German vicar-general in 1853, but the office lapsed with Raffeiner's death in 1861 and was not reestablished until 1875. Despite being thus left to their own devices, the Germans established seven Catholic churches in New York City before the Civil War.[11]

The strong community basis of the German Catholic churches led to problems when conflicts arose between the priests and the important laymen who had paid for the church building and held legal title to it. Such "trusteeism" conflicts commonly plagued the early Catholic Church in America.[12] Disputes with his parishioners at St. Nicholas Kirche led Johann Raffeiner to abandon the parish in 1840. His successors over the next two years were quick to follow suit when they found that they were expected to defer to the lay trustees. Bishop Hughes then turned the problem over to the European-based order of Redemptorists in 1842 and they installed a "fighting" priest, Gabriel Rumpler. Rumpler demanded "subjugation, obedience and a spirit of peace," but he found no peace at St. Nicholas. After two years of battle, Rumpler finally led his supporters out of St. Nicholas to found a new church, Most Holy Redeemer, two blocks away. Similar struggles took place in many other German Catholic churches and there was even an attempt in 1846–47 to establish a German-American Catholic Church independent of Rome.[13]

Kleindeutschland's Most Holy Redeemer became the leading German Catholic church in New York City, though it remained less influential than Johann Raffeiner's Holy Trinity across the river in Brooklyn.[14] The Redemptorists made Most Holy Redeemer a showplace for their missions in America and they maintained seven priests and numerous religious brothers in the parish.[15] In 1851, seven years after they founded the new church, its wooden structure was replaced by a magnificent stone edifice that the Germans called their "cathedral."[16] Its 250-foot tower, though modified, still dominates that part of New York's Lower East Side as it once dominated all of Kleindeutschland.

The Redemptorists were a missionary order and their activities extended beyond the usual ministering to their parish. They held periodic revival meetings (comparable to the extravaganzas of their American Protestant contemporaries) designed to bring lapsed Catholics back into the church. These revivals stressed such flamboyant preaching that the vivid description of the fires of hell by one of Most Holy Redeemer's pastors reportedly brought out the local fire company.[17] The revivals were aggressively extended beyond the Catholic community and every effort was made to achieve Protestant conversions as well as Catholic renewal.[18]

Another element in the success of Most Holy Redeemer was the Redemptorists' promotion of the cult of Mary. That had been one of the bases of the order's popularity in Germany and it was particularly effective in providing a sense of continuity and security for Catholic women immigrants (though Marian devotion was characteristic of nineteenth-century Catholicism generally and women immigrants of all nationalities found refuge in its comforts). Marianism did not appeal only to women, though, and hundreds of men took active roles in parish societies like the Archconfraternity of the Immaculate Heart of Mary.[19]

Organized parish activities were the major defense of the German Catholic community against the threat raised by German ethnicity (and its subversive associations with Protestantism and republicanism). Nativism and the danger of Irish domination of the church were unifying factors within the community as it battled against outside forces, but German ethnicity was a subversive force from within. It could be countered most successfully by as much segregation as possible from non-Catholic Germans and their contaminating influences. The German Catholic churches thus encouraged the formation of large numbers of Catholic associations to provide alternatives to the innumerable non-Catholic *Vereine* of Kleindeutschland. In addition to the usual religious confraternities and parish relief societies, Most Holy Redeemer sponsored numerous mutual aid societies, singing societies, and even militia companies like the Jägercompagnie and the Henry Henning Guards. In effect, an effort was made to create a parallel Catholic community within Kleindeutschland, free of the influences of Protestantism, republicanism (either of the German or the American variety), and socialism.[20]

The Catholic church community was often very much out of step with the rest of Kleindeutschland in these matters. When most of the Germans in New York were electrified by the news of the German revolutions of 1848–50 and rallied around the red, black, and gold flag of a German republic, the German Catholic press denounced the "red republicans with blood on their hands."[21] The monarchies of Austria and Bavaria were, after all, among the primary supports of Catholicism in Germany—and of German Catholicism in America.[22] The militant antirepublicanism of the German church effectively alienated many liberals and republicans who had been raised as Catholics but who could not accept the church's politics. One such was Jacob Uhl, the son of a Bavarian army officer and a lapsed Catholic. He was the owner/editor of the New Yorker *Staats-Zeitung,* which was the leading German paper in the city and was demonstrably hostile to Catholicism.[23] Another lapsed Catholic was the notorious atheist Karl Heinzen, who had started training to be a Jesuit in his youth but who had become a leading republican agitator and advocate of tyrannicide before seeking refuge in New York.[24]

Nor were the ordinary artisans and workers of Kleindeutschland drawn closer to the church when a Father Müller, of Most Holy Redeemer, told striking tailors in 1850 that it was their religious duty to return to work—and then had the members of a tailors' committee who came to remonstrate with him arrested.[25]

This same Father Müller was also notorious for his zeal in collecting pew rents, though he was not alone in being accused of "cupidity for money."[26] Immigrants from Catholic Germany were accustomed to a state-supported church and often resented the frequent pleas for funds that emanated from a clergy dependent upon voluntary contributions. These factors reinforced an anticlerical tradition with deep roots in Catholic Germany. Kleindeutschland's Catholics were divided into two groups—one active in and loyal to the church and the other indifferent (or even hostile) to it.

Protestants

Protestantism seems to have had an even weaker hold on the immigrants to Kleindeutschland than Catholicism did. A Reformed Church minister said in 1856 that "if all the German churches of New York were full, of 100,000 Germans no more than 15,000 would be in them."[27] When the representatives of twenty-five Protestant organizations proposed to establish a German Protestant newspaper for the New York area in 1860, they estimated that of New York's "85,000" Germans, 28,000 were Catholic, 7,000 were Jewish, 42,000 were unaffiliated and only 8,000 were Protestant.[28] Given the great numbers who had immigrated from Protestant areas of Germany, these estimates would seem at first to be much too low, but church records indicate that they are not far off. A generous tabulation of the memberships of New York's German Lutheran churches in 1871 totals only twelve to seventeen thousand. With the addition of perhaps four to five thousand German members of the other Protestant churches, that still adds up to only sixteen to twenty-one thousand committed German Protestants out of over 280,000 German-American

New Yorkers.[29] German New York was apparently too secular a city for the more religious German Protestants (as for the more religious German Catholics)—it either repelled them or it weaned them from their faith.

That is not to say that there were no islands of Protestant, church-oriented Germans in Kleindeutschland. There were a few Lutheran congregations of over one thousand members each, and there were many smaller congregations of other denominations that averaged two to four hundred members.[30] These congregations, like their Catholic counterparts, provided refuge and comfort for the pious in the strange and wicked New World. But also like their Catholic counterparts in New York, they failed to develop into central ethnic community institutions the way German churches reportedly did in many other German-American centers.[31]

Germans had been welcome in New York's Dutch Reformed Church since the days of New Amsterdam. In fact half the services of New York's Dutch church had been performed in German around the time of the American Revolution.[32] The Reformed Church particularly appealed to immigrants from those parts of the Rhineland and northwest Germany that were Calvinist ("Reformed"), but immigrants from Lutheran Germany were also often willing to join this well-established, aggressively proselytizing, and financially secure Protestant denomination—especially in the early years of the great migration. There was, however, a tendency for congregations of former Lutherans to sever their ties to the Reformed Church after they were well established (and no longer needed outside financial support). Then they either became independent congregations or joined a Lutheran synod.[33]

In addition to several small congregations in Kleindeutschland, the Reformed Church maintained an evangelical mission on Houston Street, which was particularly active in recruiting converts and new members for the church. Although its membership never rose much above three hundred, the mission's activities involved many more people. Its youth organization, the Christliche Jugend Verein, had over six hundred members in the mid-1850s and it was only one of the mission's auxiliary organizations.[34] After 1860, the mission was in the hands of Julius Geyer, a particularly capable minister and a leading spokesman for Kleindeutschland's Protestants. He was also reputed to have won many converts—from Lutheranism.[35]

German Lutheranism also had roots that went far back in New York's history. By 1750, Germans had become the predominant element in St. Matthew's, New York City's Lutheran parish, and they made German the official language of the church. Although the German language was abandoned early in the nineteenth century, it was reestablished at St. Matthew's in 1837, when the great migration from Germany was first getting underway.[36] St. Matthew's Church, on Mott Street to the west of Kleindeutschland, was an important community center for the early settlers of the German East Side. In 1837, the German Widows and Orphans Society was organized around the parish. It met in the church and the minister was ex officio one of the directors of the society.[37] The Deutsche Gesellschaft, or German Society of New York, also used the church as a meeting place, though it was in no way affiliated with the church.[38] As Kleindeutschland grew, however, St. Matthew's and the other German Lutheran churches became less and less central to community life.

The German Lutheran ministers who led the New York churches tended to be extremely conservative in both religion and politics. This appealed to those who were most likely to support the church, but it isolated them from the rest of Kleindeutschland. It was typical of these ministers that Carl Stohlmann, the pastor of St. Matthew's, condemned the German revolutions of 1848. He attacked the hero of the Baden revolt, Friedrich Hecker, as "an enemy of religion, order and peace."[39] This aroused the ire of much of Kleindeutschland's populace and served to further isolate Stohlmann and his supporters in the German Lutheran community. In the 1850s many of the religious Lutherans of the New York area moved to new parishes in Brooklyn and other outlying districts, away from the community with which they were so much out of sympathy. There, not too far away from the German Catholics' Holy Trinity parish, they established their own communities, which flourished in the 1860s and 1870s.[40]

Not all Lutherans were quite so conservative, though. In 1839 a group of Old Lutherans from Silesia (members of a normally very conservative sect) formed a congregation that became rather innovative. After a split in the congregation in the late 1840s, one faction followed their pastor to the California goldfields. The other faction, meanwhile, joined the "Neo-Israelites," who were known for the length of their beards and their aggressive proselytizing—both on the streets of Kleindeutschland and on the docks where the immigrant ships arrived.[41]

Freethinkers

A third major religious community of Kleindeutschland was a child of the Enlightenment and often claimed not to be religious at all. The Universal Christians, Rationalists, Secularisten, Freidenker, Frei Gemeinden, and Freimännervereine covered a spectrum that started with something approximating Unitarianism/Universalism, extended through rationalism, deism, and secularism, and included an extremist current of crusading atheism. They had their own churches (though they often called them meeting halls), Sunday schools, parochial schools, "Anti-Revivals," and holidays (like Tom Paine's birthday). In the mid-1840s, the German Rationalists and the Universal Christians were even listed as churches in the city directory (though this was later considered inappropriate).[42]

The Freethinkers were not a major religious group as a result of great numbers: in fact, they probably never numbered more than a few thousand. They did, however, include in their membership a large proportion of Kleindeutschland's intellectuals, radical republicans, and (especially in the 1850s) community leaders. Philipp Merkle, for example, was speaker of the Universal Christian Church on Christie Street in 1845 and was later active in Kleindeutschland's leading Frei Gemeinde. He was also active in the New York Democratic party (where he was a leader of the successful effort to keep the Republican party from making significant inroads in the New York German vote in 1856 and 1860) and in several organizations promoting democratic revolutions in Germany.[43] His real importance for Kleindeutschland, though, was as founder and president of the Harugari, the largest German fraternal order in America (with 5,119 members in 1854 and over 20,000 by 1871).[44] A fellow Frei Gemeinde associate and the publisher of the antireligious paper *Asträa* was Jacob Uhl, publisher of the *Staats-Zeitung* and a leading figure in Kleindeutschland until his death in 1852.[45] Rudolph Dulon, the well-known speaker of the Kleindeutschland Frei Gemeinde in the 1850s and the principal of the German-American School, was also the father-in-law of Turnverein leader and Civil War general Franz Sigel.[46] Another forty-eighter, F. Adolf Sorge, was active in the secret Secularistenbund in the 1850s and a member of several German revolutionary societies, the New York Kommunisten Klub, and numerous musical societies (he was a music teacher). In the 1860s and 1870s he was America's leading socialist, first directing the activities of the First International in the United States and later taking Karl Marx's place as its German Secretary when its headquarters were moved to New York.[47] Such activity illustrates a leading characteristic of many Freethinkers—they were inveterate joiners who often took leadership positions in several organizations. Thus they had a very important place in the leadership structure of Kleindeutschland and other German-American communities.

The Freethinker societies were less conspicuous in post-Civil War Kleindeutschland, though they remained active as middle-class supporters of reform. While some participated in the Liberal Republican movement of 1872, others formed a Freethinkers' section of the First International. Despite the developing tendency toward moderation and away from their radical roots, all the Frei Gemeinden joined together in protest against the

1874 police attack on a workers' eight-hour demonstration in Tompkins Square Park.[48] They also continued their active participation in community affairs, with Frei Gemeinde members (like their speaker Dr. Lilienthal) taking leading positions in other community organizations, including the Deutsche Gesellschaft, the Turnverein, and various singing societies.[49]

Just as the Freidenkers' influence was beginning to fade among their original supporters in Kleindeutschland, it was revived by liberal elements within the German-Jewish community of New York. In 1876, Felix Adler founded the Ethical Culture Society, which continued to promote the Freethinkers' ideals and a social gospel for another century.[50]

Jews

German Jews were a conspicuous portion of Kleindeutschland's population. Theodor Griesinger, a thoroughgoing anti-Semite, was shocked to discover that such bastions of German culture as New York's German theaters were dependent on Jewish theatergoers.[51] German Jews were also reported as participants in all kinds of community activities (though they were frequently identified only as Germans).[52] Their numbers, however, are difficult to ascertain. Estimates from contemporary sources often varied widely—even for the same year. While the *Commercial Advertiser* estimated that there were 7,000 German Jews in the city in 1860 and Isaac Lesser figured 9,000 for the same year, the Board of Delegates of American Israelites and several other sources give a much higher estimate of about 20,000 (and even this is probably too low).[53]

Part of the difficulty stems from the fact that a majority of German Jews were "unaffiliated" in the religious sense. Despite this, many of the "unaffiliated" were still very much a part of a distinctive German-Jewish community (this was more true of "unaffiliated" German Jews than it was of "unaffiliated" German Catholics and Protestants, but there was some tendency in that direction for them too). Even a self-proclaimed deist, when of Jewish origin, could take a prominent place in the explicitly Jewish German community, as was demonstrated by Abraham Chailly's vice presidency of the Maimonides Library Association.[54] Many other deists, agnostics, and atheists of Jewish origin didn't participate in the recognized Jewish community, but they socialized heavily with others of similar origins, encouraged their children to marry others of Jewish descent, and had themselves buried in Jewish cemeteries. In other words, they were Jewish deists, Jewish agnostics, and Jewish atheists.

Anshe Chesed, the first German-dominated synagogue in New York, had been established in 1828 and was a purely German congregation by the late 1830s. By 1845, two other orthodox German synagogues had

Table 13
German-Jewish Population of
New York City, 1846–85

Year	Population
1846	7,000
1850	10,000
1855	15,000
1860	20,000
1871	35–45,000
1885	85,000

Note: Again, most of these figures are adjusted from estimates of the total Jewish population corrected to exclude non-German Jews.

Sources: Hyman Grinstein, *The Rise of the Jewish Community of New York, 1654–1860,* pp. 23, 469–71, 528–29; New Yorker *Staats-Zeitung,* 10/25/1860; New York *Times,* 12/18/1870; Rudolph Glanz, *Jews in Relation to the Cultural Milieu of the Germans in America up to the 1880s,* p. 27; *Jahrbücher der Deutschen in Amerika, 1873,* p. 98.

been formed in Kleindeutschland and, for a short time, Anshe Chesed and Rodeph Shalom had shared the services of New York's first real rabbi, Leo Merzbacher. When Merzbacher left the orthodox congregations to join a group of reform advocates in the creation of Temple Emanu-El in 1845, the orthodox invited another Bavarian rabbi, Max Lilienthal, to come to New York. They designated Lilienthal chief rabbi and he served all three orthodox synagogues of the "united German Jewish community" until the end of 1847. Then Lilienthal resigned, after coming into conflict with the synagogues' trustees, and the "united German Jewish community" dissolved—never to revive.[55]

The reformers of Temple Emanu-El were the heirs of the Jewish Enlightenment in Germany and their reforms were intended to modernize Judaism so that it might, in their words, "occupy a position of greater respect."[56] They began their reforms with superficial changes in the form of the service, starting with a choir and German hymns. Then they introduced a sermon, a shortened and simplified service, an organ, and even the seating of men and women together.[57] In effect they moved steadily in the direction of a Jewish church that would be distinguishable from its neighbors only by the details of its theology. Indeed, in 1876 Felix Adler (the son of Rabbi Samuel Adler of Temple Emanu-El) took the final step of abandoning even the theology when he established the Ethical Culture Society.[58] While their "benighted" orthodox coreligionists continued to maintain something of the cultural separation that had distinguished German Jews since the Middle Ages, the Reform Jews joined their secular compatriots in opting wholeheartedly for a complete identification with German *Kultur*. Their self-identification as Jewish-American Germans was made clear by Rabbi Felsenthal of Chicago: "Racially I am a Jew, for I have been born among the Jewish nation. Politically I am an American as patriotic, as enthusiastic, as devoted an American citizen as it is possible to be. But spiritually I am a German, for my inner life has been profoundly influenced by Schiller, Goethe, Kant and the other intellectual giants of Germany."[59] This was, indeed, a formula which would have been fully acceptable to most of the unaffiliated and secularized among the German Jews of New York. To the orthodox, however, it was anathema. Attracted by the prestige associated with *Kultur* or repelled by its threat to Jewish orthodoxy, they would all have stressed that they were German-American Jews, Jewish in spirit as well as "race."

After growing slowly in its first decade, Temple Emanu-El became the elite German synagogue in New York by the 1860s. Hostility between the Reform Jews and their "Finsterlinge" (obscurantist) opponents among the orthodox divided the religious Jews of Kleindeutschland into two separate communities and they avoided common social action when possible.[60] Separated by enormous hostility and relatively free from pressure to unite in defense against anti-Semitism, the strongest tie between them was their common sense of superiority over the "lesser orders" of Jews from eastern Europe.[61]

Outside the synagogues, the Jews of Kleindeutschland joined their compatriots in forming numerous mutual aid societies, fraternal orders, and other social organizations. The best known of these is the fraternal order of B'nai B'rith, which was founded in New York in 1843. It had ten lodges and one thousand members in the city by 1860 and was closely followed in size by the Free Sons of Israel. The latter was started by B'nai B'rith dissidents in 1849 and had eight New York City lodges in 1860. These (and other) fraternal orders provided mutual aid and burial benefits along with their fraternal ties and became central institutions for the Jews of Kleindeutschland.[62]

The mutual aid societies, *Landsmannschaften*, fraternal orders, library associations, and other *Vereine* of Kleindeutschland's Jews were generally distinguishable from their non-Jewish equivalents only by the Jewish origins of their members. Otherwise they carried on the same sorts of activities, in the same language and with similar rituals. The Jewish organizations did place a somewhat greater emphasis on burial benefits (so that their members would be eligible for burial in Jewish cemeteries even if they were not synagogue members), but this did not reduce their overall similarity. Many of Kleindeutschland's Jews participated in the broader-based German political and cultural organizations, but may have turned to the Jewish *Vereine* for more social activities. There were also organizations that were not exclusively Jewish but had predominantly Jewish memberships (like the Orpheus Gesangverein).[63] Of course some of the more "elite" *Vereine* of Kleindeutschland may have excluded Jews. The Arion Gesangverein blackballed a prospective Jewish member in 1870 in what may have been an act of anti-Semitism (it also may not have been anti-Semitism, since the blackballed candidate was the son of a founding member of the *Verein*), but the Arion's action was widely condemned by the city's German press and community leaders. If it was anti-Semitism, it was the only case of conspicuous public anti-Semitism found in mid-nineteenth-century German New York.[64]

Some Jewish German-Americans were, indeed, widely recognized as leaders of the German community. Sigismund Kaufmann, for example, was not only the speaker of the New Yorker Socialistischer Turnverein from its founding in the 1850s to the 1870s but also an officer of the Deutsche Gesellschaft from 1858 through the 1880s and was president of the society in 1873 and from 1876 to 1879.[65] The leading German physician in New York was Abraham Jacobi, the "father of pediatrics" in America. He was a prominent doctor at the German Hospital (and at Mt. Sinai Hospital, New York Medical College, and the Columbia College of Physicians and Surgeons as well) and was an influential figure in Kleindeutschland long before he was elected president of the American Medical Association in 1912.[66] Many other German-American Jews played leading roles in Kleindeutschland, whether as playwrights like Max Cohnheim, businessmen like the Seligman brothers and Jacob Schiff, social reformers like Charles Schiff, or labor leaders like tailors Jacob Morstadt and Charles Miller or cigar makers Adolph Strasser and Louis Berliner.[67] Nonetheless, few of those recognized as leaders of the broader community had retained really close ties to the community of religious Jews. We may note, in this regard, that while the Hessen-Darmstädters were proud to claim Felix Adler as a native son, they made no mention of his father, the well-known rabbi.[68]

When Kleindeutschlanders mobilized in support of the German revolutions of 1848, a number of German Jewish societies marched in the grand parade, and the Harmony Society (a German-Jewish library association) held a public poetry *Fest* for German freedom.[69] That appears, however, to have been the last time that the specifically Jewish societies marched with the rest of Kleindeutschland. This may not indicate any increasing division between the Jews and non-Jews of Kleindeutschland, but rather an increasing integration of the more secular Jews into the nondenominational cultural and political societies (like Julius M. Cohen of the Independent Germania Schützen-Corps and the Plattdeutschen Volksfest-Verein, or Fred Levy and Richard Lehmann of the Eichenkranz Gesangverein).[70] With the failure of the 1848 revolutions, the more or less religiously oriented Jewish societies seem to have turned back inwards toward a more narrowly defined German-Jewish community—and to have had little to do with the rest of Kleindeutschland.

Conclusion

The German sociolinguist Heinz Kloss divided nineteenth-century German-America into two groups, the *Kirchendeutschen*—or church Germans—and the *Vereinsdeutschen.*[71] Viewed against this analytical scale the vast majority of Kleindeutschlanders were in the second camp (which we shall turn to in Chapter 6). The most successful religious groups (in terms of involving large numbers in church activities) were those that sponsored their own *Vereine* to compete for the loyalty of the *Vereinsdeutschen* populace. Although each religious community had its penumbra of denominational *Vereine,* only the Catholic *Vereine* developed a true mass following (and even they only involved a minority of Kleindeutschland's Catholics in their parallel *Vereine*-world). The minority religious communities of *Kirchendeutschen* tended to withdraw into themselves and frequently withdrew physically from Kleindeutschland—forming homogeneous settlements of their own in outlying districts of the city or its suburbs. Brooklyn, as we have seen, was the favored site for *Kirchendeutschen* settlements and Eduard Pelz voiced a common majority sentiment when he described it in his 1867 German guidebook to New York City: "On Sundays Brooklyn is especially dead, a contribution of its many churches. Anyone who wants to avoid the long faces of bored churchgoers flees the place on the Sabbath, and the ferryboats are full of passengers until late at night."[72]

Kleindeutschland was basically a secular community where religion played a far from central role. As we shall see in the following chapters, dialect and region of origin were often as significant as denominational differences in the organization of social life. While religious differences remained important for some aspects of social life, they gradually ceased being the major sources of social conflict within the German community. Changes in the economic structure of German New York generated class-based ideologies that replaced religion as the motor of social conflict within the German-American community.[73]

CHAPTER SIX

Social Life

> In New York no adequate German theater can maintain itself, in New York no German opera can prosper, in New York no German lecture series can be successful, in New York no worthwhile German newspaper can establish itself; but there is a German beer hall in New York that cost $120,000 to build. There you have German New York!
>
> Karl Heinzen, in *Pionier* (Jan. 4, 1857)

> Beer, Dance, Business—that is the world of the German "Volkes" in New York. It is like living in Buffalo!
>
> Karl Heinzen, in *Pionier* (Aug. 1, 1858)

Karl Heinzen was a cultural snob and not easily satisfied, but there was certainly an element of truth in his vitriolic condemnation of the cultural level of the German populace of Kleindeutschland. The Germans did like their beer inordinately well and there is no question but that, fond as they were of fine music, many preferred a good dance tune to a symphony. By the same token, they preferred comedies and light drama to the classics when they went to the theater. While this left Karl Heinzen and some other intellectuals sneering, it suited the hard-working Kleindeutschlanders. For those of us less committed than Heinzen to the glories of German *Kultur,* the popular culture of German New York remains a testament to the extent to which an immigrant community could create a satisfactory and comfortable social life under difficult conditions.

Kleindeutschland boasted thousands of beer halls, saloons, wine gardens, concert halls, club rooms, and other places where wine and beer were sold. Some streets, like Avenue A and the Bowery, were almost entirely devoted to such places. It was said that "on the Bowery you can count three dozen in the space of a hundred paces, often three in one house: a basement, a store and a saloon; the saloon, or *Lokal,* being up on the first floor."[1] Here an immigrant could meet his friends and relax, away from the dark and crowded tenements. The "basements with friendly service" catered to the rougher elements and to single men looking for easy girls—or outright prostitutes. These basements provided crude but gaudy quarters for crude but gaudy amusements.

They were avoided by the more respectable elements of Kleindeutschland.[2]

The local, on the other hand, was the place for the respectable immigrant to relax after work or in the evening: "If you go in the evening to the Bowery or stroll along the eastern streets where so many Germans live, you will come across, here and there, brightly lit locals which are very lively. Through the shop window you see the German worker sitting around a large table with his whole family—and ranting about politics. The little boy, who is just tall enough to reach the table edge, has a mighty tankard of 'lager' . . . in front of him and the Herr Papa views his youngest with satisfaction while the Frau Mama stuffs his mouth with pretzels and refreshes herself with a cool drink."[3] These saloons often catered to specialized clienteles, residents of a local neighborhood, workers in a particular trade, immigrants from a particular locality in Germany, church members, or political radicals. They provided meeting rooms for *Vereine* whose meetings brought in a steady flow of customers—who came in early and had some beer or wine, drank steadily through the meeting, and then stayed on to socialize and drink with friends after the meeting ended. Some of the more popular *Lokale,* like Hillenbrand's on Hester Street, the Concordia on Avenue A, and the Germania on the Bowery, grew into large conglomerations of meeting halls, bars, ballrooms, billiard rooms, and bowling alleys. Some of the larger *Vereine,* like the Social Reformers, the Turners, and the shooting associations opened their own meeting quarters with similar facilities.[4] Between the many *Lokale* and the large meeting halls, the number of organizations that could meet at once in Kleindeutschland was phenomenal, but the Germans must have met the challenge as few halls failed to prosper—or at least survive.

Even the largest and most elaborate of the meeting halls was put to shame by the great beer halls, which Heinzen found so offensive. These were indeed the pride of Kleindeutschland; elaborate halls where whole families went on Sundays to meet with friends, drink beer, listen to music, and dance. A leading hall of the mid-century was described as

> an immense room on the second story, elaborately, and gaudily painted in fresco with scenes from the Dutch [*sic*] mythology (at least not from any other), in which naked goddesses, grim knights, terrific monsters and American eagles, are like Shelley's immortal combatants—"Feather and scale inextricably blended". The floor, on ordinary occasions, is filled with rough tables and wooden benches, and partly across one end runs a balconied platform by way of orchestra. Every Sunday night at this establishment a grand German and English concert, vocal and instrumental, takes place. Several female singers, with those marvelous guttural alternating voices resembling the compound creaking of a dry grindstone, or the

> cry of a guinea-hen, are regularly engaged here and perform in both German and English. The orchestra consists of a gigantic seraphina, two violins, a flute and a fagotto, all played by Germans, and of course played well. These concerts are regularly attended by the respectable German men and women residing in the city, to the number of from twelve to seventeen hundred. In pleasant weather the audience seldom falls below fifteen hundred. The price of admission is one shilling—which we believe, . . . includes a drink of Rhine wine or a swig of bierish. At any rate there are immense quantities of these liquids phlegmatically engulphed in the Germanesque oesophigi of the visitors, both male and female. Everything, however, is carried on in excellent order and there are very seldom any disturbances here. The audiences are not at all nice [*sic*], and are easily pleased—and in fact the performances themselves, so far at least as the instrumental music is concerned, are very respectable. Next to the orchestra a pretty large stage, with proscenium, drop-curtain and scenery, is constructed, at which during the week regular dramatic performances take place.[5]

There were a number of these magnificent establishments (like the Deutsches Volksgarten, the Atlantic Gardens, Nieblo's Saloon, Magar's Concert Hall, and Lindenmuller's Odeon) that provided Kleindeutschland with flourishing centers for popular culture. The owners of such emporia were leading members of Kleindeutschland's elite in the 1850s and we have seen how one of them, Gustav Lindenmuller of Lindenmuller's Odeon, was hailed as the social superior of the respectable merchant Gustav Schwab in "the Case of the Two Gustavs" in 1860.

While the beer halls would remain the place to go for music and amateur theatricals, by the early 1850s professional theater began to establish itself in Kleindeutschland. In 1854, the old Bowery Amphitheater was rebuilt as a proper theater seating 2,500 and renamed the Stadttheater. Mixing occasional offerings of classic drama with large doses of popular comedies, musicals, melodramas, and farces, the Stadttheater established German theater in New York on an enduring basis. Intellectuals like Heinzen deplored the paucity of classical productions, but the chronicler of the New York German theater reports that "Quantitatively . . . it would seem that the New York Stadttheater compares very favorably with that of the Court Theater at Dresden. Moreover an examination of both lists shows that no great qualitative differences existed, on the whole. A considerable portion of the inferior products that were seen on New York's German stage was also inflicted on the Dresden public."[6] In fact, the Stadttheater provided just what one might expect of a vigorous popular theater—popular entertainment that catered to the nineteenth-century popular taste for melodrama and farce.

Summer's heat closed the theaters, but the open-air beer gardens behind the beer halls kept up the pace of popular entertainments. Theatrical and musical performances of all kinds flourished there. The very streets of Kleindeutschland became music halls on hot summer nights:

> Even the children devoted their complete attention to the band of musicians in the middle of the block which treated everyone to a death defying performance of every piece in its well known repertoire. The young people, despite the heat of the evening, roused themselves to an impromptu dance everytime the band struck up a waltz. The boys and girls would dance through the openings in the ranks of spectators. It was the kind of night the musicians loved—when people shuddered at the thought of bed and, as long as their tired eyes held out, camped out in the open air of the streets where, along with the pleasures of music and dance, the beer jug made the rounds. On such nights the beer sellers and street musicians were in clover.[7]

Nonetheless, the city was no place to be in the summer and excursions and picnics were the order of the day. Family outings to Jones' Wood in upper Manhattan, or to the Sommertheater in Hoboken, or by boat to Egg Harbor on Long Island, were popular. Even more popular among the gregarious Kleindeutschlanders were large organized excursions and festivals. The Social Reform Association set the pace in 1846 when it organized an excursion up the Hudson to Rockland Lake. Eight or nine hundred Kleindeutschlanders went along and the *Staats-Zeitung* stressed the Germanness of the occasion.[8] The countryside near Hoboken was soon established as the most popular location for such festivals (though its supremacy was later challenged by Jones' Wood when an elaborate beer garden was established there). The New Jersey festival grounds were especially popular because the Jersey ferries left from docks on the side of Manhattan opposite Kleindeutschland, thus providing an excuse for a grand parade through the city.

The 1850 *Maifest* (May Day festival) of the Society of Germans for Decisive Progress was a typical example, though it was dwarfed in size by the festivals of later years: "Several thousand went over to Hoboken for the festival and only bad weather kept it from being the largest *Volksfest* ever held in New York. At 10 A.M. they assembled [the Turners, the Teacher's Battalion of the Social Reformers, the Freethinkers, the Society for Decisive Progress, the Social Reform Association, and the German Men's Choral Society] at City Hall Park. They marched with two bands from the park through the city to the Hudson ferry, and again from Hoboken to the festival site."[9] By the end of the 1850s, attendance at the larger festivals frequently ran to the tens of thousands (a New Yorker Musikfest at Jones' Wood in 1858 reportedly attracted over 50,000 participants).[10] The grand *Volksfeste* of the 1870s were even larger, with the first Plattdeutschen Volksfest in 1875 drawing 150,000 to Schützen Park in New Jersey after a massive parade from Tompkins Square Park to the Christopher Street ferry on the Hudson.[11] The festivals themselves followed a general pattern, typified by the following description of a small festival held during the Civil War:

SUMMER NIGHT'S FESTIVAL AT JONES' WOOD

> A peaceful scene was afforded, last evening, by one of the festivals peculiar to the Germans, and naturally located at the Jones' Wood. The Liederkranz Society had there a reunion, with singing and dancing, refreshments and kindly feelings, undisturbed by the rude noise of war. The amenities of peace as these people practice them have much in their favor, and put the noblest strife at a discount.
>
> It was a good night for sport in the open air, and hundreds of the brightest ornaments of German society—wholesome fraulines, the prettiest blondes, whitely dressed, their followers and also their parents ready to sympathize, but not to interfere—could be counted. The moon got up before the exercises began, and played upon the river flowing by, and lit the sails that glanced past right under the trees that spread their branches from the brink. This gentle luminary was assisted by many colored transparencies hung about the spacious platform, and among the leaves; and the young and the old sat in the bowers that were shaded for them, and in the pleasant breeze and moonlight, enjoyed each other's happiness, and cakes and beer unlimited.
>
> The time before dancing was filled with an admirable concert, both vocal and instrumental. The orchestra was well adjusted, and Mr. Joseph Noll led it, and selections from Rossini, Schumann, Schubert, Verdi, and other composers were performed. The voices of the choristers sounded very sweetly, joining in melodies that are full of feeling. After which the true gaiety of the occasion was introduced, and it would be madness to attempt to describe the picturesque effects produced by the dancers, or the simplicity and heartiness of their behavior, with the moon above and the lanterns below shining upon them.[12]

Just add a grand parade and gymnastic exhibitions, or sharpshooting contests, or poetry readings, or dramatic speeches and the description fits most of the festivals over several decades.[13]

While the *Tribune* said it would be madness to attempt to describe the dance, a less charitable colleague on the *Herald* provided this detailed, if hostile, description of the dance at a *Turnfest:*

THE GERMAN DANCE

> Several fine bands of music were in attendance yesterday, as on Monday, and afforded a fine opportunity for a . . . German dance. Unlike the constrained etiquette of other ball rooms, the German custom authorizes any gent present to ask a lady to dance, the lady of course assenting or

declining at her option. The music strikes up, and instantly on that spot, whether level or sloping is not material, a ring is formed, and a dozen couples whirl around with a peculiar hopping motion, which is always the same and perfectly regardless of the time. Fatness being a peculiarly attractive portion of the German beauties, the fat girls with low necked dresses generally get plenty of partners and hop off in the shaking style. Though order may be heaven's first law, it is decidedly not the law of the German dance, especially on a side hill [hillside?]. Bump they go against one another, the more the merrier, and the oftener the better. An unsophisticated gent observes the freedom of the dance, and the charming liberty of asking whomsoever he pleases to take a hop. His heart bounding with admiration of a beautiful fat girl, and implicitly believing her a German princess in disguise, he asks her to dance. She says nothing but "yaw," takes off her hat, hands her parasol to the nearest bystander, modestly stuffs her handkerchief down her neck, and complies. Round and round go the novice and the fat girl. Bump, thump, tumble, roll and sweat, till the fat girl takes out her handkerchief and puts it in her pocket. Round again they go, gent rather tired, fat girl blowing hard, but good for several rounds yet. Finally gent gives in, wondering at the remarkable physical endurance of his princess, who, as she tenderly takes leave of him, gives him a card similar to the following:

M. Klopfel

LAGERBIER AND OYSTER SALOON
No. ___ Delancey Street,
New York[14]

While May to September was the season for excursions and picnics, German New York had other social seasons as well. December and January were the "Carnival" season when every organization in Kleindeutschland, or so it seemed, held some sort of celebration. In one week in 1856, the *Staats-Zeitung* noted that there was a production at the playhouse, the Arion Society was giving a concert, the Teutonia Männerchor was holding a masked ball, and both the Social Reform Verein and the German Liederkranz were having social evenings at the Chinese Assembly Rooms.[15] Then there was another round of social affairs in late spring, that being the season for celebrating organizational anniversaries.[16]

Vereine and German-American Solidarity

The associations, or *Vereine,* of Kleindeutschland were legion. The Germans banded together for all kinds of ostensible purposes—or for none at all—and they did so on the basis of almost any shared characteristic—even down to a German Bald-headed Men's Verein.[17] Their mania for forming *Vereine* extended down to the very young, though *Vereine* for teenagers did not advertise in the newspapers. Samuel Gompers recalled from his childhood that he and his fourteen-year-old friends organized the Arion Base Ball and Social Club (which they later transformed into an Odd Fellows' lodge).[18] The *Verein* way of life, or *Vereinswesen,* dominated social life in Kleindeutschland as it did in most large German-American communities. That said, it is worthwhile to examine some of the main categories further.

The *Unterstützungsverein,* or sickness and death benefit society, was probably the most common form of *Verein* in Kleindeutschland. It could be organized around an occupation or a place of origin in Germany, but its ostensible function was to provide a form of cheap mutual assistance fund. An initiation fee of two or three dollars and a monthly payment of 12½ to 25 cents a month provided the members of such *Vereine* with a minimal income of two or three dollars a week if they got sick and a payment of perhaps $15.00 toward their funeral.[19] It also provided a reason for men of similar origins or status to socialize together regularly.

Unterstützungsvereine organized around a common occupation prevailed in the 1850s, when they also served some of the functions of trade unions,[20] but those organized around local origins proliferated in the 1860s and 1870s.[21] We may attribute this shift in organizational basis to a discovery that common origin was more reliable than common occupation in keeping the *Verein* treasurer honest in a new world where it was easy to change your name and occupation. Hometowners, or *Landsleute,* had been known since childhood and they couldn't run off with the treasury without the disgrace affecting their families. Furthermore, they would have to cut themselves off from their kin to avoid apprehension, raising the cost of dishonesty yet further. Common origin thus provided the source of mutual trust that was essential for the *Unterstützungsvereine* to operate.

These *Landsmannschaften,* as they were called, also provided formal mechanisms for strengthening local and regional ties from Germany. A decade after the first great wave of migration, just when particularism might have begun to weaken, German New Yorkers created formal organizations designed to strengthen local ties. Social activities—meetings, dances, and picnics—brought hometowners and their families together several times a year, while the mutual support provided in times of sickness and death deepened their emotional ties. When death intruded, the benefits went beyond financial and emotional support; *Landsmannschaft* membership assured the good turnout at funerals that symbolized and was an essential aspect of respectability. Beyond the funeral, the *Landsmannschaften* often held joint burial plots in cemeteries. They thereby established a permanent and more than symbolic bond between their members. In the long run, the *Landsmannschaften* transformed a nostalgic sense of identity with a place in Germany into a living social network that provided friendship, mutual aid, and solace in the present along with a sense of continuity with the past.

An *Unterstützungsverein* might have as few as sixteen members (though such a small *Verein* would have been very vulnerable to disaster) or it might have over three hundred members, but most seem to have had between fifty and one hundred members.[22] The ideal size would appear to have been large enough to provide financial stability and ensure a good turnout at funerals but small enough to provide a relaxed atmosphere where all the members knew each other.[23]

The *Unterstützungsvereine* and the *Landsmannschaften* provided mutual aid and fellowship, but many German New Yorkers craved something with more exotic rituals as well. Germany had boasted many a secret order and guild organization with elaborate rituals and pageantry, and the immigrants wanted this in their new home too. The first German Masonic lodge in New York was formed in 1819 and affiliated with the Prussian Grand Lodge in Germany. By 1871 there were eighteen German Masonic lodges in New York City, seventeen affiliated with Prussia and one with Hamburg (Masonic orders were, of course, forbidden in the Catholic German states).[24] Although these Masonic lodges were fairly numerous, they were clearly reserved for the well-to-do, at least by the 1870s. In the depression year of 1876, for example, the initiation fee for one lodge was $50, a figure far beyond the reach of ordinary German New Yorkers.[25] Other fraternal orders, like the Druids with their $5 initiation fee, would have had a broader appeal.[26]

While some German-speaking lodges affiliated with orders based in Germany and others attached themselves to American orders (Masons, Druids, Odd Fellows, Foresters, and Redmen), these orders generally provided little opportunity for German-Americans to rise to their more exalted positions. The solution was found in purely German-American orders. In the summer of 1840 a German section of New York's Odd Fellows broke away from the parent organization and established the order of Hermannssöhne.[27] In the next decade, German-American orders proliferated with the formation of the Vereinigte Deutscher Brüder, the Harugari, the Templars, the Freiheitssöhne, the B'nai B'rith, and the Free Sons of Israel (among others).[28]

The largest of the independent German-American fraternal orders was the Harugari, founded in 1847 by the well-known Freethinker Philipp Merkle. Although led by a Freethinker who was a factional leader in the Democratic party, the order formally prohibited the discussion of religious, political, or social questions. Instead, it was dedicated to the promotion of German language, culture, unity, and freedom—and to the fraternal ideals of "friendship, affection and humanity." The order grew rapidly and Merkle abandoned his freethought congregation to pursue essentially similar goals through promoting the Harugari. Merkle saw the order as an outgrowth of the radical artisan tradition in Germany and was proud of the fact that it attracted most of its members from "the working classes."[29] By the 1870s the Harugari had become a significant force in German-America (with over three hundred lodges), and they had sixty-two lodges with six or seven thousand members in the New York City area.[30] Although they suffered some membership decline in the depression years of the 1870s, the Harugari recovered and were still operating (though not growing) well into the twentieth century.[31]

Kleindeutschland's fraternal orders were even more significant than an analysis of their continuing social role as promoters of community solidarity would suggest. That is because they were key participants in the events that led to Kleindeutschland's first self-conscious identification of itself as a community. Before 1848, the German press of New York City essentially ignored its public (as news) and focused on events in other places (with a heavy concentration on Germany). It was the organized response to the German revolutions of 1848 that first brought Kleindeutschland into the pages of its own press and kept it there long enough for the *Staats-Zeitung* and the other papers to turn regular attention to news about the German community (an attention that then continued to foster a sense of self-identity). The fraternal orders took a leading role in organizing the community response to the revolutionary events in Germany. In May of 1848, the Hermannssöhne, Germania, Teutonia, and Solon lodges joined with the Templars, the Druids, the Steuben Society, the Jackson Society, and the Freiheitssöhne to organize a grand parade to support the German revolution, the first real communitywide effort in Kleindeutschland's history.[32] The fraternal orders continued their revolutionary agitation for years, and the Harugari, Templars, and Freiheitssöhne raised money for Kossuth and the Hungarian freedom fighters as well as for the German revolutionaries.[33] Their activities thus contributed a great deal toward Kleindeutschland's self-consciousness in the early years of its existence.

While the fraternal orders were the rage in the 1840s and continued to expand in later years, the fashion in the 1850s was to form Guards, militia companies, and *Schützenvereine* (shooting clubs). New York's Germans had formed some militia companies of their own as early as the 1830s (there were four German companies with some 320 men by 1840),[34] but it took the nativist attacks of the early 1850s to prompt the kind of popularity for militia companies in German New York that they already enjoyed in the city's Irish districts.[35] By 1853, some seventeen hundred Germans constituted 28 percent of the city's militiamen,[36] but that was only the beginning. By the late 1850s every conceivable group in Kleindeutschland appeared to have discovered the social possibilities of having its own Guard. By this time most of them specialized in beer drinking and partying (Civil War general Franz Sigel characterized the 5th New York Militia Regiment, where he had been the adjutant, as a "social club").[37] Some companies were simply groups of friends or drinking buddies, with the company named after their captain, while others were based on occupation or place of origin (like the Mechanics' Guard, the Union Bakers', the Tailors', the Guttenburg Guard, and the Bayerisches [Bavarian] Militia Club).[38] Before the end of the decade the Union Bakers' Guard was joined by a Journeymen Bakers' Guard, an Independent Journeymen Bakers' Guard, and an Empire City Bakers' Guard.[39] Leading saloons like Hillenbrand's and Lindenmuller's Odeon had their own Guards companies and there was even a Gin Cocktail Guard.[40]

The militia companies lost some of their popularity after the outbreak of the Civil War (though many companies served with distinction in the war), but their tradition was carried on by the many *Schützenvereine*, which continued to expand after the war. Although they retained a certain degree of popular appeal, many of the later *Schützenvereine* were basically middle-class organizations (like the merchant-organized New Yorker Schützen-Corps) and they lacked the broader appeal of the Guards companies of the 1850s.[41] By the 1870s, in fact, many of the *Schützenvereine* were located in the middle-class German suburbs and their only association with Kleindeutschland was with the *Schützenbund* central hall on St. Mark's Place.[42]

Given the alacrity with which the Germans took to organizing militia companies, it is surprising that they failed to organize volunteer fire companies as well, since they too were popular uniformed organizations and played a prominent place in the civic life of Anglo-American New Yorkers. The "fire laddies" retain a conspicuous place in the history of New York City,[43] but they seem to have made little headway in Kleindeutschland. That is not to say that there were no German fire companies. There were some, but they failed to take an important place in the social life of the community. They seem to have been ignored by New York's German press and are mentioned only in government reports.[44]

The most conspicuous of the many small *Vereine* of Kleindeutschland were the *Gesangvereine* (singing societies), which began on an informal basis back in the 1830s and continued an old German tradition.[45] As Kleindeutschland expanded in the 1840s, more permanent *Gesangvereine* were organized and rapidly became regular participants in all sorts of social and political events—in addition to their own concerts. The Deutscher Liederkranz (established in 1847 and later an elite singing society with nearly aristocratic pretensions) sang on the dock as the Social Reform Verein leader and former communist Hermann Kriege sailed off to join the German revolution in the spring of 1848, while the Social Reform Gesangverein performed at meetings of the Deutschen Revolutions-Verein.[46] Both marched in the Revolutionary Memorial parade that May, along with the Liedertafel, the Concordia Gesangverein, and the Rheinischen Sängerbund.[47]

Most of the singing societies soon dropped their political activities and concentrated on their concerts and *Sängerfeste* (choral festivals), though distinguished forty-eighters continued to be given prominent places in *Sänger* activities through the 1870s.[48] In 1851, five New York singing societies sent choruses to the second national German *Sängerfest* in Baltimore and the New York societies hosted the thousands who attended the third festival in 1852.[49] Even the local *Sängerfeste* grew into mammoth affairs, absorbing all the energies of the singing societies for months at a time.

These singing societies were credited with providing a sort of social cement that held Kleindeutschland and other German-American communities together. The *Staats-Zeitung* editorialized that their "cultural historical mission" to America united "the worker, the businessman and the politician . . . [and] erases the social distinctions which divide the German element."[50] While the *Gesangvereine* may have blurred the still-weak distinctions between social classes in the Kleindeutschland of the 1850s, this did not last. Even in the 1850s, the Deutscher Liederkranz had something of an elite identification, though its low initiation fees and dues ($5 each in 1859) hardly restricted its membership to the very wealthy.[51]

The succeeding decades saw the rapid development of a German-American upper class in New York, and this was mirrored in the singing societies of Kleindeutschland. The prime example was, of course, the Liederkranz. Under the leadership of *Staats-Zeitung* publisher Oswald Ottendorfer and piano manufacturer William Steinway, the Liederkranz raised its initiation fees from $5 to $10, and then to $25 and even to $50 by 1867 (raising its annual dues to $24 that same year).[52] This rising cost did little to inhibit membership growth, however, as the Liederkranz grew from 355 members in 1859 to over one thousand in 1869.[53] In 1863, the Liederkranz also moved from its rented rooms in Pythagoras Hall on Canal Street to its own Liederkranz Halle on East Fourth Street. As the German-American upper class continued to prosper mightily (and to move to more fashionable quarters uptown), the old Liederkranz Halle began to appear dingy and out of the way. The Liederkranz therefore decided to build a new and more sumptuous Liederkranz Halle uptown on East Fifty-eighth Street. This 1881 clubhouse was designed to demonstrate that the German-American upper class of New York was fully prepared to match the opulent life-style of its Anglo-American contemporaries. Needless to say, all thought of erasing social distinctions had been thoroughly abandoned.

The Arion Gesangverein, which split off from the Deutscher Liederkranz in 1854,[54] became the other really upper-class club for German New York. (It was described in 1892 as "the leading German social organization of the United States.")[55] It followed in the footsteps of the Liederkranz by renting its former rooms in Pythagoras Hall from 1865 to 1871, and then bought its own clubhouse in Kleindeutschland (after it had absorbed the Teutonia Männerchor in 1870).[56] As its members were also growing wealthy, the Arion sought preeminence by importing the director of the Breslau Philharmonic, Leopold Damrosch, to direct the Arion Chorus.[57] By the 1880s the Arion too found that its members had moved uptown and felt that the old hall was too far away. In 1885, therefore, it followed the Liederkranz out of Kleindeutschland to the upper east side.[58] Despite the Arion's thoroughly upper-class character, it did maintain the socialist leader F. A. Sorge as an honorary member from at least 1880 through the 1890s.[59]

There were also solidly upper-middle-class *Gesangvereine* for German New Yorkers who didn't fit in with the real elite. The Beethoven Männerchor was one such counterpart of the Liederkranz and Arion societies. It was founded in 1859 to specialize in the production of Beethoven's music and it met in a saloon for its first half-decade.[60] This may not appear very classy, but it was the saloon of the well-known German Catholic lay activist Joseph Dolger and thus quite respectable.[61] In 1864 a Beethoven Halle was built for the Männerchor, but it was rapidly "outgrown" in the prosperity of the late 1860s. A new Beethoven Halle was therefore built in 1870, on a scale more nearly comparable to the Kleindeutschland homes of the Liederkranz and the Arion (though vastly less sumptuous than their later quarters uptown). Where the Männerchor parted ways most significantly with its wealthier musical rivals was in remaining in its Kleindeutschland hall for the rest of the century, which suggests that many of its members had also remained residents of Kleindeutschland.[62]

Few of the many other German singing societies in New York were wealthy enough to buy or build their own halls, but there was never a shortage of meeting halls in Kleindeutschland. The New Yorker Sängerrunde, for example, met at Eugen Liever's Shakespeare Hotel in the late

1840s, moved on to Erhard Richter's saloon in the mid-1850s and 1860s, and then on to the Germania Assembly Rooms in the 1870s (a steady northward migration through Kleindeutschland).[63] The Gesang-Verein Schiller-Bund and the Mainzer Carneval-Verein (which specialized in humorous and nonsensical sketches) both ended their peregrinations by settling in the new Turn Halle after 1871.[64] While there is no real evidence as to the broader membership of these more typical singing societies, there is the strong suggestion that most of them drew many of their members from the skilled workers and artisans who formed the most numerous sector of Kleindeutschland.

While the *Gesangvereine* failed to suppress the growing social divisions in German New York (and, indeed, became new forums for expressing them), they continued to play a major role in Kleindeutschland's social life. "The worker, the businessman and the politician" no longer belonged to the same organizations, but they still shared a common culture and they all identified with whichever societies went on to represent New York in the national competitions. They thus contributed to maintaining some community cohesion in the face of the growing class divisions in the Kleindeutschland of the 1860s and 1870s.[65]

Kleindeutschland's *Unterstützungsvereine*, fraternal lodges, singing and shooting clubs, and even some Protestant churches were often segregated by German region of origin, even when they were not explicitly *Landsmannschaft* organizations.[66] This may have resulted from an informal process of social selection rather than from conscious design (particularly when mutually unintelligible dialects were concerned). As time went on, however, it often became a strongly felt aspect of these organizations. This aspect of their identity grew ever more significant, linking them to a temporally ever more distant homeland (especially after 1871, when their homeland was submerged in the rising German Empire). In order to help maintain their members' sense of self-identity (and pass it on to their children) these organizations banded together to form New York's regional *Volksfestvereine*. Swabians, Bavarians, Plattdeutschen, and Hessians, each group in turn formed a *Volksfestverein* that sponsored a massive regional festival every year to promote the dialect, customs, and community of its home region in Germany.[67] In line with the general neglect of subnational ethnicity, the widespread phenomenon of the *Volksfestvereine* has attracted almost no attention, but such groups were created in at least the large nineteenth-century German-American centers of New York, Philadelphia, Cincinnati, and Chicago.[68]

The nineteenth-century German emigration began in Württemberg and the Württembergers of New York were the first group to focus their identity through the creation of a regional festival (they did so before many of the other German groups had even begun to organize *Landsmannschaften*). They held their first Cannstatter Volksfest in 1862 and continued to hold it annually for over a century.[69] Their *Volksfestverein* became the focal point of Swabian activities and organizations throughout the New York metropolitan region. After 1877 they even had their own press in the New York *Schwäbisches Wochenblatt* (Swabian Weekly). The depth of their particularism is indicated by the fact that the *Verein* raised funds for the relief of Württemberg in the postwar crisis of 1920—not for the relief of Germany.[70]

It was not until 1874 that the Bavarians of New York followed the Swabian example and established a second *Volksfestverein*. This was taken as a challenge by the north Germans, who organized a Plattdeutschen Volksfest-Verein the next year. Forty *Landsmannschaften* and *Vereine* joined to organize the first Plattdeutschen Volksfest in 1875. Their celebration attracted some 150,000 people and became an annual event.[71] In latter years, Hessians, Saxons, Thuringians, Hessen-Darmstädters, and even Lichtensteiners organized their own *Volksfestvereine* in New York.[72]

The large numbers involved in creating and attending the massive *Volksfeste* display the breadth of the appeal of regional particularism for German New York. But to appreciate the depth of its appeal truly, we must turn to that most characteristic form of expression for the nineteenth-century German soul, romantic poetry. Here are some selected excerpts from a mass of such material published in various dialect and regional publications, starting with a Plattdeutsch example:

> That which honors the old homeland
> the speech which our mothers taught us
> O, here in this foreign land
> still learned and preserved with heart and soul.
>
> That is what this banner stands for
> that is why we hold it holy
> Proudly we shall show the world
> we are, from our deepest hearts, Plattdeutsch![73]

A favorite theme was loyalty to the homeland unto death:

> And when at last my lips shall shake
> when care shall close my eyes
> My heart will soar yet one more time
> into your sunny light
> As last salute, in final hour
> my dying mouth will breath:
> I salute you with heart and hand
> you sun-filled, blissful Hessenland.[74]

Or, for some Bavarian-Americans, even beyond:

When at last we must part,
When the death bell tolls
And the loyal Bavarian friends
carry us to our final rest
We shall rest well in foreign earth
far from our Bavarian home
For over our graves, the heavens will be spanned
with Bavaria's colors, white and blue.[75]

It was the *Volksfestvereine*, the organized expression of such sentiments, that institutionalized and preserved German particularism for generations of German-American New Yorkers.

The Sociable Reformers

Two other *Vereine* served as central social and political organizations for thousands of Kleindeutschlanders. One began as a radical political association and the other as a sports club with political overtones, but both the Social Reform Association and the Socialist Turnverein developed into broad-based multifunction organizations. Their large memberships engaged in a wide range of social, political, and cultural activities and they were the leading popular societies in Kleindeutschland for many years.

The Sozialreformverein was founded late in 1845, as the public arm of a secret German-American branch of the European communist League of the Just (later renamed the Communist League and famous for its publication of the *Communist Manifesto* in 1848).[76] It thus might claim the distinction of being the first "communist front" in American history. It was set up as a workers' political association to promote independent political activity among the German workers of New York and to agitate for the passage of a law giving free land to settlers in the western territories (later known as the Homestead Act but then going under the rubric of "land reform"). Under the leadership of Hermann Kriege (who also edited the Social Reformers' short-lived newspaper, the *Volkstribun*),[77] the association took an eclectic approach to reform that soon led to its expulsion from the League of the Just.[78] Kriege's sentimentalist appeals and the Reformers' stress on "land reform" offended Karl Marx and his colleagues in the league, but they seem to have suited the workers of Kleindeutschland in the mid-1840s. The association attracted some four hundred to six hundred members right away and there was soon a New York Social Reform Association No. 2, with 345 members.[79]

The Social Reformers rapidly came to terms with the American political environment. In May of 1846 Kriege called on the association to establish itself as "the left wing of Tammany Hall" and on July 4 the *Volkstribun* dropped the slogan "Up with Labor! Down with Capital" from its masthead and declared that the association was no longer communist.[80] Deciding that America was the "asylum of the oppressed, land of the workers and free farmers," they became intensely patriotic and took a strongly anti-English stand in the dispute over the Oregon boundary in 1846.[81] Then, when war broke out with Mexico, the Social Reform Association organized a volunteer company of "Young American Riflemen." Fifty of New York's German Social Reformers marched off to fight—in a war condemned by both the American National Reform Association (with which the Social Reform Association was affiliated) and the European left.[82] With this descent into the pit of national chauvinism, the Social Reform Association is written off by the historians of the labor movement and essentially disappears from the history books.[83]

It hardly disappeared from Kleindeutschland, however. The Social Reform Gesangverein (founded shortly after the parent body) was one of the leading choral groups in Kleindeutschland for a decade, while the Social Reformers' excursions, picnics, masked balls, and banquets continued to draw thousands of Kleindeutschlanders into their activities every year. Despite its alleged "bourgeois" status, the association remained active in the German labor movement all through the 1850s and was an organizational member of most of the German citywide central labor councils formed before 1860.[84] It is true that the Social Reformers were less conspicuous in Kleindeutschland's social life by the end of the 1850s, but that seems to have been only a relative decline, as there were then seven divisions of the Sozialreformverein in the city, each with its own meeting hall.[85] The main Social Reform Halle on Grand Street continued to be one of Kleindeutschland's most important public meeting places for decades. In the 1860s it was still a center for trade union activities. Hundreds of striking tailors met there in 1864, as did the German United Cabinetmakers' Union, the upholsterers' union, and the cigar makers' union during the labor movement upsurge of 1868.[86] The Social Reform Association did eventually decline into a minor social organization, held together only by its mutual benefit fund, but that was only long after its broader community functions had been taken over by the rising Turnverein.

The Turnverein, or Gymnastics Union, had its roots in a nationalistic physical culture movement that arose in Napoleonic Germany. By mid-century the German movement had added republicanism and free thought to its ideology and thousands of its proponents were active in the German revolutions of 1848–50. When the revolutions failed, many of the

Turners (as they were called) joined comrades of theirs who had emigrated to the United States in earlier years. Together they formed the German-American Turner Movement.[87]

The first step toward establishing a Turner movement in New York came in 1846, when the *Staats-Zeitung* ran a long story on the founder of the German movement, "Father Jahn."[88] It was another two years, however, before the Turners in New York set up a small Turngemeinde, or Gymnastics Society.[89] The Turngemeinde members practiced their gymnastics and took a minor place in the social life of Kleindeutschland for two years. Then the society was disrupted by an influx of more revolutionary Turners who had recently fled from Germany. These radicals pushed for a more active and political operation of the organization, and, when their proposals were not accepted, they withdrew to form their own organization—the New Yorker Socialistischen (Socialist) Turnverein.[90]

As recent refugees, they naturally threw their efforts into preparing for a new revolutionary outbreak in Europe, but they also expanded the scope of local Turner activities. The first addition was a singing society (of course), followed by a drama society, a German school, a rifle company, and a chess club. Before long it was possible for a resident of Kleindeutschland to carry on an active *Vereinsleben* without ever leaving the Turnverein. About two hundred Kleindeutschlanders joined the new *Verein* in its first year and it had over five hundred members by 1853.[91]

The Turners first attracted widespread attention when they participated in the Mayfest of 1851. The Turner contingent, with their sharply pressed white uniforms, impressed the crowds along the route to the ferry, but it was across the river in New Jersey that the real action took place. The festival-goers were attacked on the outskirts of Hoboken by a crowd of rowdies, including the Short Boys (a notorious fighting gang with nativist sympathies). The Turner contingent turned the tables on the nativists with a disciplined counterattack that beat them off.[92] After that, Turner contingents marched at the head and tail of almost all of Kleindeutschland's parades (except for religious processions) and they continued to do so for many years.[93]

The Turners soon returned to Hoboken to hold their own *Turnfest* (gymnastics festival), demonstrating that they were not afraid of the nativists.[94] This was the first of what were to become annual festivals for Kleindeutschland, and the *Turnfest* quickly became one of the most popular events of the year for German New Yorkers. By the end of the decade, the Turnverein was able to purchase a former church on Orchard Street for its headquarters and Turnhalle; while several other German neighborhoods were supporting their own Turnvereine and halls.[95]

The republican principles of the Turners carried many of them into the struggle against slavery, and eventually into the Republican party. Their renown as effective fighters brought them out of Kleindeutschland to act as defense squads for antislavery meetings in English-speaking sections of the city.[96] The Turners' main struggle lay within the German community, though. There they had to combat the active proslavery propaganda of the *Staats-Zeitung* and the efforts of the Democratic party machine (which included the Social Reformers and some of the fraternal orders).[97] Whatever success they may have had in generating antislavery sentiment, and they claimed a great deal, it was never translated into a Republican majority in Kleindeutschland. They were sufficiently successful, however, to lay claim to a fair amount of Republican patronage in later years. Leading Turners filled posts in the county coroner's office and the New York office of the Internal Revenue, among other places.[98]

The New York Socialistischen Turnverein (like its fellow *Turnvereine* in other cities) nearly dissolved into the Union army when its members enlisted en masse and formed a Turner regiment at the outbreak of the Civil War.[99] After serving with distinction, they had reestablished the Turnverein before the war's end and they were raising money for a new and larger Turnhalle by 1866. The grand new hall built in 1871 may still be seen on Fourth Street. It included a theater, two saloons, and several bowling alleys, in addition to the gyms and meeting rooms that were central to the Turnverein activities.[100]

The postwar Turnverein was more accurately characterized as radical republican than socialist (indeed, as we shall see below, even their "socialism" was often more populist than socialist), but the Turners remained interested and involved in labor reform and trade unionism. The Turnhalle was open for union meetings and the *Verein* provided support for striking workers—as in the cap makers' strike of 1869.[101] When Conrad Kuhn, president of the cigar makers' union and former head of the German central labor council (the Arbeiter Union), was blacklisted from his trade after the eight-hours' strikes of 1872, it was the Turners who found him a job in another trade.[102] Two years later, in 1874, it was the Turners who led the public outcry against the brutal police attack on a workers' mass meeting in Tompkins Square Park.[103]

While the reform impetus of the Social Reformers and the Turners lost much of its strength after their first years, these two successful social organizations were tremendously important in establishing and maintaining a generally proradical climate of opinion in Kleindeutschland. It was in this atmosphere that the German-American trade union movement of New York flourished and socialism established its first real roots in America.

CHAPTER SEVEN

Politics, Classes, and Unions in the Formative Years

German New York's political evolution paralleled its economic and social development. The community began in the 1840s as a small and undifferentiated mass of mostly recent immigrants who had little group identity or political consciousness. Some immigrants quickly attached themselves to the dominant political factions and parties of Anglo New York (especially when the Americans were spending money to attract German votes for upcoming elections), but this had little impact on the community as a whole. As Kleindeutschland grew larger, greater social and economic complexity combined with familiarity with American conditions to increase both political consciousness and internal differentiation. This process led, in the end, to the formation of two relatively distinct political worlds, one working-class and one middle-class, but it did so by fits and starts. It was molded by the frequent ups and downs of an erratic business cycle that gave rise to and then destroyed labor movements with startling rapidity.

The division of German New York into distinct political worlds was foreshadowed in the mid-1840s. When Hermann Kriege and the Social Reform Association began their paper, the *Volkstribun*, in 1846, they ran the slogan "Up with Labor! Down with Capital!" on the masthead and advocated a "communism" that would protect producers from capitalist exploitation.[1] Hardly had the *Volkstribun* appeared when it was attacked by German New York's leading daily, the *Staats-Zeitung*, for distorting reality by its depiction of poverty-stricken workers living in an America divided by hard-and-fast class lines.[2] This attack was followed by many more, including a very effective polemic by Karl Guskow that ridiculed the utopianism of these "communists."[3] While, as we have seen, the *Volkstribun* and the Social Reformers soon abandoned their advocacy of class struggle and "communism," some of Kleindeutschland's workers began the first stirring of labor organization. Just as the *Volkstribun* first appeared, the German handweavers met to protest the decline in their wages from $4 to $2.50 a week (in just over a year).[4] By the end of the summer they had organized a carpet weavers' union (with their English-speaking coworkers) that had over one thousand members in thirty-one factories and declared itself ready to strike if necessary.[5] That was the first brief expression of the German labor movement in New York.

Wilhelm Weitling, the famous German utopian communist and Hermann Kriege's mentor, had been invited to come to America by the Social Reform Association when it began its agitation in the spring of 1846. By the time he arrived at the beginning of 1847, the union movement had ended, the Social Reformers had abandoned communism, and the *Volkstribun* was bankrupt. Little daunted, Weitling soon hit upon the idea of setting up a communist fraternal order, the Befreiungsbund or League of Deliverance. Weitling's new league had little impact on Kleindeutschland, though it is of interest to note that a leading member was Eugen Lievre, owner of the Shakespeare Hotel and later host to a generation of radical activities. What ended Weitling's agitation was the news of the outbreak of the German revolutions of 1848. The New York lodge of the Befreiungsbund, turning its attention to a real revolution, sent Weitling to Berlin to organize the workers of Germany for the league.[6]

The German revolutions dominated the politics of German New York for the remainder of the decade. Revolutionary organizations, fraternal orders, singing societies, newspapers, and the vast majority of German New Yorkers seem to have thrown all their organized activity into celebration of, or support for, the revolutionaries in the homeland. Political thought focused on Berlin, Vienna, and Frankfurt—a German constitution and German politics—rather than on New York and American conditions. This revolutionary agitation continued well into the 1850s, especially in the social circles of the postrevolution refugees—the real "forty-eighters." It totally dominated the political life of Kleindeutschland, however, only as long as the revolutions themselves appeared to have serious prospects for success.

The labor movement that had appeared so briefly in 1846 returned to Kleindeutschland as a serious force in 1850. Industry was booming and the expected influx of gold from the California goldfields contributed to a rapid increase in prices. While prices were rising, employers were attempting to continue their accustomed practice, from the deflationary 1840s, of cutting wages. Meetings were called to protest wage cuts or to demand higher wages (leading to strike calls and the formation of trade unions) and the German workers were in the forefront. The first to go out on strike, at the end of February, were the cabinetmakers, who were resisting a wage cut. It was reported that a large number, representing all the nationalities of the trade, were participating. It was also reported that their leader, union president F. Steffen, came from Hamburg, the German furniture-manufacturing center. When Steffen spoke before a meeting of striking workers, he called first for unity but he then went on to address longer-term solutions to their plight, solutions that make it clear that he was a follower of the communist tailor, Wilhelm Weitling.[7]

Weitling himself had returned to New York at the end of 1849, having fled his last German revolutionary agitation in Hamburg only hours before the police arrived to arrest him.[8] He had lost no time in reviving his New York contacts and was able to get out the first issue of his new newspaper, *Die Republik der Arbeiter* (Workers' Republic), in January of 1850. He was again preaching his distinctive form of utopian communism to the workers of America (that is, to those who could read German). Unlike Owen, Fourier, and Proudhon, with their classless utopianism, Weitling appealed to the workers to make their own revolution. On the other hand, he included petty employers who had "once been workers themselves" in his scheme for social reorganization. He supported unions and strikes as means of organizing workers, but saw their potential for raising wages as limited; real success, he argued, could only lead to an inflationary spiral that would then eat up the gains.[9] Producers' cooperatives were an important element in his scheme, but only when organized into his master conception, the *Gewerbetauschbank* or trade-exchange bank. He described the bank in the first issue of his paper:

> The founding of a Trade Exchange Bank, if it is to serve its intended purpose, requires the issuing of a new workers' paper money and the opening of stores and warehouses. In these warehouses (or to their agents) workers, employers and farmers can sell their products at any time for workers' paper-money. With this paper-money they can buy whatever they need in return, so that with the founding of this Exchange Bank, each member always has work and can always sell and buy his products without appealing to the capitalists and middlemen and submitting to their swindling. Everyone will always, by the exchange-rules of this Trade-Exchange Bank, receive the full value of his expenses and labor.

Weitling went on to describe how the bank would produce massive profits that would finance cooperative factories and utopian colonies.[10]

Part of the idiosyncratic flavor of Weitling's communism lay in his appeal to Christian principles when his fellow radicals were flaming atheists. An especially fine example was a poem he wrote for young communists, which was sometimes recited at gatherings of his followers:

> Ich bin ein kleiner Kommunist
> Und frage nicht nach Geld,
> Da unser Meister Jesus Christ
> Davon ja auch nichts hält.

Ich bin ein kleiner Kommunist
Und bins mit Lieb und Treu,
Und trete einst als treuer Christ
Dem Arbeitsbunde bei.[11]

I am a little communist
and do not ask for cash,
because our master Jesus Christ
has no regard for wealth.

I am a little communist
and am with love and faith,
and as a faithful Christian, I
support the Workers' League.

Back in 1846, Weitling's followers had been ridiculed by *Staats-Zeitung* owner/editor Jacob Uhl for suggesting such utopian schemes. Now Weitling was a hero of the German revolution (at least a minor one, anyway) and deserved respect. The *Staats-Zeitung* thus expressed sympathy with Weitling's goals, but gently suggested that the trade-exchange bank was thoroughly impractical. Uhl also pointed out that without the bank's profits, producers' cooperatives were possible only for the few elite workers who had the money needed to finance them. Cooperatives would therefore be of no use to the majority of workers unless they received state support (an argument that would appear to show that he was familiar with the state-sponsored socialism of Louis Blanc and the Paris workers' movement of 1848). Uhl concluded by stressing the possibilities for promoting the worker's interests through electoral politics in a democracy (the *Staats-Zeitung* had long been identified with the Democratic party). This shift to the left by the *Staats-Zeitung* didn't last very long, but it might have been expected in the newspaper that had just become the New York agent of the *Neue Rheinische Zeitung* of "Carl Marx."[12]

With Weitling and even the *Staats-Zeitung* urging them on, the German workers organized rapidly. The cabinetmakers were only the first, and the house carpenters immediately followed their example. Even as they prepared to strike, the German carpenters met with the cabinetmakers and with a shoemakers' organizing committee. They agreed to unite their organizations on a "social basis" and lead their joint membership of over one thousand in an attempt to implement Weitling's program.[13] The next day the German shoemakers held a mass meeting at the Shakespeare Hotel to organize an association.[14] German unions, German workers' associations, and German sections of multilingual unions were also formed by upholsterers, carvers, paperhangers, shade painters, varnishers, polishers, clockmakers, cigar makers, and bakers.[15] Weitling took credit for all this activity, claiming that his agitation had led to strikes in twenty trades, which achieved wage increases averaging 25 percent. The communist tailor was especially proud of New York's German tailors, who (he reported) signed up two thousand members in only one day in March. He also claimed that the German example provided the impetus for the organization in New York of English-speaking unions with sixty to eighty thousand members.[16]

Weitling immediately proposed a central labor body for the unions and was selected by his fellow tailors to represent their union in organizing one. At the end of April they succeeded in organizing the Central Commission of the United Trades for German workers in fifteen trades. Weitling then represented the Central Commission in the industrial congress set up by the English-speaking workers the next month.[17] The United Trades had about twenty-four hundred members, most of them from the unions—though it also had representatives from the Social Reformers and an "Economic Exchange-Association."[18] Weitling's influence soon waned, however, as it became clear that his program focused on the exchange bank and that he didn't really support either trade unions or cooperatives for their own sakes. The fact that Weitling seemed to demand complete deference to his leadership also generated conflict, and he resigned from the Central Commission in October. He concluded his resignation by saying: "Under the existing circumstances it would be more damaging than useful to the movement which I lead in spirit, should I continue to let my feelings be abused at your meetings." The United Trades replied "that we feel strong enough to guide the movement of our brothers and . . . we need no spiritual leader which Weitling pretends to be."[19]

The most dramatic events of 1850 were precipitated by the Irish tailors calling a strike in July. The German tailors also walked out, with the support of most of Kleindeutschland—including the moderate *Staats-Zeitung,* which attacked the exploitative putting-out system. Father Müller of Most Holy Redeemer, however, attacked the strike as antireligious. He even called the police when a tailors' committee came to remonstrate with him. The *Staats-Zeitung* was outraged at the arrests, but the antiforeigner New York *Herald* (which had long delighted in attacking all of the Germans as communists) was overjoyed and claimed that the committee had gone to burn the church down. A few days later a group of sixty to eighty tailors, "apparently all Germans," tried to picket the uptown home of an employer. Again the German and English papers covered the events very differently. The *Staats-Zeitung* reported that the tailors were attacked by the police and an armed mob of "loafers and niggers [*sic*]," leading to many injuries and arrests. The English papers reported that the tailors rioted, breaking windows and fighting the police, leading to about forty arrests. The police denied reports that three tailors had died of their wounds. In the end, thirty-nine tailors were convicted of rioting and served prison sentences.[20] The *Staats-Zeitung* concluded that it was proud of the leading role the Germans had played, but perhaps a cooperative might be better than a strike.[21]

The tailors and many of the other German unionists seem to have agreed with the *Staats-Zeitung*. The majority of those workers who had won their strikes soon drifted out of the unions because they saw no further need for the organizations (a common weakness of early trade unions). The majority of those who remained turned enthusiastically to the creation of cooperative workshops. These projects then absorbed the energies of both the unions and the Central Commission for the remainder of their existence; but the Central Commission and many of the unions soon collapsed, often from the recriminations and disillusionment that followed the failure of the cooperatives.

The Germans' preference for forming cooperatives was predictable. Not only were cooperatives generally the rage in labor circles, including Horace Greeley's New York *Tribune*, they were also the natural choice of proletarianized artisans—a fair description of most of New York's organized German workers. These artisans had no objections to a petty-producer capitalism where workers had a reasonable chance of becoming their own masters. What they resented was the prospect of indefinite servitude. Cooperative workshops offered them the renewed hope of becoming their own masters, and did so with an appeal to the artisan ethic of cooperation rather than through the alien notions of competition and conflict. Because cooperative workshops seemed such an obvious solution to artisan proletarianization, the ideal survived the failure of the 1850 cooperatives and was resuscitated nearly every time there was a labor movement revival in small-scale industries.

For another four years Weitling himself continued his agitation through the Workers' League and his *Republik der Arbeiter*. For a while he continued to have hundreds of followers among New York's German workers and he promoted his vision of cooperatives, the trade-exchange bank, and a utopian colony at Communia, Iowa. Indeed, the New York local of the Workers' League was prosperous enough in October 1852 to open an *Arbeiter Halle* that provided the usual range of German social activities—theater, singing, dancing, bowling, and beer. The league began to fade in New York with the creation of a Marxist rival in the spring of 1853 and then finally collapsed in 1854 as charges flew concerning the bankruptcy of the utopian colony at Communia. Fighting accusations of dishonesty, Weitling tried to keep the league alive and continued publishing his newspaper until July of 1855. It was a bitter end. In later years Sorge, Weitling's friend, continued to defend his honesty as "above suspicion" and honored him as a founder of the German-American labor movement.[22]

Full employment and satisfaction with the gains of 1850 had proved the downfall of most of the German unions, which were seen by many of their members as temporary organizations designed to achieve immediate goals. The continuing boom offered little incentive to further organization in 1851 and 1852, but continued inflation began to reduce the value of wages and the rate of inflation began to increase sharply toward the end of 1852. By the beginning of 1854, New York newspapers reported that the cost of necessities had increased 30 percent in eight months.[23] As the situation worsened, first the *Staats-Zeitung* and then the New York *Times* urged employers to raise wages voluntarily in order to avoid provoking strikes.[24]

Everyone was concerned about the effects of inflation, but most of the respectable elements in New York were more worried about unions and strikes than about the workers' living conditions. Even Weitling and his Workers' League, now saying that communism was the only solution to the workers' plight, had joined the opposition to wage-conscious unions and strikes.[25] There was, however, a new faction in Kleindeutschland ready to urge militant action. A close political associate of Karl Marx, Joseph Weydemeyer by name, had arrived in New York in November 1851. He was determined to create a revolutionary workers' movement by spreading the new ideas of "scientific" socialism to America. A former army officer converted to socialism, Weydemeyer had had extensive editorial experience during the German revolution and he plunged into leftist journalism in New York. Only two months off the boat, he took over a small atheist paper, *Luzifer,* and renamed it *Die Revolution.* It died after two issues. Weydemeyer had also, however, begun to write for the new Socialistischer Turnverein paper, the *Turn-Zeitung,* and he was able to reach many German workers through its pages. While the "socialist" Turners defined socialism as antimonopoly rather than anticapitalist, they were soon publishing Weydemeyer on the dictatorship of the proletariat and the meaning of "class consciousness."[26] Weydemeyer, like all good Marxists in those years, stressed the importance of trade unions and strikes as basic forms of class struggle.

Weydemeyer also moved to generate a political organization. He considered trying to take over the Workers' League, but Marx had advised him to avoid Weitling,[27] so he joined the Social Reform Association instead. In six months he had enough followers to set up a small Marxist club called the Proletarierbund, which he said was influential in Turner circles.[28] He became even better known when he became the leading publicist for the defendants in the notorious Cologne anticommunist trial of 1852–53 and was given access to the pages of the literary *Belletristisches Journal* for his campaign. By the spring of 1853, therefore, he was an influential journalist with a small organized following in the reviving labor movement, and was ready to try to create a new militant labor organization.

The German trade unionists, who had allowed their unions to lapse into dormancy or had maintained them only as mutual benefit societies, began to plan a spring organizing campaign during the winter of 1852–53. While the Workers' League planned a fund-raising banquet for a renewal of the German revolution (the *Staats-Zeitung* reported that they "spent more on beer than on revolution"),[29] the Marxists were meeting with the trade union leaders. Even as the first strikes were getting underway, they planned to set up a new central body for the German workers. The unions and strikes that followed involved dozens of trades, starting with the German hatmakers' unsuccessful strike for a 12 percent raise. The carpenters and other construction workers were more successful, as were the gilders, typesetters, piano makers, gold workers, and engravers. The tailors again had the best organization, with shop and district committees in addition to the central office. Even the German waiters organized a union with six or seven hundred members and won a raise from $15 to $18 a month. Eighteen fifty-three was also the year the German cigar makers organized their first real trade union, even setting up an English-speaking section at the request of the Marxists, who wanted to organize the English-speaking workers too. All of the new and revived unions had a much more clearly trade union/wage-oriented character than their predecessors, which had stressed cooperatives and mutual benefits.[30]

On March 15, 1853, Weydemeyer and his colleagues put out a call: "To the Workers of All Trades! For a broad workers' alliance. Not only to win a wage increase in each work place or to forge a purely political union. No, now is the time to create a platform on a modern basis and recommend practical ways to achieve our goals."[31]

Some eight hundred German-American workers responded to the call for a "practical" organization—including a large number of Weitling's followers.[32] On March 21, they founded the American Workers' League (originally the General Workers' League) in close association with the trade unions (the house painters', tailors', shoemakers', cabinetmakers', and cigar makers' unions participated), the Social Reformers, and the Turners.[33] Proclaiming the irreconcilability of capital and labor, the "practical" platform focused on ten-hour and child-labor laws, a homestead act, the creation of a mechanic's lien law to protect workers, and similar reforms to be implemented by a Labor party.[34] Weitling denounced this platform as reformist, having nothing to do with "the real emancipation of the workers." Even the Marxist historian Hermann Schlüter was forced to conclude that the new program "poured a goodly portion of petty-bourgeois water into the proletarian wine."[35] Despite the watering of the wine, it seems to have been just what the German proletariat of New York ordered and they flocked to the table of the American Workers' League.

The new league actively encouraged the unions and participated in some of the strikes that followed in the spring and summer. Despite the influence of the Marxists, however, it was forced to contend with a strong strain of sentimental reformism (typical of nineteenth-century romanticism). Weydemeyer reported to Marx that he had had to smuggle himself into a meeting of the committee drafting the organization's constitution, to oppose "as far as possible" the sentimentality of the proposed draft, "so that the final product wouldn't be too pitiful [*jämmerlich*]."[36] The sentimental tide was only temporarily stemmed. The American Workers' League suffered heavy membership losses about a month later, when many of the sentimentalists went over to a newly formed Freethinkers' Society. German unions, however, continued to form and to affiliate with the league, until both were brought down by the economic crisis of 1854–55. By late 1854 Weydemeyer and the Marxists were trying to get the league and the German-speaking unions to merge with their English-speaking equivalents, but the slogan "workers of all tongues unite" carried unity too far for German-American workers. After all, they would have been reduced to a tongue-tied minority in such a union. Weydemeyer resigned in disgust and soon left New York, but by that time an economic crisis had wiped out most of the unions, and the league was being kept alive only by its mutual benefit and singing societies.[37]

This time the labor movement in Kleindeutschland had not died of lack of interest. It had been crushed by mass unemployment on a scale that made survival rather than organization the most pressing concern for New York's German workers. The *Staats-Zeitung* reported that there were over three thousand unemployed skilled workers in the Eleventh Ward alone and called for public works projects.[38]

The radical saloonkeeper Erhard Richter and the freethinker leaders, doctors Schramm and Försch, addressed a large protest meeting of the unemployed in City Hall Park. There they too called for a broad municipal public works program to alleviate the mass suffering.[39] Weitling waxed eloquent in his protest: "Need pounds with heavy fists on the door of public attention, which has offered only beggars-soup in response. Beggars-soup! Beggars-soup!! In America it has already come to that."[40]

In America, as the *Staats-Zeitung* had already reminded Weitling, there was also an electoral political arena. As Kleindeutschland grew larger in the early 1850s, the German vote became an important potential resource for the political parties that dominated New York politics. The Democratic party had long been committed to promoting the rights of immigrants (mostly Irish) in return for immigrant votes, and those German New Yorkers who voted had generally voted Democratic. In 1852 the Whigs mounted a serious attempt to develop German support and the Democrats responded with their first nomination of a German candidate—for the Board of Governors of the Poor House.[41] Not that there was a great threat of defections, but loyalty required some reward (the Democrats carried all the German wards quite handily that year). When the new Democratic administration of Franklin Pierce appointed August Belmont chargé d'affaires at the U.S. embassy in the Netherlands, the Germans remembered that Belmont's name had originally been Schönberg and they defended his appointment against nativist attacks.[42]

The German vote was safely in the Democratic camp (at least for a while), but the real question of municipal politics was "who gets the spoils?" With native and Irish politicians dividing the patronage rewards for Germans' votes, some Germans tried to take over the local Democratic organization in the Seventeenth Ward in 1853.[43] They had some success on their own, but solidified their position through an alliance with the Democratic faction led by native-born Captain Isaiah Rynders (later known as the boss of the Tenth Ward but then boss of the "Bloody Sixth"). This native-German alliance, against the native-Irish alliance that dominated Tammany Hall, proved to be a precedent that outlasted the principles (or the lack thereof) that underlay the maneuver of 1853. Always lagging behind the Irish in numbers, organization, or political talent, New York's German politicians consistently sought native allies. These German-American politicians of 1853 were already clearly distinguishable from their labor and socialist contemporaries. Even Dr. Philipp Merkle, who was proud to head a workers' fraternal order (the Harugari), was far from being a worker himself. Neither were his colleagues and fellow freethinkers, Dr. Schramm and Dr. Försch, nor Magnus Gross (at that time a *Staats-Zeitung* editor, he was later known as "the German school commissioner").[44]

Some of these German Democrats soon made the Germans the laughingstock of the city. Early in 1854 they held a mass meeting to try to form a united German political organization, but the attempt at unity collapsed at the begining when they fell out over who would chair the meeting. One group united behind the candidacy of Erhard Richter. A more conservative faction, led by Anton Dugro (the first German Democrat elected to public office in New York City—member of the Board of Governors of the Poor House), pushed the candidacy of Jacob Windmüller of the Deutsche Gesellschaft. The two sides tried to shout each other down and finally came to blows. The meeting ended in a brawl, with chair legs being wielded as clubs, much to the amusement of some of the English-language papers. The *Staats-Zeitung* joined in condemning the fiasco, contemptuously pointing out that most of the brawlers, having only recently arrived in the United States, were not even eligible to vote.[45] The next month Richter, Försch, and the staff of the New York *Demokrat* led a protest against the Kansas-Nebraska Act, beginning the conspicuous antislavery activity that would draw them all into the Republican party.[46]

In the mid-1850s, the most important issue for the masses of German voters was neither slavery nor wage slavery but rather the defense of their right to recreation. Evangelical Protestant reformers were influential in American politics and two of their favorite reforms, temperance and the "Puritan" Sabbath, threatened the staples of German-American life—beer and Sunday social activities. First came the suggestion, in 1853, that the Crystal Palace exhibition hall be closed on Sundays, then it was suggested that Jones' Wood and Central Park also be closed.[47] The workers of New York, who had only Sundays for recreation, were strongly opposed and the proposals were dropped. The antiliquor, anti-immigrant, anti-Sabbath-breaking, anticity forces were much stronger on the state level, however, and in 1855 they succeeded in passing a state law against the sale of liquor and beer on Sundays. (We may join the city's beer and liquor drinkers in noting the exclusion of the upstaters' favorite drinks, hard cider and wine.) Mayor Fernando Wood sabotaged the enforcement of this act, winning himself a reputation as the saloonkeepers' mayor but also making himself very popular in Kleindeutschland (not that he hadn't already had the support of the *Staats-Zeitung* and the *Criminal-Zeitung und Belletristisches Journal*).[48] He was the savior of the "continental Sunday."

Wood continued to appeal to immigrant voters, and won reelection with their support in 1856, but this brought the full power of the new Republican state government down on the city administration. The Republicans believed that the Wood machine was based on the mayor's control over the Municipal Police and decided to break that power by abolishing the Municipal Police force and replacing it with a state-controlled Metropolitan Police. After a brief cold war and the famous "battle of the bulls" between the two forces, the Metropolitans took over the city in July of 1857.[49] They were, however, an outside force imposed upon the city by the Republican state administration and they met with a violent reception from the native and Irish fighting gangs that had long been associated with municipal politics.[50] Isolated, embattled, and suspicious, the Metropolitan Police force was ill equipped to patrol the totally foreign territory of Kleindeutschland.

The result was a series of riots on July 12 and 13, 1857. The Metropolitan Police reported that two of their men had been attacked by a mob of Germans in the Seventeenth Ward when they tried to break up a fight, that four of the first ten reinforcements had been injured by the stone-throwing mob, and that a German bystander had been killed by a sniper when shooting broke out between the second group of reinforcements and the mob. They also said that "interested parties" (meaning former Municipals and supporters of Mayor Wood) had incited the crowd.[51] Furthermore, they reported, the next afternoon a hostile crowd had attacked the precinct captain near the home of the deceased German, and growing mobs had battled the police and rioted through the afternoon and evening, until the police were compelled to call out the militia. Once again there were reports of former Municipals and Wood supporters inciting the crowd with denunciations of Governor King and his "damned Black Republican" Metropolitans. (They were also said to have spread rumors that the Metropolitans were going to stop the sale of beer on Sundays, were going to prevent Germans from voting, and were even planning to assault the German Catholic church on Third Street.)[52] That the Germans had a different version of events was indicated by a woman "agitator" who was quoted as saying, "This is what we can expect now, we shall be shot down like dogs. When our husbands go out in the mornings we do not know if they will ever come home again."[53]

The Germans' version of events came out at the coroner's inquest on the death of Johann Müller, the passerby who had been killed while walking home with his wife and child. Jacob Dryfuss testified that he had been watching from his window when a fight (mostly verbal) attracted a crowd. Two policemen (Metropolitans) had come along and ordered the crowd to disperse. When a man objected, a policeman knocked him off the sidewalk and a scuffle ensued, which ended with the man's being clubbed. Dryfuss reported that others separated the two and that the policeman then set off in pursuit of one of the original disputants, who had run off. He caught the man in front of a beer garden and clubbed him down in the doorway. As the crowd had grown to two or three thousand by this time, the other officer had run back to the station for help. Dryfuss said that a squad of reinforcements arrived and "they commenced firing the minute they got to the corner . . . the people on the corner were at the time laughing at the policeman who had run away" and that the police had fired eighteen or more shots at three or four paces. Dryfuss denied that anything had been thrown at the police before they had opened fire and added that a dozen officers had then waded into the dispersing crowd with flailing clubs and continued firing their guns. After that, he said, there were no further crowds that night, but the police were visible, attacking random pedestrians—including one inoffensive old man that Dryfuss saw clubbed to the sidewalk (after which he said he was too disgusted to watch further).[54] A large number of other witnesses corroborated Dryfuss's version of events, a version consistent with the *Tribune*'s reports that the second night's rioting was the action of a large crowd that had taken up arms to defend the quarter against an expected attack by the police and/or the militia.[55]

The German version of events was credible enough to convince six of the seven members of the coroner's jury to endorse the following report:

> The Jury condemn the resort to firearms, and find no legal authority to sustain its employment. . . .
>
> We find that the riot commenced through the indiscreet conduct of an officer by the name of Peter Cook, in attempting to disperse an inoffensive and peaceable assembly by unnecessarily arresting a man and beating him with a club, which provoked the gathering of a large crowd. That said Cook unjustifiably sounded the alarm rap, which brought the police in contact with a miscellaneous crowd of men, women and children. That said police did not act with prudence, but, under great excitement, committed acts of brutal violence.
>
> That John Muller was feloniously killed by a police officer of the Seventeenth Ward, whose name is to the Jurors unknown.[56]

It is hard to escape the conclusion that the riots were the result of the imposition on New York City and Kleindeutschland of an alien and alienated police force.[57]

German Democrats were quick to take advantage of this opportunity to counter the pro-Republican efforts of a large group of forty-eighters who saw the antislavery principles of the Republican party as an extension of their own republicanism and were leading many of their fellow German-Americans (especially in the midwestern states) into the new party.[58] The day after the riots, the Seventeenth Ward Democratic Association (German supporters of Mayor Wood) called a protest meeting at the Fourth Street Deutsches Volks Theater—in the center of the riot district.

The stage was draped with a black banner that read "Opfer der Metropolitan Polis" (victim of the Metropolitan Police). The German Democrats entered the hall in a body, led by Councilman Schappert and former coroner Dr. Wilhelm.[59] Dr. Wilhelm took the chair by acclamation and the denunciations began. They started with mild sarcasm, referring to the "so-called 'Party of Freedom' " that was responsible for the death of the inoffensive Johann Müller, but they got more inflammatory as the evening wore on. The rhetorical peak was reached when one speaker cried out, "It would seem that the City of New York was singled out as a target by the Black Republican Legislature for obnoxious laws that would make Berlin or Munich swim in blood [cheers]. Great God what did we come here for if such things can be in the land of the brave and the home of the free [cheers]."[60]

Inflammatory as the speeches were, with references to cities swimming in blood, the action they proposed was far from a call for further violence. The speakers concluded their remarks with the observation that there was no way to defeat the Metropolitans except to turn out "on the first Tuesday in the coming November . . . [and] to stick with the Democratic party until the last Republican was buried and all that belonged to them obliterated."[61]

In the election campaign of the year before, the German Republicans had appeared to get off to a good start. Former Whigs like Friedrich Kapp joined with moderate forty-eighters like Rudolph Lexow (editor of the *Belletristisches Journal*) and communist forty-eighters like Fritz Jacobi to hold an impressive rally, which the *Tribune* claimed attracted nearly four thousand Germans. Thirty-four notables, including the aforementioned and Julius Fröbel of the Frankfurt parliament; Max Cohnheim, the playwright; Franz Sigel, the Turner (and Civil War general-to-be); and Julius Brill, Kleindeutschland's leading photographer, were elected officers of the meeting: "At this junction the German Turnverein arrived, bearing the American flag, followed by the red flag of their association. Their appearance was the signal for a general uprising among the audience, and for several minutes the enthusiasm was uncontrollable."[62] In October, more than twice as many (the *Tribune* claimed ten thousand) turned out for a Republican rally at the Academy of Music, where they were addressed by the German revolutionary hero Friedrich Hecker.[63] This massive display of support, however, was still dwarfed by the German Democrats' rally of twenty thousand that same week.[64] In November, the Republican candidate Frémont got fewer than four thousand votes in Kleindeutschland (compared to somewhere between five and ten thousand for Buchanan and the Democrats).[65] Although not the victory the German Republicans aimed for, it had been a substantial start in winning the German vote; but their hopes for 1860 were badly damaged by the actions of the Republican-organized Metropolitan Police in July of 1857.

While the German Democrats had followed Mayor Wood in 1856, he had lost the support of Tammany Hall's sachems. Wood withdrew to a new headquarters at Mozart Hall in 1857 and retained the bulk of the German and Irish votes in his narrow 1857 defeat. Most significant for Kleindeutschland's political future, Tammany Hall ran a largely Irish ticket (for the first time) in 1858 to win back the Irish vote, leaving the Wood machine nearly entirely dependent on the German vote for his successful comeback in 1859.[66] This newly enhanced position for the German Democrats virtually assured the loyalty of Kleindeutschland in 1860 (especially when combined with the generally anti-immigrant reputation of the eastern Republicans and the actions of the Metropolitan Police). Indeed, while Lincoln reportedly won the German-American vote in the Midwest, he lost the mostly German wards of Kleindeutschland by nearly two to one (14,167 to 7,441).[67]

CHAPTER EIGHT

Politics, Classes, and Unions in the German-American Metropolis

While the Democrats and Republicans fought for the German vote, German New York was in the throes of economic and social flux. Independent artisans and small factory owners who survived the panic of 1854–55 were faced with another major panic in 1857. Many businesses did not survive and their owners were driven down into the ranks of the wage earners (though many still hoped to rise again). Panics were times of opportunity as well as disaster, however, and those German merchants and manufacturers who had cash on hand were able to expand their business at bargain prices (picking clean the corpses of their failed rivals). By the end of the decade, many of the more successful businessmen from Kleindeutschland had accumulated substantial fortunes and had risen well above the nebulous line that divides the middle from the upper classes. In the 1860s they would move to assume the social and political prerogatives that they felt were theirs by virtue of their new status.

The short prosperity after 1855 did little to revive the German labor movement, and the slavery question absorbed most of the energies of those who were reform activists. The second panic of the decade did stimulate something of a revival of labor reform organizations, though. In October of 1857, Albert Komp gathered some of his friends and fellow radical forty-eighters (including the freethinker Adolph Sorge, who seems to have moved toward Marxism through this association) into a Kommunisten Klub (Communist Club), dedicated to freethought and the equality of all mankind.[1] The thirty members of the new club joined with the English-speaking labor leader James Maguire in organizing mass demonstrations of the unemployed. On November 5, fifteen thousand unemployed English- and German-speaking workers marched from Tompkins Square to Wall Street carrying banners reading "Work-Arbeit" and chanting "we want work."[2] With this encouragement, the Communist Club took the lead in reviving the dormant American Workers' League, but the revived league was much more successful in attracting all sorts of reformers (including a contingent of Fourierist utopian socialists) than it was in appealing to the German workers of New York. Without

Weydemeyer's leadership, the Marxists found themselves with little influence in the increasingly reformist-dominated league. They even had to accept the addition of an anticommunist declaration to the league platform in 1859. By that time the league included both a Republican club and a consumer cooperative union, but it had failed to attract any of the trade unions that had begun to revive with the return of prosperity. It reportedly died from lack of relevance.[3]

The unions had been slow to revive even after the economy recovered from the 1857 panic. All that was left of the militant cabinetmakers' union in the spring of 1858 was a small mutual benefit society with forty to forty-five members, and the cigar makers were similarly reduced.[4] This time it was the old Social Reform Association that took the lead and called on the workers of all trades to meet in its hall. The piano makers and furniture makers were first to heed the call and soon there were German trade unions and associations flourishing in New York once more.[5] Once again, however, a short economic boom was followed by a period of widespread unemployment, this time as the country drifted into civil war. The newly revived German trade unions were too feeble to withstand the shock and quickly collapsed (although this time there were four survivors—the cap makers', cigar packers', tailors', and shoemakers' organizations).[6]

The Civil War economic crisis had spelled the end for the unions, temporarily, but the threat of taxation to pay for the war spurred the employers to organize their own associations. In November of 1862, the German employers organized the Boss Bakers' Association, the Brewery Owners' Association, the Cigar Manufacturers' Association, and the Boss Cabinetmakers' Association, among others.[7] They were formed to oppose taxes on their products, but they soon turned to defending their members' profits against an even more serious threat, the trade unions that were reviving once more.[8]

After the economic paralysis that accompanied the outbreak of war, the war created its own demands for production. The army's need for uniforms, boots, and countless other items soon reestablished full employment in many of New York's skilled trades. Then the enlistment of large numbers of German workers in the Union army created labor shortages in the German trades and war-induced inflation gave the remaining workers a strong incentive to organize their unions once more.[9] This time they met collective resistance on the part of their employers.

The Boss Cabinetmakers took the offensive in the summer of 1863. They declared that all cabinetmakers and carvers would have to keep an employment book in which their employers could make entries—to be produced on demand—or they would not be eligible for employment in their trades.[10] The next year, the Merchant Tailors' Association provoked a major strike by refusing to employ any tailors who were members of a union.[11] Both of these attempts to break the unions failed, but they demonstrated the operations of a new industrial order in German New York. The larger employers not only took the lead in these actions, they bound the smaller operators into a united front against their employees by threatening to underprice any of their number who gave in to union demands. This forced any employers who might be sympathetic to their workers, like a group of cap manufacturers in 1869, to express this sympathy by giving financial support to the unions striking their shops rather than risk the retaliation of their fellow manufacturers (and consequent bankruptcy) by granting the workers' demands.[12]

Industrial disputes were no longer a matter of one employer confronted by his own workers, or even of confrontations between temporary coalitions of workers and manufacturers. Now they were tradewide disputes, one side united behind their unions and the other behind their employers' associations. Both types of organizations were intended to be permanent fixtures on the social landscape, and, in many of the more rapidly mechanizing trades, ever fewer workers were able to cross the boundary that separated the two. In 1858, Weydemeyer had written to Karl Marx that in America "the workers are incipient Bourgeois and feel themselves to be such," so that the prospects for "proletarian propaganda" were poor.[13] The new social conditions of the mid-1860s might have led him to revise that judgment, as his notions of class struggle and class solidarity began to take on a new reality for New York's German workers.

Despite the opposition of the new employers' associations, the later war years were good for unions. The economy was booming and employers were reluctant to forgo the profits that would be lost by long strikes. The German labor movement, therefore, flourished. From the meager four unions that survived the beginning years of the war, the movement grew to at least twenty four unions in 1863 and twenty six in 1864.[14] Among the leading German unions were those of the furniture trades, the piano makers, the tailors, the shoemakers, the cigar makers, and the bakers.[15] A number of successful strikes were carried out in those years by the varnishers and polishers, the tailors, the cabinetmakers, the piano makers, the carvers, the upholsterers, and the clothing cutters.[16]

Once again, the success of the trade unions encouraged them to establish a central body, this time called the Arbeiter Union (after the English-speakers' central body, the Workingmen's Union).[17] Founded to unite the trades "for the defense of their rights and the promotion of the interests of the working class," the Arbeiter Union had hardly gotten off the ground when a postwar slump suspended its activities.[18] Although the central body became dormant and the German unions called few strikes in the immediate postwar period, the fact that the unions generally survived the slump indicates the greatly increased strength of trade unionism in Kleindeutschland.

Even before the trade union revival of 1868, it was clear that the German-speaking unions were now among the leading unions in New York City. They not only accounted for a large portion of the organized workers in the city, they also began to take the lead in the move to create a national labor organization. By the time of the 1867 National Labor Congress, the convention of the National Labor Union, four of the seven New York City unions represented were German (the piano makers', German varnishers', carvers', and cabinetmakers' unions). In addition, two of the six national unions at this convention were German-led and based in New York (the cigar makers' and the tailors' unions).[19]

The year 1868 got off to a bad start. It was reportedly the worst winter since 1857–58, with over 100,000 workers unemployed in New York City.[20] The earliest activity reported for a German union was the carvers' resolution to fight any wage cuts of over 10 percent—not exactly a sign of great militancy.[21] But business picked up in the spring, and in May the bricklayers' union (English-speaking) led the way with a strike for the eight-hour day. At almost the same time, the strongest German unions, in the furniture and piano-making trades, struck for higher wages.[22] By summer, it was clear that 1868 was the beginning of a major economic boom and both the English- and the German-speaking workers began their most successful organizing drive in New York's history, one that raised the strength of organized labor in the city to seventy thousand by 1870.[23]

Hardly had the boom begun, than the cabinetmakers' union called for a joint effort by the German unions to sponsor their own newspaper. They were joined by the piano makers', the carvers', and the varnishers' unions in an Association of United Workers and began to lay their plans. Soon the cigar makers' union joined them and they all called for a mass meeting on June 5 to launch their project. Conrad Kuhn, president of the cigar makers' union, was chosen as president of the new Association of United Workers—often known by the name of the newspaper it sponsored, the *Arbeiter Union* (though it was not an actual revival of the earlier organization with the same name). The weekly *Arbeiter Union* soon made its first appearance (on June 13) and the German labor movement had a voice.

At first, the new paper was edited by a lawyer named Landsberg whose social perspective could best be described as Malthusian. Under his editorship the *Arbeiter Union* focused on "the practical, not the theoretical," but it was currency reform that Landsberg considered practical, not trade unionism. When the unionists protested, Landsberg resigned and the editorship went to Adolf Douai (a well-known forty-eighter who had been driven out of Texas in the 1850s because he had been publishing an abolitionist newspaper; he had become a Republican party activist and was now a leader of the Freethinkers' League). Douai was also something of a currency reform enthusiast, favoring the doctrines of Edward Kellogg as adopted by the National Labor Union in 1867.[24]

While Douai was still primarily a currency reformer, he wasted no time before he began serializing excerpts from a new book that had impressed him—*Das Kapital* by Karl Marx.[25] By the next May, the *Arbeiter Union* was featuring a debate on currency reform between Douai (still a defender of Kellogg) and Konrad Carl, a Marxist tailor.[26] Douai was not yet a convert to Marxism, but the very next issue of the *Arbeiter Union* came out for government expropriation of all monopolies and large factories. The *Arbeiter Union* had thus taken the first major step away from reformism and utopian socialism toward Marxian socialism.[27] It was also in May that the *Arbeiter Union* became a daily, for the German-American labor movement in New York was now large enough to support a daily paper. The extent of the active support for the new labor daily is indicated by the report that fifteen to twenty thousand workers and their family members turned out for the *Arbeiter Union* picnic and festival that June.[28]

The revival of labor activity naturally encouraged the German-American socialists to resume their activities as well. A small group of Lassallean émigrés, with their notions of state-sponsored socialism and their disdain for trade unions, had formed an Allgemeine Deutscher Arbeiterverein (General German Workers' Union) in 1865, but the organization had little influence. Then, in 1867, the Kommunisten Klub, with its mix of freethought and Marxism, was revived in response to the labor activity of recent years. The Kommunisten opened negotiations with the Lassalleans to form a socialist political party, leading to the formation of the Social Party for New York City and Vicinity in January of 1868. The provisional president of the new party was Kommunisten Klub member F. Adolf Sorge. Wilhelm Weitling, still a popular figure among Kleindeutschland's workers and Sorge's old friend, was invited to join the executive committee, but he declined. A friendly coal dealer financed a spring campaign for them in the municipal elections, but they only got about two thousand votes.

The Social party had a few union activists among its members, but it had no direct ties to the unions that were so active that spring. The socialists concluded that they could not reach the workers without active union support, so they gave up their electoral pretensions and changed their organization's name back to the General German Workers' Union. Then they moved to reach out to the workers by joining the National Labor Union (which had just called for the formation of a labor reform party). They were soon chartered as NLU Local 5. By the end of 1869, when they also joined the International Workingmen's Association as Section 1 for North America, they still numbered only about fifty members, but they had become influential with the *Arbeiter Union* and its supporting unions (especially the cigar makers' union).[29]

The socialists' rise to a position of greater influence in the German labor movement of New York was spurred by another fall in the business cycle. As business declined through the second half of 1869 and unemployment increased, the unions were once more thrown onto the defensive. The strikes of late 1869 started with a series of only partially successful attempts to win wage increases, but the year ended with the unions striking against wage cuts and 1870 opened with an anti-union offensive by the employers.[30] Times were hard, but not hard enough to break the unions and this seems to have been the perfect environment for making the trade unionists receptive to Marxian socialist ideas. While Kelloggism had completely taken over the National Labor Union as the economy declined, it was displaced from the pages of the *Arbeiter Union*, where Marxism now occupied the field. Many of the leaders of the German-speaking unions had either joined Section 1 of the International Workingmen's Association or were drawn increasingly close to its doctrines. With Konrad Carl (president of the Tailors' Central Union), Karl Speyer (leader of the United Cabinetmakers' Union), and a large proportion of the leaders of the increasingly influential Cigar Makers' International Union all adhering to Section 1, the most purely Marxist section in the entire International, it is hard to escape Samuel Gompers' conclusion: "Unquestionably, in those early days of the 'seventies the International dominated the labor movement of New York City."[31]

Unfortunately for the Internationalists, their rise to leadership was immediately followed by the outbreak of hostilities between France and Germany. As members of an organization dedicated to international proletarian solidarity, and with both German and French sections in New York City, the Internationalists enlisted the *Arbeiter Union* in their opposition to the "unjust war, provoked only for the benefits of despotic rulers." Their campaign against the war culminated in November with a mass antiwar meeting at Cooper Union. The meeting was cosponsored by the International Workingmen's Association's New York sections, the Association of United Workers (known by this time as the Arbeiter Union), the Workingmen's Union (its English-speaking equivalent), the League of Freethinkers, and several reform organizations. Adolf Sorge chaired the meeting and was the lead speaker for the crowd of about two thousand. He spoke in English and then translated his eloquent denunciation of the war into German and French. Konrad Carl spoke for the trade unions, Adolf Douai spoke for the Freethinkers, and greetings were read from Senator Charles Sumner. The meeting attracted widespread, indeed international, attention and was accounted a "perfect success."[32] It was, however, denounced as "unpatriotic" by all five German-language dailies in New York and by all but one of the weeklies.[33]

That was indeed a problem. We may note that the November meeting was not sponsored by the *Arbeiter Union* newspaper. Kleindeutschland was swept up in a flood of German patriotism during the war (after all, even Marx and Engels had hedged as long as it appeared that Germany was fighting a defensive war), and the *Arbeiter Union*'s antiwar stance had not gone over well. German nationalism had had a greater appeal for the German proletarians of New York than did proletarian internationalism, and they had stopped buying the *Arbeiter Union*, which folded in September. The Internationalists and the German labor movement thus lost their major means of reaching the German workers of New York, just as it had become a reliable instrument of socialist propaganda.

Despite this setback, the Internationalists continued to lead the German unions and the German unions were soon back in the forefront of the New York labor movement. The building-trades workers (mostly English speakers) renewed their demand for the eight-hour working day early in May 1872 and the German furniture makers followed suit within a few days. It was the beginning of a busy season after a slow year and many employers gave in quickly, spurring more and more workers to demand the eight-hour day.[34] By May 25, there were about 20,000 workers reported out on strike, with about 6,000 in the mostly German furniture trades.[35] The United Cabinetmakers' Union then set up the Eight Hour League with the gilders, brass finishers, and photographic instrument makers (all German organizations), and the Germans took over the leadership of the eight-hour movement.[36] A week later there were 40,000 out on strike, and before the summer of 1872 ended more than 100,000 workers took part in the eight-hour strikes in New York City.[37] Even the German masons, who had split off from the bricklayers' union in 1868 because they preferred higher wages to the union's demand for eight hours, now joined the move for the eight-hour day.[38]

The influence of socialist ideas quickly made itself apparent. On May 27 there was an eight-hour demonstration in City Hall Park with a separate speaker's platform for the German workers, who comprised half the crowd. Conrad Kuhn gave the major address, concluding: "Let the capitalists make us those concessions which we have asked for, and which are certainly fair, and there will be no war between the two classes." President Siebert of the Pianoforte Makers' Union said that the workingmen were chained by the capitalists. "Let us break these chains, let us cast off these shackles. We want to work, we want to be industrious: but, first of all, we want to be freemen [enthusiastic applause]."[39] The small-producer ideology of earlier years, with its opposition of working classes and idle classes, had given way to a two-class, working class versus capitalist, conception of society.

The strikers were rolling up victory after victory, primarily in the trades dominated by small employers, but they met firmer resistance from the larger manufacturers. Piano manufacturer William Steinway took the lead by rallying the Piano Manufacturers' Association against the workers' demands. He explained his position to his dealers:

> Although satisfied that the workmen will triumph at the end of the strike . . . we are compelled to oppose the movement with all the means and perseverance in our power, no matter what may be the danger to our lives and property, and the magnitude of our losses.
>
> By holding out we may obtain more moderate terms; besides, unless the workmen are subjected to a long strike in enforcing their demands, they will in a few months again demand and strike for higher wages.[40]

Steinway could be very persuasive and soon talked his workers into accepting a 10 percent wage increase and nine hours instead of the eight-hour day, having convinced them that he would otherwise have to raise his prices by one-third and that this would so reduce his market that many of his workers would have to be laid off.[41] The next day fifteen hundred piano makers and two thousand other strikers picketed the Steinway factory and only one-quarter of the Steinway workers showed up for work. In line with his expressed fears of "danger to our lives and property," Steinway was apparently convinced that only fear of union violence kept his workers from remaining loyal—though he had arranged for three hundred policemen to guard his factory gates against possible union violence.[42] He redoubled his anti-union efforts among the employers' associations and got his friend Oswald Ottendorfer (German Democratic Club leader and owner/editor of the *Staats-Zeitung*) to join him in a campaign to portray the strikers as being manipulated by a violence-prone minority of union agitators and communists.[43] They thus laid the basis for the employers' increasing reliance upon the police to defeat the strikers.

Steinway may have relied upon force to defeat the strikers, but he was circumspect in his public announcements. Ignoring his earlier concession that the strikers were bound to win, he told the *Times:* "The fact is that the piano men have struck in the commencement of the dull season, and like the cabinetmakers have outwitted themselves. Business will not be brisk for three months, and the manufacturers would only have been making stock to keep their hands going, so that this strike is a god-send to most of us. It is the same with the cabinetmakers, who can make holiday, if they desire it, for three months, for their bosses do not want them. But the question ought to be settled now, so that there will be no strike when business becomes brisk again."[44]

As the employers' associations were publicly mobilizing for a counter-attack against the unions, the Eight Hour League called for a demonstration of strength—an eight-hour-day parade. The league confidently predicted that thirty five thousand workers of all nationalities would march on June 10. The next day the *Sun* reported:

> The principal thoroughfares of the city rang with cheers yesterday. The workingmen's parade attracted crowds of spectators in the Bowery, in Broadway, in Fourteenth street and Twenty-third street, and all the other streets through which the procession passed. The houses in the Bowery near where the procession was formed displayed flags and the whole street was gay with the colors of the United States and Germany. As the majority of the workingmen in the parade are Germans, so the greater part of the spectators seemed to be of Teutonic origin. It was a gala day for the workingmen of New York. Thousands who did not march in the procession stood on the sidewalks and attested the interest they felt in the parade by enthusiastic cheering.

It would appear to have been a glorious sight as the procession marched off from the Germania Assembly Rooms. "The bands playing the Marseillaise and the Wacht am Rhein; the flags flying; the voices of the spectators shouting and cheering; the marshals, arrayed in their best, galloping to and fro; the whole army of workingmen marching gaily ahead; waving of handkerchiefs and the cries of 'Vivat' and 'Hurrah' —the spectacle was one worth witnessing. The workingmen seemed to feel the power of their numbers—they seemed cheerful and buoyant as they marched on under the cheering of the multitude."

Section 1 of the International marched right behind the cabinetmakers, carrying a red flag and a banner reading "Those who would be free / Themselves must strike the first blow." An unidentified German union carried some "ancient German poetry" on its banner:

> God, who let iron grow,
> did not want men to be slaves;
> therefore he gave us swords and spears,
> so that we can fight for our rights as freemen.

The *Sun* reported that the Eight Hour League claimed that twenty thousand had participated and that the demonstration was a success.[45] The *Times* and the *Tribune* reported that only four or five thousand marched, mostly Germans. The anti-union *Times* even claimed that some of the marchers were there only "under compulsion." These antistrike papers presented the march as a total fiasco, and focused on the threatening tone of a banner carried by an English-speakers' section of the International that read "Peacefully if we can / Forcibly if we must."[46] The papers associated this with the specter of the recent Paris Commune and waxed hysterical.

As newspapers focused on the threat of violence, the "failure" of the eight-hour-day parade, and the fact that no new victories had been won, some of the strikes started weakening and some strikers began to return to work. Once again the Steinway factory was the symbol of resistance. Four hundred strikers assembled near the Steinway factory early on the morning of June 15 to discourage Steinway's workers from going back to work. They were confronted by an equal number of policemen. The *Staats-Zeitung* reported that when the strikers were heard making threats against men who showed up for work, the police ordered them to disperse and enforced the order vigorously with their clubs.[47] The *Times*'s report was more in keeping with its anti-union fear campaign, saying that the strikers had attempted to assault the factory and attributing the violence to the evil influence of the International Workingmen's Association upon the unions.[48] In any case, William Steinway announced that all but sixty of his workers had come in to work after the picketers had been driven off.[49]

Two hours later, the police detachment left their post at the Steinway factory and marched down to Forty-second Street, where two hundred furniture makers were trying to keep a group of strikebreakers imported from Newark from entering a factory. Once again, the police moved in with swinging clubs and cleared the area.[50] A new policy was now apparent. Two days later there was a third major police incident. This time it was a crowd of sugar refiners who were trying to prevent some colleagues from returning to work. "The police, in their onslaught struck the men with their clubs, regardless of anything but the order they had received and the poor wretches scattered, groaning and bleeding."[51] That same day the authorities threatened to arrest the president of the Eight Hour League (cabinetmaker Richard Schlüter) on conspiracy charges.[52]

The Steinway victory and the militancy of the police encouraged many employers who had been hanging back from the struggle to join (or rejoin) the fray. On June 18 employers from all trades formed a central employers' association to prepare for a major confrontation. They declared that it was intolerable that there were still seventy thousand workers out on strike in New York City and that order had to be restored. To that end they resolved not to employ anybody unwilling to work ten hours a day or anybody belonging to any organization that sought "to interpose itself between employers and employees" (i.e., unions and eight-hour leagues).[53] In the short confrontation between the eight-hour movement and the united employers' association, the German workers of New York experienced the struggle of class against class that the socialists had called for but were unable to win.

In the next few days the newspapers reported numerous clashes between strikers and police as the police continued to break up the strikers' gatherings.[54] To reinforce the message that the strikes would be broken by any means necessary, the police board was reported to be considering plans to bring in troops to back up the police actions against the eight-hour men.[55] The pressure mounted, and the strikers, many of whom were already suffering severely from the effects of being out on strike for weeks without strike benefits, began to cave in. No new victories were being announced, and then came some major defeats. The added pressure of the police violence convinced them that they had no hope of winning. Day after day the papers reported the failure of strikes in trade after trade.[56] On the last day of June, the united employers' association met and declared the eight-hour movement vanquished.

Even after the defeat of the eight-hour movement, the employers hounded their adversaries. Leading trade unionists, like Conrad Kuhn of the cigar makers' union, were blacklisted—unable to find work in their trades.[57] Anyone suspected of union agitation was subject to immediate dismissal, in accordance with the resolution of the united employers. In those trades where the eight-hour day had been won, it was taken back by fiat—knowing that nobody would dare resist.[58] By October of 1872, there were only about fifteen thousand workers in New York City and Brooklyn still working only eight hours a day.[59] As for the socialists, they had divided into two competing "Internationals" and were increasingly bogged down in internecine warfare.[60]

The employers' victory rested on more than their determination to hold out against a long strike. It also depended on their ability to mobilize the repressive apparatus of the government, that is, the police and the threat of the militia, against the strikers. Neither of the popular immigrant-based political machines that had ruled New York City for the preceding two decades, Mozart and Tammany halls, would have been easily persuaded to identify itself as the enemy of the workingmen.[61] Mozart Hall was long dead, however, and Tammany had just been overthrown by an elite native-German alliance. The eight-hour movement had the misfortune to be opposed by a business community that was taking back control of the city government for the first time in decades.

The assorted collection of doctors, journalists, middle-class professionals, and saloonkeepers that had dominated the German factions of the Democratic party of New York City in the mid-1850s began to give way to a rising German-American business elite by the early 1860s. The key transitional figure was Oswald Ottendorfer. He had been a republican revolutionary in the German revolutions of 1848–50, but had rapidly adapted his political perspective to the Jacksonian republicanism of his new employer, the New Yorker *Staats-Zeitung.* In the late 1850s he was an editor of the *Staats-Zeitung* and a Democratic party activist (along with his fellow editor Magnus Gross). Then, in 1859, he married his employer, Jacob Uhl's widow, Anna.[62] He thus became owner-editor of the *Staats-Zeitung,* New York's largest German-language newspaper, and crossed the boundary between middle-class professional and member of the developing German-American elite. Ottendorfer was now as wealthy as any contemporary German-American piano manufacturer or brewer prince and met with them as social equals. He also became the undisputed leader of the newly important German Democracy (which had just helped Fernando Wood recapture the mayor's office).

The *Staats-Zeitung* had always had a largely middle-class readership, but it lost a significant portion of its professional support after its vituperative attacks on the German Republicans and their antislavery politics. At the same time, the growing prosperity of German-American businessmen in New York made it ever more attractive for the paper to identify itself as the newspaper of and for New York's numerous German businessmen and shopkeepers. Under Ottendorfer's editorship, the *Staats-Zeitung* became firmly established as the newspaper of "all the German shopkeeping community," and Ottendorfer joined forces in the German Democracy with merchants like Otto Sackersdorf and Louis Bamberger.[63]

The German Democrats were then the mainstay of Mozart Hall, Fernando Wood's political organization. This, however, turned out to be an extremely awkward position when the South seceded from the Union in 1861. Wood had been allied in national Democratic party politics with several factions led by Southern politicians. When the South seceded, Wood had publicly considered the idea of pulling New York City and Long Island out of the Union to form the free city of Tri-Insula. Later he vacillated between lukewarm support of the war effort and blaming the war on the Republican administration.[64] Wood's less-than-patriotic leadership had no great attraction for the developing ethnic business and political elite, which was composed of recent immigrants who felt compelled to demonstrate their loyalty conspicuously. They were further alienated from Wood because the organized German community of the *Vereine* was rapidly mobilizing behind the war effort and the German Republicans were trying to capture the German vote by portraying the Democratic party as subversive. It was essential for the German Democracy to abandon Wood.

Tammany Hall made the break with Wood easy by nominating Godfrey Gunther for mayor. Gunther was the son of German immigrants, so the German Democrats were able to claim ethnic solidarity and principle (in addition to expedience) as the basis for abandoning the cause of their leader. Ottendorfer led the German Democrats out of Mozart Hall and into the creation of a new German Democratic Union party, which then endorsed the "German" Gunther.[65] The ethnic appeal even brought some German Republicans back to the Democratic party as they abandoned the Republican candidate, Opdyke, for Gunther.[66] When the votes were counted, Opdyke won the mayor's office by a narrow plurality, but Gunther had also edged out Wood by some six hundred votes (and had displayed a commanding lead in the Kleindeutschland wards).[67] The German Democratic Union party had thus demonstrated that it continued to command the loyalty of the German voters and might easily swing an election.

The Civil War had an effect on the German-American press similar to that of the 1848 German revolution. News became more important and circulation increased rapidly. Now it wasn't just news of the distant homeland either. There were some thirty-six thousand German New Yorkers fighting in the Union army, so friends and family members off at the front were subjects of pressing concern.[68] The German regiments and German generals in the Union army were all local heroes. Were nativists in the army and the Republican administration denying the German regiments the opportunity to display their skill and heroism? Why wasn't General Franz Sigel given command of the Army of the West? These were important wartime issues in Kleindeutschland and the German press played them for all the circulation they were worth.[69] As the largest German-language paper, the *Staats-Zeitung* reaped the greatest benefit from this boom and by 1870 it ranked with the *Times* and *Tribune* in circulation (about forty five thousand).[70] The wealth and influence of its owner, Oswald Ottendorfer (and of his German Democratic Union party), rose accordingly.

The German Democratic Union party did especially well in the mayoral election of 1863. Ottendorfer built a "reform" coalition around its basic strength in the German wards. Together with their allies in the McKeon

Democracy, they nominated Gunther for mayor once more. This time, a disaffected Tammany chieftain, "Honest John" Kelly, led a portion of the Irish vote from the Tammany wigwam over to the Germans. With no other candidate able to tap strong German support (which Wood had still had two years earlier), Gunther was elected mayor and Ottendorfer was kingmaker.[71] The Germans were no match for a united Tammany, though, and they lost badly in the next election. Nonetheless, the 1863 election had demonstrated their independent power and their importance in the incredibly complex factionalism of New York's Democratic party politics.[72]

There was one other important legacy of the Civil War years for the political development of German New York. The national Democratic party had been virtually destroyed by the secession crisis and the outbreak of war. It was rebuilt by its new national chairman, a wealthy and powerful New York banker with long-standing ties to the national Democratic party organization, the German-born August Belmont.[73] Belmont avoided stressing his German background and had married a prominent American socialite (Commodore Perry's daughter), but he had always gotten the support of the *Staats-Zeitung.* Either in the course of his social rise or directly through politics, Oswald Ottendorfer made Belmont's acquaintance and they became political allies. In 1864 the Democrats needed German-speaking organizers to work for General McClellan's presidential campaign in Pennsylvania and Belmont turned to Ottendorfer for assistance.[74] Belmont provided the rising German-American elite of New York with political contacts among their English-speaking social equivalents, who were destined to be close political allies at the beginning of the 1870s.

The rise of the Irish-based Tweed machine in the late 1860s pulled the rug out from under the German Democrats. Suddenly they were effectively excluded from both power and patronage. Once more they sought native allies against the Irish and this time they found them among the social elite of New York. The Tweed machine based its success on providing needed services for nearly every constituency, but this proved very expensive (and would have been even if there hadn't been widespread corruption). In four years of rule, the machine tripled New York's municipal debt, and the substantial property owners of the city (both English- and German-speaking) began to fear that massive tax hikes would inevitably follow.[75] Tweed also made the mistake of attempting to unseat August Belmont as chairman of the Democratic National Committee in 1869, and Belmont responded by taking a hand in promoting an anti-Tweed alliance.[76]

Even before the formal founding of a property owner's anti-Tweed alliance in 1871, the German Democrats and their allies were taking steps to move against the Tweed machine. In November of 1870 a grand jury was impaneled to investigate graft and corruption in the municipal government and the various opponents of Tweed and Tammany Hall made sure that they had their representatives on the grand jury. Lucius S. Comstock, a reformer and antivice crusader, was foreman of the grand jury, which began to expose the scandalous condition of the city's finances. The jury also contained a number of German New Yorkers, including Oswald Ottendorfer's close friend and associate, the publisher Ernst Steiger.[77] The highly politicized grand jury leaked testimony and evidence to Tweed's opponents, and there was soon a major newspaper campaign against the "Tweed Ring," led by the *Times* and the *Staats-Zeitung*.

When the stories broke with reports of the precarious state of New York City's finances, the city's creditors refused to lend it any more money "while the city is controlled by its present management."[78] This was the signal for the property owners of New York to organize. On September 4, 1871, a mass meeting of "tax-payers and citizens of New York" was held at Cooper Union and resolved that the municipal government should be turned over to "the wisest and best citizens," meaning themselves. Among the vice presidents of the meeting were the bankers Abraham Kuhn and Jessie and Joseph Seligman, the merchant Gustav Schwab, and "the German school commissioner" Magnus Gross. Oswald Ottendorfer was listed as an organizer of the gathering and he was one of six featured speakers that evening. He said that "the tax-payer of New York had to furnish the corruption fund which kept the machines of both parties going" and called for a nonpartisan city government to save the property owners' money. Indeed, the *Times* reported that all the speakers "touched the hearer in what has been called the tenderest spot—the pocket." Among the members of the executive committee selected to direct the cleansing of the municipal administration was Ottendorfer's good friend and political associate, Theodore Steinway.[79]

The *Staats-Zeitung* reported the meeting as representative of the whole population: "Side by side with the millionaire, the rich banker, the merchant, the educated man, the journalist, was represented the simple workman, the skilled worker, the retail shop-keeper; a common interest had brought them together."[80] This was a rather disingenuous description of a meeting dominated by millionaires, rich bankers, and merchants, but in Kleindeutschland (as in the city as a whole) these were the men who were attempting to define their interests as the "common interest." The anti-Tweed forces in Kleindeutschland were united when Ottendorfer set up a German Independent Citizens Organization to draw the German Republicans into an electoral coalition for the fall elections.[81] Tweed and Tammany were smashed and the business- and property-owning classes were in charge of the city administration—just in time for the eight-hour strikes of 1872. The fact that the anti-Tweed forces did particularly well in the German districts gave the German leaders like Ottendorfer and Steinway a great deal of influence over how the strikes would be handled.[82]

Even as class politics were being worked out in the streets between the German workers and their German employers (with the assistance of the police), Ottendorfer and the German-American businessmen who led the German Democracy made an attempt to dominate the mayor's office. On June 15, 1872, they formed a German Reform party and nominated former mayor (and descendant of German immigrants) William Havemeyer as their candidate. With fifty-seven thousand enrolled members, the new reform party's support gave Havemeyer a leading position in the race for the support of the rest of the reform movement.[83] Havemeyer thus won general support from the various reform factions and was elected mayor that fall. He was insensitive to the needs of his constituency, however, and soon alienated most of his supporters.[84] The Germans were particularly put out when the mayor, who owed his position to their early support, discriminated against all immigrants in filling municipal patronage positions. (He was only supposed to keep out the Irish). Havemeyer even appointed an Anglo-American to the "German" seat on the Board of Commissioners of Emigration.[85] When the next election approached, nobody even considered renominating Havemeyer.

Ottendorfer and his German Reform party had fallen out with the native American reformers before the 1874 election, so they resolved to try to elect Ottendorfer mayor. This split the reform vote because a "reformed" Tammany Hall nominated a leading member of the good government Committee of Seventy as its candidate.[86] It also split the German vote because August Belmont and Augustus Schell (both German-born) were now part of the reform leadership of the Tammany organization, along with "Honest John" Kelly.[87] Patronage was promised to German-American politicians who stuck with Tammany, and many of them did. As a result, Ottendorfer carried only one of Kleindeutschland's wards and suffered a dismal defeat.[88] This experience with popular democracy at work soured Ottendorfer and his allies on democracy. By 1877 they had reached the conclusion that the only way to end municipal corruption and high taxes was essentially to disenfranchise everyone who didn't pay taxes on property worth over $500 or a rent of $250 a year.[89] In this proposal they joined many of their fellow "reformers" who were also disenchanted with democratic politics. They thereby reunited the property owners' coalition around the most blatantly class-oriented proposals since the German radicals' publication of the "Communist Manifesto."

Back in the labor movement, the severe depression after the panic of

1873 brought down most of the organizations built over the preceding decade. Even the workers' fraternal orders, the Harugari, the Druids, and the Hermannssöhne, were hard hit by the depression and lost many members.[90] The International Workingmen's Association survived long enough to help organize a mass protest of the unemployed at the beginning of 1874, however. German New York was then treated to a most convincing demonstration of the socialist maxim that the state is the executive committee of the ruling class.[91] The night before the demonstrators were to assemble in the heart of Kleindeutschland, at Tompkin's Square Park, their permit was canceled. The cancellation was poorly publicized, though, and demonstrators assembled by the thousands the next day. With some ten thousand men, women, and children in the park by 10:30 that morning, the police moved in to attack. Samuel Gompers remembered that scene vividly:

> a group of workers marched into the park from Avenue A. They carried a banner bearing the words "TENTH WARD UNION LABOR." Just after they entered the park the police sergeant led the attack on them. He was followed by police mounted and on foot with drawn night-sticks. Without a word of warning they swept down the defenseless workers, striking down the standard-bearer and using their clubs right and left indiscriminately on the heads of all they could reach.
>
> Shortly afterwards the mounted police charged the crowd on Eighth Street, riding them down and attacking men, women and children without discrimination. It was an orgy of brutality. I was caught in the crowd on the street and barely saved my head from being cracked by jumping down a cellarway. . . . A reign of terror gripped that section of the city [Kleindeutschland].[92]

All pretense of legality was then abandoned as the police invaded private indoor meetings and dispersed their would-be participants.[93] Rumors that the Internationalists were plotting to turn New York into another Paris Commune again circulated through the city and the police were given a free hand.[94] The labor and socialist organizations of Kleindeutschland were already reeling from the effects of the economic collapse, and many now gave up entirely and closed down. The International Workingmen's Association didn't give up the ghost for a while longer, but it was rent by further factionalism severe enough to make its activities insignificant.[95]

Although the German labor movement was virtually paralyzed for the rest of the decade by the depression, the experiences of the late 1860s and early 1870s appear to have established a fundamental political division within German New York, which persisted for a generation. Two politically separate worlds coexisted beyond the rest of the century, one for the middle classes and one for the workers. The middle classes were hard money reform Democrats or liberal Mugwump Republicans (mostly the former) and rallied around the *Staats-Zeitung* and Oswald Ottendorfer's elite-dominated political organization. The German workers rallied around the United German Trades, followed socialist union leaders, read the new socialist paper, the New Yorker *Volks-Zeitung,* and even began to vote for the new Socialist Labor party. While the socialist vote was never overwhelming, the *Volks-Zeitung* came to rival the *Staats-Zeitung* for the honor of being German New York's leading journal. It is clear, then, that in one fundamental respect class divisions had come to replace religious differences as the most significant dividing lines within German New York.

CHAPTER NINE

Particularism, Class Consciousness, and Community

A major American immigrant settlement like Kleindeutschland offers a constant challenge to the investigator: to work out the nature and structure of the social order that underlay the apparent anarchy of the ethnic metropolis. In this work I have sketched out the main lines of Kleindeutschland's social organization and introduced some of its major social groups. Rather than attempt to produce a complete compendium of all facets of New York's German-American life, a project that would fill many volumes, I have endeavored to bring out those elements that gave it structure and coherence, and made Kleindeutschland one of the most interesting ethnic communities in American history.

The study began with an exploration of the roots of Kleindeutschland's complexity in the social order of a fragmented German Europe. In the first two-thirds of the nineteenth century German Europe was divided into the thirty-nine states and free cities of the German Confederation, German Switzerland, Alsace, East and West Prussia, and the many German-speaking cities and districts from Bohemia to the Ukraine and Transylvania.[1] The Prussian state hammered most of the German Confederation into a new German Empire in the years between 1866 and 1871 (losing the Austrian Germans in the process), but it was an empire of princes and not a nation-state. The creation of a German nation-state was to take another generation or two, led to two world wars, and is now back on the historical agenda. In the nineteenth century, both before and after 1871, cultural, religious, and linguistic boundaries cut across those of states and customs unions, dividing German Europe into a multitude of small cultural and linguistic regions.[2] I have made it clear that these regions, and not a mythical German nation, were the source of the German emigration that created Kleindeutschland.

Having noted the dominance of particularism in German Europe, it was clearly necessary to begin looking for evidence of particularism in German America. Even a cursory exploration of German migration and settlement patterns in the United States made it obvious that particularism was an important element in the development of German America and, having demonstrated the pattern on a national level, I then examined the settlement patterns of German New York. There, it turned out that German immigrants not only settled in dense concentrations, which they dominated to the near exclusion of other ethnic groups, but that they ordered their neighborhoods around subnational criteria that often approximated their region of origin in Germany.

Despite these findings, German-American settlement patterns and residential concentrations could still be viewed as merely the inevitable result of a process of chain migration. Assuming that social networks based on kinship and common origin were major factors in an immigrant's initial choice of a place to settle and the immigrant's ability to secure a job and find a home, then the apparent persistence of German-American particularism could be merely a residual feature of the migration process rather than a long-term German-American pattern. After all, a constant stream of fresh immigration could suffice to explain the continued existence of regional settlements, even in the face of strong tendencies toward assimilation into a more homogeneous German-American community. This has indeed been the traditional approach to German-America. When we considered other forms of social interaction, however, we found that they too exhibited regional patterns, and that these patterns are not so easily explained by references to continuing processes of chain migration.

Marriage is the one form of social interaction that probably reveals more about people's perceptions of social distance than any other, and our examination of the marriage patterns of Kleindeutschland provided us with further evidence of the enduring strength of German particularism. First-generation immigrants from Germany consistently displayed a strong tendency toward regional or subnational endogamy, choosing spouses from either their own state of origin in Germany or from an adjacent state in the same region. Even more striking was that the patterns of restricted marriage choices continued to operate for Kleindeutschlanders born and raised in New York City. In 1880, 43 percent of the married American-born children of Bavarian immigrants were married to fellow Bavarian-Americans and another 22 percent were married to German-Americans from adjacent territories. The children of Prussian immigrants were even more exclusive, marrying other Prussian-Americans 92 percent of the time.

These patterns of state and regional endogamy, especially when they persisted into the second generation, clearly drew us beyond the realm of chain migration. Combined with the data on residential concentration by nativity, they provided evidence of a pervasive informal social separation between New Yorkers from different parts of Germany.

While marriage patterns clearly indicated that local and regional particularism were of enormous social significance, other family and household characteristics turned out to have little association with place of origin within Germany. Instead, within broad ethnic norms, both families and households varied in structure, size, and composition according to the occupational level of the head of household. This then led to an analysis of the next major axis of social differentiation in German New York, that of its economy.

In the mid-nineteenth century, some German immigrants were able to take advantage of opportunities in New York's rapidly expanding economy to become increasingly prosperous businessmen. Mercantile agents for German firms and entrepreneurial shopkeepers became founding members of a new German-American elite. Other Germans found new possibilities in the growth of manufacturing and the development of large-scale markets that they found in America. Master artisans became clearly differentiated employers; they were no longer just fellow members of a trade who had followed the normal career path and they often supervised increasing numbers of employees. Some of these former artisans became large-scale manufacturers who had less and less to do with most of their employees. Some merchants also took the lead in reorganizing production, and they too became large-scale manufacturers. These manufacturers and merchants joined together to form a business elite within German New York. The members of this rising elite, conscious of their increasing distinctiveness, then sought not so much to sever all social relations with the German-American masses of New York as to make clear their social superiority to those masses. First they created separate institutions, expensive and exclusive voluntary associations like the German Masonic Order, the Liederkranz, and the Arion Gesangverein. Later they moved their families away from the lower classes of Kleindeutschland entirely and established a more fashionable German district uptown in the vicinity of their Anglo-American counterparts. By the 1870s, then, social class divisions clearly followed the lines of economic divisions that had already developed and single-class German-American neighborhoods began to replace and transform the multiclass diversity of the old Kleindeutschland.

Having explored the structure of German New York in terms of subnational differentiation and occupation and class, it was necessary to address at last the third major axis of differentiation—that of religion. Although it was impossible to explore the ramifications of religious differences through the census the way we could with birthplace and occupation, it was still possible to explore the broader institutional outlines of German New York's distinct religious subdivisions. The broad groupings of Catholics, Protestants, and Jews were themselves composed of relatively discrete subgroups of their own (church Catholics versus liberal Catholics, Lutheran versus Reformed versus nominal Protestants, and Orthodox versus Reformed versus nominal Jews), and each contributed some members to the Freethinkers' congregations that formed yet another religious subcommunity. Individuals (or even entire congregations) sometimes passed through the permeable membranes that divided Kleindeutschland by religion, but the religious categories continued to organize the social life of New York's German-Americans.

The salience of this religious differentiation remained strong throughout the nineteenth century and into the twentieth. In fact, Andrew M. Greeley has found that German-American Catholics and Protestants remain clearly distinct groups even now on a wide variety of scales—although on other scales both groups of German-Americans stand out from their non-German-American coreligionists. Even despite a noticeable rise in anti-Semitism that began in the later 1870s (paralleling its increasing virulence in both Europe and Anglo-America), however, religious friction became relatively less significant to Kleindeutschland as the development of increasingly significant class divisions became the main focus of internal disputes within German New York.

The clearest expression of the social divisions of German New York lay in the world of its voluntary organizations. Religious differentiation was conspicuous in this realm, with several different religious communities maintaining a broad range of more or less exclusive *Vereine* to provide religious alternatives to the extensive *Vereinswesen* of secular Kleindeutschland. The most complete of these parallel associational networks was maintained by Catholics, but Jews and religious Protestants also had their own fraternal orders, benevolent associations, and singing societies. The rising business and social elite of German New York also began to set up exclusive *Vereine* as it began to establish a separate identity for itself. Upper-class fraternal lodges, singing societies, and social clubs were important arenas for displaying newly acquired wealth and for forging bonds of social solidarity between individuals of widely disparate origins. At the same time, other associations and fraternal orders took on an increasingly working-class character, while yet others clearly pitched their appeal to shopkeepers and other middle-class elements.

Perhaps the most interesting thing about the voluntary associations was the way in which they institutionalized German particularism and subnational ethnic identities in a new context. It is unlikely, after all, that informal social mechanisms could have been sufficient to transmit the values of particularism to American-born generations. The social markers of dress and dialect, which distinguished Germans from different regions, were lost as American clothing and then American English became prevalent—which was certainly the case for the second-generation German New Yorkers. Informal mechanisms simply do not appear sufficient to account for the continued strength and persistence of particularism, so it was necessary to look for formal, structured modes for transmitting a sense of German local identification to an American-born generation that had no experience of Germany. These modes were found in the world of the voluntary associations.

The *Landsmannschaft* associations, based explicitly upon local origins, began to proliferate in the 1860s, a decade after the first great wave of migration.[3] Thus, just when particularism might have begun to weaken as ties to the homeland began to attenuate, formal organizations designed to strengthen local ties took form. Social activities—meetings, dances, and picnics—brought hometowners and their families together several times a year, while sickness and death benefits (including funeral attendance) deepened their emotional ties. The *Landsmannschaften* often held joint burial plots in cemeteries and thereby established a permanent bond among their members. In each case they transformed a nostalgic sense of identity with a place in Germany into a living social network that provided friendship, mutual aid, and solace in the present along with a feeling of continuity with the past.

German particularism was not purely local, however, and the *Landsmannschaften* were not sufficient in themselves to transmit a complete sense of cultural continuity to an American-born generation. This required a more broadly focused regional network—one that the *Landsmannschaften* helped to create in the great *Volksfest Vereine*. These *Volksfest Vereine* and their associated German dialect newspapers (like the *Plattdütsche Post* and the *Schwäbisches Wochenblatt*) solidified a broad-based form of German-American particularism, one that was capable of socializing an American-born generation into subnational German identities. For the American-born generation, subnational identification never reached the fervid peaks expressed in the poetry of the parent generation, but it was strong enough to promote endogamy and group cohesion—attributes we normally associate with ethnicity. These identifications were in fact ethnic phenomena and they provided alternative versions of ethnicity that were able to compete with the standard notion of German-American identity for the primary group identification and loyalty of a large number of New York's Germans.

This raises some basic questions about the formation of American ethnic groups, because similar problems arise with non-Germans as well. Where were the boundaries that separated "our own kind" from strangers really drawn? Nobody is foolhardy enough to suggest that the English,

Welsh, Scots, and Irish immigrants to America formed a single ethnic group just because they came from the same European state and spoke the "same" language, though few have hesitated to put Plattdeutschen and Swabians, Prussians and Badeners into the same ethnic pot. The obvious fallacy of current attempts to treat "Hispanic-Americans" as if they were members of a single ethnic group should serve as a warning for those who would attempt to impose these ideological categories on a recalcitrant social reality—either in the past or in the present.

We simply cannot continue to assume that the ethnic formations that developed in the United States must have corresponded to the folk categories provided for us by nineteenth-century romantic nationalists. The easy comforts of an allegedly "natural" order of ethnicity must be rejected, along with the old shibboleths of "Americanization" and the "melting pot." What we need to do is to develop a new historical conception of ethnicity, one rooted in careful study of the complex social behavior of real people and real groups acting in different social settings.

In some ways this discussion of ethnicity as social process, in which specific ethnic consciousnesses arise out of particular historical circumstances and experiences, is reminiscent of E. P. Thompson's discourse on the nature of class and class consciousness. Indeed, these two processes are similar not only in form but in the ways in which they provide competing notions of identity for the same individuals.

While the chapter on work provided evidence for the objective existence of rapidly developing class differentiation in German New York, in the chapter on politics we were able to trace the subjective consequences of these developments. As German-American employers became more clearly differentiated from their former status as master artisans, they came into increasing conflict with their employees over wages, working conditions, and hours of work. The German-American labor movement of New York City was the workers' response to this development. It rose and fell with the economic tides, but it reached higher levels with each cycle. Employers and employees organized against each other, and Kleindeutschland was ever more sharply divided along the borders between economic classes. With opposing economic interests and little social contact, the emerging social classes of German New York developed strikingly different political perspectives. The upper and middle classes found ways to utilize the Democratic and Republican parties for their own purposes, while class conflicts and socialist agitation led many German-American workers to adopt an independent radical politics. By the 1870s, therefore, class divisions had come to overshadow religious ones as the most sharply drawn and strongly felt social boundaries within German New York.

Class consciousness took on a peculiarly ethnic form in German New York, however. Self-interest and socialist prodding brought German-American workers to the forefront of interethnic alliances, but they showed little inclination to submerge their self-identity in a pure, universalized working-class consciousness. The effective content of the German-American socialist call for "workers of all nations" to unite, when preached primarily to German-American workers in the German language, was that the German-American workers of New York should submerge *their* differences and unite. The socialists were thus more effective in subordinating subnational ethnic consciousnesses to an ethno-class consciousness than they were in creating a nonethnic class consciousness. Despite the universalistic formulation of the socialists' message, it was interpreted by German-American workers in ways that generally promoted class solidarity only within the ethnic group. Contrary to their intentions, therefore, German-American socialists found themselves effectively promoting what they wished to end, ethnic solidarity and a concomitant ethnic fragmentation of the working class.

Even as Kleindeutschland was continuing to grow in population during the 1870s, it had already begun to contract socially and physically. A substantial number of the wealthier German-American families had moved to more fashionable uptown neighborhoods as early as the 1860s. This process continued through the 1870s and 1880s, emptying Kleindeutschland of the "upper" levels of its society. Much of the rest of Kleindeutschland's population began to fill up the northern Eleventh and Seventeenth wards. By the 1870s, Kleindeutschland was abandoning the older and more crowded Tenth and Thirteenth wards to the increasing numbers of immigrants from Eastern Europe (some Bohemians and Poles but mostly Ostjuden, Jews from the Austro-Hungarian and Russian empires).

The 1870s and 1880s were also decades of building booms in which the built-up section of Manhattan expanded greatly to the north. After 1871, many better-class tenement buildings were constructed around the Yorkville section of Manhattan's upper east side (Eighty-third to Eighty-ninth streets flanking the old Boston Post Road—later Third Avenue), close to the stretch along the East River where the brewer princes had built their large new breweries in the late 1860s. Yorkville thus became the center of a new and expanding German neighborhood, which increasingly became the area of settlement for the third wave of German immigrants, who began arriving in the 1880s.

A truncated Kleindeutschland (largely confined to the Eleventh and Seventeenth wards) still contained nearly one-quarter of New York City's

German-Americans in 1890[4] and was still the German cultural and social center for the city. Its days as a German-American residential neighborhood were numbered, however. By 1910, the old Kleindeutschland contained only 10 percent of Manhattan's German-born residents. In those twenty years, Yorkville had grown into a new "little Germany" and the Jewish Lower East Side had engulfed the old Kleindeutschland.

Appendix A

Origins by German State of the German-born Population of Five U.S. Cities, 1860–80 (in percentages*)

Table 1—1860

German State	New York City	St. Louis	Chicago	Cincinnati	Milwaukee
Austria	3	8	7	1	5
Baden	15	13	10	16	4
Bavaria	30	17	20	35	15
Hamburg	—	—	—	—	—
Hanover	—	—	—	—	4
Hesse	20	15	12	11	9
Mecklenburg	—	—	—	—	13
Oldenburg	—	—	—	—	—
Prussia	21	42	45	27	31
Saxony	—	—	—	—	8
Württemberg	10	5	7	10	4
Other	—	—	—	—	7

*Rounded percentages may appear to total more or less than 100 percent.
Source: Eighth Census, *Population of the U.S.,* pp. 609, 621, 937.

Table 2—1870

German State	New York City	St. Louis	Chicago	Cincinnati	Milwaukee
Austria	4	1	2	1	3
Baden	9	10	7	11	3
Bavaria	17	11	8	20	8
Hamburg	1	1	1	—	—
Hanover	5	16	5	18	3
Hesse	11	9	5	5	5
Mecklenburg	3	—	7	—	10
Oldenburg	—	—	—	5	—
Prussia	43	43	54	31	59
Saxony	3	3	4	2	5
Württemberg	6	5	5	7	3
Other	—	1	2	—	1

Source: Ninth Census, *Statistics of the Population,* pp. 336–39, 385–89, 521.

Table 3—1880

German State	New York City	St. Louis	Chicago	Cincinnati	Milwaukee
Austria	5	3	3	1	4
Baden	11	11	5	11	3
Bavaria	18	10	6	19	7
Hamburg	2	1	1	1	—
Hanover	7	14	4	19	2
Hesse	4	7	2	4	4
Mecklenburg	1	—	4	—	8
Oldenburg	—	—	—	4	—
Prussia	40	47	70	30	66
Saxony	4	3	3	2	4
Württemberg	8	4	3	7	2
Other	—	—	—	3	—

Source: Tenth Census, *Statistics of the Population of the United States,* pp. 482–85, 520–23, 546–49.

Appendix B

Relative Concentrations of Immigrants from the German States in Kleindeutschland and Its Wards, 1860–80 (in percentages)

Table 1—1860

German State	Number from State in Sample	Klein-deutschland	10th Ward	11th Ward	13th Ward	17th Ward
Austria	21	3.0	—	6.6	—	2.7
Baden	93	13.5	14.1	16.4	13.3	10.9
Bavaria	187	27.0	16.0	28.2	31.7	32.2
Bohemia	8	1.2	—	1.9	—	1.6
Bremen	11	1.6	0.6	2.3	—	1.9
Hamburg	5	0.7	1.3	0.5	—	0.8
Hanover	31	4.5	3.2	8.9	3.3	1.9
Hesse-Nassau	99	14.4	12.2	7.5	33.3	17.1
Mecklenburg	5	0.7	1.3	0.5	—	0.8
Oldenburg	0	—	—	—	—	—
Posen	0	—	—	—	—	—
Prussia	130	19.0	36.5	10.3	11.7	17.1
Saxony	22	3.2	1.3	5.2	1.7	3.1
Schleswig-Holstein	1	0.1	0.6	—	—	—
Württemberg	74	11.0	12.8	11.7	5.0	10.1

Source: Author's census samples.

Table 2—1870

German State	Number from State in Sample	Klein-deutschland	10th Ward	11th Ward	13th Ward	17th Ward
Austria	33	3.3	5.8	5.1	0.7	2.2
Baden	122	12.1	5.8	10.2	7.7	17.0
Bavaria	178	17.6	13.0	21.3	13.4	19.4
Bohemia	4	0.4	—	0.5	—	0.6
Bremen	11	0.1	2.9	1.5	—	0.4
Hamburg	25	2.5	3.9	0.5	1.4	3.0
Hanover	44	4.4	5.8	4.6	7.0	2.8
Hesse-Nassau	124	12.3	8.2	17.3	7.0	13.6
Mecklenburg	8	0.8	1.4	0.5	—	0.9
Oldenburg	4	0.4	—	—	2.8	—
Posen	4	0.4	—	—	2.1	0.2
Prussia	311	30.8	38.6	21.3	40.1	28.4
Saxony	41	4.1	5.8	2.5	2.1	4.5
Schleswig-Holstein	7	0.7	0.5	1.0	2.8	—
Württemberg	94	9.3	8.2	13.7	12.7	6.4

Source: Author's census samples.

Table 3—1880

German State	Number from State in Sample	Klein-deutschland	10th Ward	11th Ward	13th Ward	17th Ward
Austria	37	4.8	9.7	5.5	4.1	1.8
Baden	63	8.2	9.1	7.4	12.4	6.6
Bavaria	134	17.5	9.1	18.0	12.4	24.3
Bohemia	10	1.3	—	2.3	1.7	1.1
Bremen	9	1.2	0.6	—	1.7	2.2
Hamburg	9	1.2	1.9	—	2.5	1.1
Hanover	49	6.4	3.2	3.2	15.7	6.6
Hesse-Nassau	86	11.3	7.1	13.4	6.6	14.0
Mecklenburg	4	0.5	0.6	—	0.8	0.7
Oldenburg	1	0.1	0.6	—	—	—
Posen	3	0.4	1.9	—	—	—
Prussia	275	36.0	48.7	41.9	34.7	24.6
Saxony	24	3.1	3.9	0.9	2.5	4.8
Schleswig-Holstein	1	0.1	0.6	—	—	—
Württemberg	52	6.8	1.9	7.4	3.3	10.7

Source: Author's census samples.

Appendix C

Average Age of Father at Birth of First Child, Mother at Birth of First and Last Child, and Number of Children, by Father's Occupation

Father's Occupation	Father's Age at First Birth	Mother's Age at First Birth	Mother's Age at Last Birth	Average Number of Children
Unskilled	29.4 (18)	26.1 (22)	37.9 (14)	2.8 (30)
Semiskilled	27.3 (48)	23.7 (52)	36.0 (13)	2.8 (64)
Skilled	27.8 (372)	24.4 (371)	36.8 (110)	2.9 (486)
Clerical	27.8 (25)	22.5 (26)	—	2.0 (28)
Proprietor	28.4 (200)	23.3 (202)	35.9 (70)	3.4 (259)
Professional	29.8 (34)	23.6 (35)	36.3 (14)	2.9 (48)
All occupations	28.1 (697)	24.0 (708)	36.5 (221)	3.0 (915)

Note: Figures in parentheses are base Ns for the adjacent percentages.
Source: Author's census samples.

Appendix D

Mother's Average Age at Childbearing and Average Number of Children by Mother's Nativity

German State of Origin	Mother's Age at First Birth	Mother's Age at Last Birth	Average Number of Children
Baden	24.6 (63)	39.4 (17)	2.9 (81)
Bavaria	23.5 (120)	36.2 (44)	3.1 (161)
Hesse-Nassau	23.8 (74)	34.7 (32)	3.4 (107)
Prussia	23.9 (159)	36.6 (72)	3.0 (222)
Württemberg	24.9 (53)	38.6 (18)	3.2 (68)

Note: Figures in parentheses are base Ns for the adjacent percentages.
Source: Author's census samples.

Appendix E

Occupational Distribution of Kleindeutschlanders, 1850–80
(in percentages)

Table 1—by Industry

Industry	1850 (n = 472)	1860 (n = 620)	1870 (n = 750)	1880 (n = 947)	1880-U.S. born (n = 223)
Building trades	4.0	4.0	5.0	4.0	4.5
Clothing trades	26.0	25.0	21.0	18.0	9.0
Food	11.0	5.0	5.0	6.0	3.6
Furniture and wood	8.0	7.0	8.0	5.0	6.7
Leather	1.0	0.0	1.0	0.6	0.9
Maritime	1.0	0.0	0.0	0.5	
Metal	3.0	3.0	3.0	2.3	2.7
Precious materials and instruments	1.0	1.0	2.0	2.4	3.6
Textile	0.0	0.0	0.0	0.5	0.5
Tobacco	3.0	4.0	3.0	7.7	13.5
Printing	0.0	1.0	0.0	2.0	3.6
Other trades	3.0	1.0	1.0	2.3	2.7
Transport workers	1.0	1.0	1.0	2.1	3.6
Laborers	4.0	2.0	4.0	1.6	0.5
Engineers	1.0	0.0	0.0	0.0	0.0
Machinists	1.0	1.0	1.0	1.0	2.7
Domestic servants	0.0	8.0	6.0	5.0	3.6
Service workers	0.0	2.0	4.0	4.6	0.0
White-collar workers	8.0	8.0	9.0	11.3	24.7
Government	0.0	0.0	0.0	0.2	0.0
Proprietors	0.0	0.0	2.0	1.3	3.8
Shopkeepers	14.0	12.0	12.0	12.0	4.9
Manufacturers	1.0	2.0	2.0	0.6	0.5
Merchants	2.0	1.0	2.0	0.3	0.0

Table 1—by Industry (Continued)

Industry	1850 (n = 472)	1860 (n = 620)	1870 (n = 750)	1880 (n = 947)	1880-U.S. born (n = 223)
Semiprofessionals	2.0	1.0	3.0	2.4	1.3
Professionals	2.0	1.0	2.0	1.3	1.3
Others (misc.)	2.0	5.0	1.0	2.0	3.1

Source: Author's census samples.

Table 2—by Occupational Level

Occupational Level	1850	1860	1870	1880
Unskilled	4.6	3.6	3.9	2.6
Semiskilled and service	5.0	14.4	15.1	17.1
Skilled and artisan	60.7	50.9	46.9	50.8
White-collar workers	8.3	9.7	7.3	8.9
Proprietors (worth under $1,000)	16.3	10.8	9.3	—
Proprietors (worth $1,000–$10,000)	1.3	5.7	6.3	17.0*
Proprietors (worth $10,000+)	0.0	1.4	5.8	—
Professionals	3.9	3.5	5.5	3.6

*The 1880 census does not give any property evaluations.
Source: Author's census samples.

Notes

INTRODUCTION

1. There were about 154,000 Germans and their children in New York City in 1855, with another 30,000 in Williamsburg and Brooklyn (*Census of the State of New York for 1855* (hereafter cited as *Census, N.Y.*, [*year*]), pp. xxii–iv, 103–18, and below, Chapter 2). The populations of the leading German cities in 1852 were: Vienna—477,846, Berlin—441,931, and Hamburg—148,754 (*Seventh Census of the United States, 1850*, p. liii).

2. In 1875 the population of Kleindeutschland was 152,106 (*Census, N.Y., 1875*, p. 21, and Chapter 2 below). German city populations are in *European Historical Statistics*, pp. 76–78.

3. The "New York German metropolis" is used to refer to the German-born and their families of New York City, the city of Brooklyn, and Hudson County, New Jersey. For that population figure see Chapter 2, table 3 below. For U.S. city populations see: *Eighth Census of the United States: Population of the United States in 1860*, pp. xxxi–xxxii; *Ninth Census of the United States: Statistics of the Population*, pp. 365, 385–89; *Tenth Census of the United States: Statistics of the Population of the United States*, pp. 538–41.

4. This is indicated by Samuel Gompers in his autobiography, *Seventy Years of Life and Labor.* He refers to New York City as "the cradle of the labor movement" (p. 61), after commenting that "the *Arbeiter Union*, the central body for the German workers, was the more virile and resourceful organization," in contrast to the English-speaking Workingmen's Council (p. 47). Stuart B. Kaufman devotes the bulk of his *Samuel Gompers and the Origins of the American Federation of Labor* to demonstrating the influence of New York's mostly German socialists on the development of both Gompers and the union movement. Even Bernard Mandel's more conservative interpretation of Gompers' life (*Samuel Gompers*) notes the significance of the German labor movement in New York (pp. 14–19, 21–22, 26–27, 30–31, 33–37, 70–73, 82–83, 101, 112–17). The Germans' importance is evident from their prominence throughout the text of Carl Degler's "Labor in the Economy and Politics of New York City, 1850–1860," pp. 13, 16, 22, 23, 28, 32, 34, 38, 43, 47, 53, 55, 64, 67, 80–81, 85, 87, 88, 116, 133–36, 167, 171, 179, 188–89, 195, 234, 282, 287, 299, 302–4, 307, 309, 327, and in Lawrence Costello's follow-up "The New York Labor Movement, 1861–1873." Costello stresses the point with a special survey of the German movement (pp. 165–85). The significance of the German movement is also stressed by Hermann Schlüter's *Die Anfänge der Deutschen Arbeiterbewegung in Amerika*, Friedrich A. Sorge's *The*

Labor Movement in the United States, and Selig Perlman's "Upheaval and Reorganization," pp. 203–4, 207, 209, 218, 223–26, 232, 301–9, 313–15, 399–402.

5. This is evident from all of the above-cited sources, particularly Kaufman, Schlüter, and Sorge. See also Morris Hilquit, *History of Socialism in the United States,* pp. 143–275; Daniel Bell, *Marxian Socialism in the United States,* pp. 18–24; Henry David, *The History of the Haymarket Affair,* pp. 58–157; Samuel Bernstein, *The First International in America;* and Perlman, "Upheaval," pp. 203–4, 269–300, 386–89, 399–402, 449, 456, 459–61, 514–19.

6. Ronald Sanders, *The Downtown Jews,* p. 46. See also ibid., pp. 46–48, 56–62, 90–91; Moses Rischin, *The Promised City,* pp. 76–81, 95–111, 150–51, 174–79; Morris U. Schappes, "The Political Origins of the United Hebrew Trades, 1888," pp. 13–14; and Stanley Nadel, "Jewish Race and German Soul in Nineteenth Century America." Even the vital Yiddish theater had its German roots, and New York's first Yiddish production (in 1882) took place on the stage of Kleindeutschland's *Turnhalle* (Irving Howe and Kenneth Libo, *World of Our Fathers,* pp. 461–62).

7. Even more than the Jewish community, the Czech community in New York began as a segment of Kleindeutschland—as a Czech district within the German neighborhood, with the Czechs working in the German trades and relying on German-owned meeting halls and institutions. This early Czech immigrant community, in turn, influenced Czech immigrant settlements throughout the U.S. Thomas Čapek, *The Čechs (Bohemians) in America,* pp. 125–27, 137–40, 254–61, and *The Čech (Bohemian) Community of New York,* esp. pp. 21, 49–50, 59–75.

8. Leo Schnore, "Community," pp. 84–99. Also see Roland Warren's "Towards a Reformulation of Community Theory," pp. 8–11, and *The Community in America,* pp. 4–16.

9. The block constitutes a "natural" unit because there is a high frequency of social interaction in what is effectively a bounded sociogeographic unit with only two exits. It was not unknown, however, for blocks to form two social units, each with its own exit at either end of the street (particularly in transitional situations). Each of these small neighborhoods was further divisible into subunits of one tenement building or one courtyard. These subunits sometimes had the potential for developing into new ethnic communities, as when a settlement of eleven Italian families on East Eleventh Street in 1880 turned out to be the nucleus of a new neighborhood which occupied the entire block by 1890 (Richard Lieberman, "Social Change and Political Behavior," p. 41). In *The Changing Face of Inequality,* Olivier Zunz uses this social unit (in clusters) as the basis for a highly sophisticated geographic sampling procedure designed to bring out social patterns hidden in samples drawn from more arbitrary geographic units (pp. 20–24, 407–12).

10. The actual percentages are: 1845—49 percent, 1855—51 percent, 1865—54 percent, 1875—46 percent (*Census, N.Y., 1845,* pp. 29-1 to 29-5; *Census, N.Y., 1855,* pp. xxii–xxiv, 103–4, 110–11, 117–18; *Census, N.Y., 1865,* pp. 130–31; *Census, N.Y., 1875,* pp. 21, 37–38).

11. Kleindeutschland was the central business district and central meeting place for all the Germans of the New York area, and many of the Germans who

lived in other neighborhoods still worked in Kleindeutschland or belonged to organizations that met there, and they all read the Kleindeutschland newspapers. Even after Kleindeutschland lost most of its German residents, it continued to be a center for German cultural and social activities for many years. Even now, the old Frei Leseverein (Free Library) Building on Second Avenue houses the only New York Public Library branch with a major collection of German books for circulation.

12. This at least is the major thrust of Audrey L. Olson's "St. Louis' Germans, 1850–1920." Richard Lieberman ("Social Change," pp. 30–35) questions the concept of a "little Germany" for 1880 because his block-by-block analysis shows a mixed pattern of small neighborhoods defined by a combination of ethnicity, religion, and social class (though his attributions of religious affiliation to the different German neighborhoods is based on very doubtful assumptions about the relationship between state of birth in Germany and religious affiliation—see below). Lieberman's own data, however, show his different German neighborhoods as forming a nearly contiguous block, thereby reconstructing a "little Germany" after all.

13. One suggestion as to the mechanism for this was brought to my attention by a paper by Jenny Phillips (delivered at the annual meeting of the American Anthropological Association in 1976) on "Conflict and Identity among Armenian Americans." I am borrowing the term "segmentary solidarity" from Edward Evans-Pritchard (*The Nuer,* p. 142) because I think his conception of a web of similar groups that are capable of uniting on however broad a scale as is necessary to resist outsiders (while still being capable of internal warfare between groups when not subject to outside pressure) is particularly applicable to the German-American community, with its multitudinous subgroups and its subjective and situational boundaries. It becomes even more apposite as refined by Max Gluckman (*Custom and Conflict in Africa,* pp. 1–26) to show how crosscutting ties operated to contain conflicts even as segmentary oppositions created and promoted them.

14. A good example of such subtle relationships is provided by Andrea Simon's analysis of the complex relationships surrounding the dispute between two rival Greek churches in Astoria, New York ("The Sacred Sect and the Secular Church"). She uses in-depth interviews and her own observations of personal interactions and seating patterns, among other nondocumentary sources, to relate the church conflicts to a pattern of conflict between immigrants from two different waves of migration who have found very different class positions in New York and have reached different sorts of accommodations with the broader American society. These conflicts and their roots are accessible to the participant-observer, but they frequently leave no documentary record for the historian (except for the record that there were two churches separated by obscure doctrinal differences).

15. Kathleen Conzen discusses the development of the idea of German-American identity among German-American intellectuals in "German-Americans and the Invention of Ethnicity," pp. 131–47.

16. See Handlin's discussion of the naming of Germantown, Illinois, in *The Uprooted,* pp. 166–67.

17. John Hawgood, *The Tragedy of German-America.*

18. There is, for example, no discussion of these internal relationships in such classics of immigration history as Oscar Handlin's *Boston's Immigrants* or Robert Ernst's *Immigrant Life in New York City.* Even the sophisticated work of Kathleen Neils Conzen, *Immigrant Milwaukee, 1836–1860,* with its focus on the German and Irish immigrant communities in Milwaukee, fails to take this question very far. Studies of German-America from Albert B. Faust's *The German Element in the United States* and Hawgood's *Tragedy of German-America* to the German community studies of Chicago (Andrew Townsend, *The Germans of Chicago,* and Hartmut Keil and John B. Jentz's *German Workers in Industrial Chicago, 1850–1910*), Baltimore (Dieter Cunz, *The Maryland Germans*), and St. Louis (Olson, "St. Louis' Germans") also failed to examine these relationships. Guido Dobbert's *The Disintegration of an Immigrant Community: The Cincinnati Germans, 1870–1920* pointed out the importance of regional divisions and the persistence of regional-based mutual assistance associations, but failed to explore regionalism's ramifications throughout the community. Walter Kamphoefner in *The Westfalians: From Germany to Missouri* raised the issue of regionalism in terms of migration and settlement patterns, but not in reference to community structure (probably insignificant given the homogeneity of the small communities he focused on). Since 1981, Lesley Kawaguchi ("The Making of Philadelphia's German-America") and James Bergquist ("German Communities in American Cities: An Interpretation of the Nineteenth-Century Experience") have picked up the importance of these factors in defining and structuring German-American communities.

19. Also see Heinz Kloss, *Um die Einigung des Deutschamerikanertums: Die Geschichte einer unvollendeten Volksgruppe,* and Frederick Luebke, *Immigrants and Politics* and *Bonds of Loyalty.*

20. Milton Gordon, *Assimilation in American Life,* and Nathan Glazer and Daniel P. Moynihan, *Beyond the Melting Pot.*

21. Glazer and Moynihan, for example, say that "the ethnic group in America became not a survival from the age of mass immigration, but a new social form," thus allowing for considerable transformation, but they still posit a primordial group based on originally "distinctive language, customs and culture" (*Beyond the Melting Pot,* pp. 16–17). The persistent tendency to view ethnic groups from the outsider's point of view and to treat heterogeneous groups (and even separate groups) as if they were homogeneous is often still present in the literature on ethnicity—as in Joseph Hraba's *American Ethnicity.*

22. Fredrik Barth, ed., *Ethnic Groups and Boundaries.*

23. Ibid., p. 14.

24. Barth's influence is particularly apparent in such collections as Abner Cohen, ed., *Urban Ethnicity;* Leo Despres, ed., *Ethnicity and Resource Competition in Plural Societies;* and Charles F. Keyes, ed., *Ethnic Adaptation and Identity.* In Despres's comprehensive conclusion to his own volume, "Toward a Theory of Ethnic Phenomena," he even makes humorous reference to "ethnic studies B.B. and A.B. (i.e. Before Barth and After Barth, editor, 1969)" (p. 189). Some sociologists like Donald L. Horowitz (see esp. his provocative article on "Ethnic

Identity" in Glazer and Moynihan, eds., *Ethnicity, Theory and Experience*) have been greatly influenced by Barth's conceptualization. Other sociologists, exemplified by Pierre van den Berghe (*Race and Ethnicity*) have argued that Barth's approach stresses the subjective components of ethnicity too much (it may not be coincidental that many of this latter group are trying to deal with both ethnicity and race together). The one historian who has made creative use of Barth's theoretical innovation is Werner Sollors, in his *Beyond Ethnicity.*

25. Joan Vincent, "The Structure of Ethnicity," pp. 375–79.

26. Ronald Cohen, "Ethnicity: Problem and Focus in Anthropology," p. 387.

27. Michael Hechter, "The Political Economy of Ethnic Change," pp. 1151–78.

28. The contrast between language and dialect is often more a function of cultural belief than of scientific discrimination. That Plattdeutsch and Hochdeutsch are held to be the same language, while Dutch is not, can only be explained in nonlinguistic terms. Dutch and Plattdeutsch are far closer to each other than either is to Hochdeutsch and linguists generally include both Dutch and Flemish among the varieties of Plattdeutsch. If state formation had followed linguistic lines, a hypothetical Greater Netherlands or Plattdeutschland, extending from Flanders to the borders of Lithuania, would lie between a Hochdeutsch Germany and the northern seas. Were this a political reality, the speech of the two hypothetical nations would be taken as two completely separate languages and, at least in popular parlance, the notion that they might be merely dialects of the same language would be decisively rejected. See Rudolf E. Keller, *German Dialects,* Karl Bernhardt, *Sprachkarte von Deutschland,* and H. C. Darby and Harold Fullard, eds., *The New Cambridge Modern History Atlas,* pp. 147, 178.

29. T. S. Eliot, *Notes toward the Definition of Culture,* pp. 58–60.

30. This is evident in the prominent place given German immigration in general works on American immigration like Marcus Lee Hansen's *The Atlantic Migration* and Carl Wittke's *We Who Built America.* The Germans also figured prominently in Robert Ernst's *Immigrant Life in New York* and even in Oscar Handlin's classic *Boston's Immigrants,* though the Germans never constituted a major portion of Boston's population. Last, but not least, this period also produced John Hawgood's *Tragedy of German-America.*

31. Wittke followed *We Who Built America* with *Against the Current: The Life of Karl Heinzen, The Utopian Communist, Refugees of Revolution,* and *The German Language Press in America.*

32. Luebke, *Immigrants and Politics* and *Bonds of Loyalty;* Philip Gleason, *The Conservative Reformers: German-American Catholics and the Social Order.*

33. See, for example, Alan Burstein, "Residential Distribution and Mobility of Irish and German Immigrants in Philadelphia, 1850–1880"; Nora Faires, "Ethnicity in Evolution"; Dobbert, *Disintegration;* Lawrence Glasco, "Ethnicity and Social Structure"; Kamphoefner, *Westfalians;* Kawaguchi, "Making of Philadelphia's German-America"; and Andrew Yox, "Decline of the German-American Community in Buffalo."

34. Stephan Thernstrom, *Poverty and Progress* and *The Other Bostonians.* Also, Josef Barton, *Peasants and Strangers;* John Bodnar, *Immigration and*

Industrialization; Clyde Griffen and Sally Griffen, *Natives and Newcomers;* Thomas Kessner, *The Golden Door;* Peter Knights, *The Plain People of Boston, 1830–1860;* and Humbert Nelli, *The Italians in Chicago, 1880–1930.*

35. Particularly influential were Herbert Gutman's "Class, Status and Community Power in Nineteenth Century American Industrial Cities—Paterson, New Jersey: A Case Study" and Alan Dawley's *Class and Community.*

36. Fernand Braudel, *The Mediterranean and the Mediterranean World in the Age of Philip II,* vol. 1, pp. 20–21.

37. Street addresses were not listed in the census manuscripts until the second census of 1870, and the maps that purport to show the EDs don't always have the same number of EDs shown for a ward as are listed in the census manuscripts.

38. The actual samples were: 1850—390 households/1,558 persons; 1860—397 households/1,861 persons; 1870—421 households/2,037 persons; 1880—435 households/2,177 persons, for a total sample of 1,643 households and 7,633 persons. For a further discussion of sampling methods, confidence levels, and confidence intervals see Charles M. Dollar and Richard J. Jensen, *Historian's Guide to Statistics* and John E. Freund, *Modern Elementary Statistics,* pp. 272–77, 389–90.

CHAPTER ONE

1. Norbert Krebs, *Atlas der Deutschen Lebensraumes in Mitteleuropa* and *Landeskunde von Deutschland; New Cambridge Modern History Atlas,* pp. 140–42, 147; W. O. Henderson, *The Rise of German Industrial Power, 1834–1914,* pp. 31–32; Geoffrey Barraclough, *The Origins of Modern Germany,* pp. 406–12.

2. Barraclough, *Origins of Modern Germany,* p. 411.

3. August Bebel, *Aus meinem Leben,* p. 21.

4. This cutting across state borders is a very important point for my later consideration of subnational ethnicity. It means that state of origin in Germany can only be used as a very rough approximation of identity and that a broader (or narrower) region that includes adjacent territories may prove to be our best unit of analysis.

5. Bebel, *Aus meinem Leben,* p. 425; A. J. P. Taylor, *Bismarck: The Man and the Statesman,* pp. 129–32.

6. Robert E. Dickinson, *The Regions of Germany;* R. E. Dickinson, *Germany: A General and Regional Geography,* pp. 306–66; Gerhard Lüdtke and Lutz Mackensen, *Deutscher Kulturatlas;* Keller, *German Dialects;* Bernhardt, *Sprachkarte.*

7. See Handlin, *Uprooted,* pp. 7–36, for a particularly strong example. See also Hansen, *Atlantic Migration,* pp. 4–9, 128; Barton, *Peasants and Strangers,* pp. 27–47; Hawgood, *Tragedy of German-America,* p. 33; and Ernst, *Immigrant Life,* pp. 1–11.

8. For an extended essay on the origins of serfdom (and further references) see Perry Anderson, *Passages from Antiquity to Feudalism.* Also see Marc Bloch, *Feudal Society,* pp. 241–79.

9. The original Prussians were a non-Christian Slavic people who were essentially exterminated by the Teutonic Order in the thirteenth century (William H. McNeil, *The Rise of the West*, pp. 545–46; C. W. Previté-Orton, *Shorter Cambridge Medieval History*, pp. 573–74, 745–46, 796–97).

10. Previté-Orton, *Shorter Cambridge Medieval History*, p. 743; M. M. Posten, "Economic Relations between Eastern and Western Europe," p. 169.

11. For modern (nineteenth-century) German migrations to Russia see Mack Walker, *Germany and the Emigration, 1816–1885*, pp. 10, 31; and Hansen, *Atlantic Migration*, pp. 109–12.

12. Mack Walker focuses on the exclusivity of the guilds in his excellent study *German Home Towns: Community, State and General Estate, 1648–1871.*

13. John F. Hayward, "English Swords 1600–1650," pp. 158–61. Hayward refers to an English tradition of importing German arms makers going back to Henry VIII's settlement of "Almain" armorers in Greenwich.

14. Estimated at 80,000 or more by Arnold Ruge, *Zwei Jahre in Paris*, pp. 53 and 431; and Karl Gutzkow, *Pariser Briefe*, p. 276.

15. Wittke, *Utopian Communist*, pp. 11–133; Schlüter, *Anfänge der Deutschen Arbeiterbewegung*, pp. 17–18, 30, 38; and Stanley Nadel, "From the Barricades of Paris to the Sidewalks of New York."

16. In fact the German piano makers' union of New York City boasted that they possessed a flag that had been carried by the journeymen piano makers of Paris "upon the barricades during the stormy days of the French Revolution" (*National Workman*, 10/27/1866).

17. Walker, *German Home Towns;* Andrew Griessinger, *Das Symbolische Kapital der Ehre*, pp. 302–30; Michael J. Neufeld, *The Skilled Metalworkers of Nuremberg: Craft and Class in the Industrial Revolution*, chap. 2. Neufeld and others also describe the repression of the independent journeymen's associations throughout Germany, and this might have been an added incentive for radical journeymen to emigrate.

18. Henderson, *Rise of German Industrial Power*, pp. 53–70; Walker, *Germany and the Emigration*, pp. 3, 50.

19. Henderson, *Rise of German Industrial Power*, pp. 62–64, 68–69.

20. Walker, *Germany and the Emigration*, pp. 4–10, 26, 31.

21. Ibid., pp. 46, 50, 74, 87–89; Hansen, *Atlantic Migration*, pp. 239–41.

22. Walker, *Germany and the Emigration*, pp. 42–45, 48–49, 160; and Hansen, *Atlantic Migration*, pp. 211–18.

23. Jacob Toury, "Manual Labor and Emigration," p. 61. Conditions in the various Rhenish provinces differed considerably, so the transport capabilities of the Rhine would appear to have been of major significance in determining the extent of emigration from those parts of Germany in the 1830s. We may also note that Bavarian Franconia was heavily Protestant—it is thus a serious error (though a common one) to assume that immigrants from Bavaria were necessarily Catholics.

24. Rhenish Prussia was largely Catholic—again contradicting the common assumption that "Prussian" immigrants were necessarily Protestants.

25. Walker, *Germany and the Emigration*, pp. 55–56.

26. Wittke, *Refugees of Revolution*, p. 25.

27. Walker, *Germany and the Emigration,* p. 73.

28. Adolph Zucker (*The Forty-eighters*) says that there were only about 4,000 real forty-eighters among the immigrants to the U.S., and Hansen (*Atlantic Migration,* pp. 272–78) says that they were only a few thousand, but Wittke (*Refugees,* pp. 3–4) allows more leeway and claims that larger numbers could be fairly characterized as forty-eighters.

29. Frederick H. Bultman, Memoirs, typescript in family archive, 1912.

30. Walker, *Germany and the Emigration,* p. 68; Hansen, *Atlantic Migration,* p. 147.

31. Walker, *Germany and the Emigration,* pp. 157–58.

32. Eighth Census, *Population of the U.S.,* pp. 609, 621, 957.

33. Hansen, *Atlantic Migration,* p. 289; Olson, "St. Louis' Germans," p. 10.

34. Hansen, *Atlantic Migration,* pp. 293–94; and Walker, *Germany and the Emigration,* p. 219.

35. See Map 1.

36. See Map 1. Figures for the second wave are estimates derived by subtracting the figures for the German-born from each German state given in the 1860 U.S. census (Eighth Census, *Population of the U.S.,* pp. 609, 621) from the highest figure for the same state in the 1870 census (Ninth Census, *Statistics of the Population,* pp. 336–39, 386–89) or the 1880 census (Tenth Census, *Statistics of the Population of the United States,* pp. 482–85, 546–49). The Prussian category could contain some ethnic Poles, but the census manuscripts show that many Poles got the census takers to record their place of birth as Poland—even though there was no Polish state in those years. In later years the U.S. census tabulations even came to distinguish between German, Austrian, and Russian Poland.

37. Walker, *Germany and the Emigration,* pp. 184–85, 219.

38. Hansen, *Atlantic Migration,* p. 293; Olson, "St. Louis' Germans," pp. 67–70; Anton Eickhoff, *In der Neuen Heimath,* pp. 372–73. A major portion of the latter work's section on Wisconsin is devoted to a listing of such settlements. Some of this needed research has been begun by Walter Kamphoefner in his *Westfalians,* pp. 109–51.

39. Eighth Census, *Population of the U.S.,* pp. 609, 621; Tenth Census, *Statistics of the Population of the United States,* pp. 482–85, 546–49; Richard B. Morris, *Encyclopedia of American History,* p. 442.

40. John E. Knodel, *The Decline of Fertility in Germany, 1871–1939,* p. 143.

41. This high degree of urbanization is generally taken for granted for other immigrant groups. Often, however, German-Americans are presented as having been almost entirely rural simply because they were so much more so than groups like the Irish, the Italians, or the Eastern European Jews.

42. See Appendix A. The Mecklenburg figures may be attributable to the high demand for unskilled labor in these cities at the time, as the immigrants from Mecklenburg were mostly displaced farm laborers with low skill and capital resources. Kamphoefner (*Westfalians,* pp. 122–25) suggests that these cities were way stations, where the Mecklenburgers raised the money to buy farms in the German-settled rural hinterlands of these cities.

43. These are only a few of the illustrations that might be drawn from the U.S. censuses of 1860–80. See Appendix A for more data on this.

44. Recent studies of Philadelphia are most prominent, among them are Caroline Golab, *Immigrant Destinations*, and studies associated with the Philadelphia Social History Project: Burstein, "Residential Distribution," and Stephanie Greenberg, "Industrialization in Philadelphia: The Relationship between Industrial Location and Residential Patterns, 1880–1930."

45. Theodor Griesinger, *Land und Leute in Amerika*, p. 54.

46. They were overrepresented in New York by 28 percent in 1860, 24 percent in 1870, and 47 percent in 1880 (Eighth Census, *Population of the U.S.*, pp. 609, 937; Ninth Census, *Statistics of the Population*, p. 521; Tenth Census, *Statistics of the Population of the United States*, pp. 546–48).

47. They were overrepresented by 33 percent in 1860 and 18 percent in 1870, but were underrepresented by 22 percent in 1880 (ibid.).

48. Ibid.

49. They were underrepresented by 32 percent in 1860, overrepresented by 6 percent in 1870, and again underrepresented by 14 percent in 1880.

50. They were overrepresented by 58 percent in 1870 and 150 percent in 1880. In the same decade their absolute size increase was only fifty fewer than the total for the United States.

51. That is, the demographic structure of the German-born of Kleindeutschland as revealed by the author's sample.

52. Walker, *Germany and the Emigration*, pp. 46, 50, 74, 87–89; Hansen, *Atlantic Migration*, pp. 211–18, 296–97; Conzen, *Immigrant Milwaukee*, p. 51; Olson, "St. Louis' Germans," p. 10; Hawgood, *Tragedy of German-America*, p. 26.

53. This is most important when it is a matter of trying to contrast the German and Irish migrations (as is frequently done). Carol Groneman Pernicone ("The 'Bloody Ould Sixth' ") has shown that the Irish of New York's Sixth Ward had reconstituted their families through a process of chain migration. Thus, the Irish migration may turn out to have been more of a family migration than that of the Germans to the urban U.S.

CHAPTER TWO

1. As in David Ward, "The Emergence of Central Immigrant Ghettoes in American Cities: 1840–1920," pp. 343–59; Howard P. Chudacoff, "A New Look at Ethnic Neighborhoods: Residential Dispersion and the Concept of Visibility in a Medium-Sized American City," pp. 76–93; and Thernstrom, *Other Bostonians*, pp. 39–41.

2. For a thorough examination of mid-nineteenth-century Philadelphia see Alan Burstein, "Immigrants and Residential Mobility," and Stephanie Greenberg, "Industrial Location and Ethnic Residential Patterns," and for Milwaukee see Conzen, *Immigrant Milwaukee*, pp. 126–53. For a rough comparison of six cities see ibid., p. 132, and below.

3. The index is a measure of the deviation from a random distribution of the members of a nationality group. A randomly distributed (i.e., unsegregated)

group would have a theoretical index of 0, while a totally segregated group would have a theoretical index of 100. The formula used to calculate the index was:

$$I = \frac{\Sigma\, Xi}{X} - \frac{\Sigma \sim Xi}{\sim X}$$

(where I equals the index, Xi equals the number of members of group X in a district where their proportion of the district population equals or exceeds their proportion of the city as a whole, and X equals their total numbers). The index is a rough measure because it varies with the size of the district—increasing as the district being considered is made smaller and decreasing as the district is made larger. Its degree of discrimination is thus dependent on the size of the ward, and some of New York's wards were larger than most contemporary cities.

4. The index for the Irish was 17.1 in 1855, 19.2 in 1865, and 14.8 in 1875; for the Germans it was 28.9 in 1855, 31.4 in 1865, and 27.2 in 1875.

5. The revised figure was 32.2 in 1855, 36.0 in 1865, and 34.9 in 1875. This is the figure to use in comparing New York's Germans to those of other cities because it is more nearly comparable to those calculated from samples of heads of households (the most common procedure for getting around the problem of American-born children living with foreign-born parents). Conzen (*Immigrant Milwaukee*, p. 132) gives German segregation indices of about 44 for Milwaukee in 1860, 31 for St. Louis in 1860, 35 for Philadelphia in 1860, and 33 for Boston in 1855. The index is a poor guide, however. It can fluctuate even for the same city and time depending on the size of the unit selected (Conzen, for example, gives two very different indices for the Germans of Milwaukee in 1860, when she calculates them both for five wards [1850 boundaries] and nine wards [1860 boundaries]; 36.2 and 45.0 respectively [p. 130]). Thus, because these cities varied greatly in the size and number of their wards, these figures are not strictly comparable—only very rough indicators. In *Changing Face of Inequality* (chaps. 2, 6, and 13 and appendix 4), Zunz uses a sophisticated small area sampling technique to get around some of the limitations of the index of segregation and substitutes the more precise conception of ethnic dominance for the cruder formulation of segregation. His conclusion, that ethnicity was the primary factor in the selection of residence in late nineteenth-century Detroit, is much more compatible with the New York data than the analyses of the Philadelphia Social History Project, which are effectively predisposed against finding ethnic concentration as a predominant mode of residential selection.

6. "Dutch" was a corruption of the German "Deutsch," meaning German, and "Dutchman" was the popular mode of reference to Germans in mid-nineteenth-century America (though the phrase "damned Dutchman" was probably as common).

7. Robert Ernst (*Immigrant Life*), follows Frederick Leuchs (*Early German Theater in New York*) in placing the center solidly in the western portion of the Tenth Ward. This is not, however, compatible with the 1845 New York State Census figures. These show that the German-born population of the Eleventh Ward was more than twice as large as that of the Tenth and that it also comprised

a much larger percentage of the ward's total population (17 percent vs. 11 percent (*Census, N.Y., 1845*, p. 29-1).

8. *Census, N.Y., 1845*, pp. 29-1 to 29-5.

9. Robert G. Albion, *Rise of the Port of New York*.

10. *Census, N.Y., 1845*, pp. 29-1 to 29-5.

11. The percent-German figures are corrected versions of the statistics given in *Census, N.Y., 1855*, pp. 225–40. The corrections are based on the German-born:born-elsewhere ratio calculated for the German-Americans of New York in the analysis of population size later in this chapter—see table 3.

12. *Census, N.Y., 1875*, pp. 21, 37–38 (corrected as above).

13. Johann Frei, *Drei Monat in New York*, p. 56.

14. Lord and Taylor opened their large new department store on the corner of Grand and Christie in 1852 (*Wochenblatt der New Yorker Staats-Zeitung* [hereafter NYSZw], 5/14/1852).

15. See the Industrial Statistics sheets in the 1855 New York State Census manuscripts.

16. NYSZw, 2/22/1856.

17. Census of the State of New York, 1855, manuscripts.

18. NYSZw, 4/19/1856.

19. Gompers, *Seventy Years*, p. 24.

20. NYSZw, 4/9/1856.

21. Griesinger, *Land und Leute*, pp. 551–52.

22. See the New York *Tribune*, 12/28/1884; New York Association for the Improvement of the Condition of the Poor, *Forty-third Annual Report* (1886), pp. 43f.; Allen Forman, "Some Adopted Americans," pp. 51–52; *Report of the Tenement House Committee of 1894*, pp. 8, 12, 104.

23. *Census, N.Y., 1875*, pp. 114–47.

24. Otto Lohr, "Das New York Deutschtum der Vergangenheit," p. 12.

25. Griesinger, *Land und Leute*, p. 594.

26. Ernst Steiger, *Dreiundfunfzig Jahre Buchhändler in Deutschland und Amerika*, p. 342.

27. Dobbert, *Disintegration*, p. 78.

28. NYSZ, 5/3/1852, 5/4/1855.

29. These and following calculations are based on the tables in Appendix B.

30. See in this regard Olson, "St. Louis' Germans," pp. 49–72 (and note the contrast between the data she presents on p. 59 and her conclusions on settlement patterns), and Lieberman, "Social Change," pp. 96–98, 247–48, 265–68, and 290–97. Conzen's *Immigrant Milwaukee* does not make a major attempt to discern any internal structure based on origin within Milwaukee's German community.

31. James Fenimore Cooper, *Correspondence*, p. 693.

32. Slang for safecracker (*Oxford English Dictionary*, p. 3854).

33. Bultman Memoirs.

34. Groneman Pernicone, " 'Bloody Ould Sixth,' " p. 63.

35. Theodor Griesinger, *Lebende Bilder aus Amerika*, pp. 231–32.

36. James S. Lapham, "The German-Americans of New York City, 1860–1890," pp. 63–67, 114–17, 260–61.

37. Aaron Singer, "Labor-Management Relations at Steinway and Sons, 1853–1896," pp. 89–105.

38. New York *Times*, 3/21/1855. See also Citizens Association of New York, *Report of the Council of Hygiene and Public Health*, p. 286; and Charles L. Brace, *Dangerous Classes of New York*, p. 152.

39. Ira Rosenwaike, *The Population History of New York City*, pp. 42, 67.

40. 371,223—*Census, N.Y., 1845*, p. 29-1.

41. *European Historical Statistics*, pp. 76–78. In 1870 Berlin had 826,000 residents and Vienna 834,000. In 1880 they each had about 1.1 million, while fourth-place Hamburg (with 290,000 residents) was little more than half the size of the New York German metropolis (53 percent).

42. This figure of 32 percent is comparable to the 33 percent of the white population of the U.S. under ten years old in 1820. When it is remembered that the U.S. in 1820 was primarily rural and had a great need for child and adolescent labor, while Kleindeutschland was urban and (as we shall see) did not depend on child labor, the high fertility of the German immigrants becomes even more striking.

43. See figures 3–5.

44. See Conzen, *Immigrant Milwaukee*, pp. 39–41, 254; and Glasco, "Ethnicity and Social Structure," pp. 51–52. As for step-migration within the United States that ended in New York, the only significant source outside the New York area was Pennsylvania, running about 1 percent to 1.5 percent from 1850 to 1870 and then dropping to .5 percent by 1880. Nonetheless, there were a few families like the Schmidts, who had gone to Chicago from Prussia with their new daughter around the early 1870s, stayed to have three children, and then moved to New York by the time their fifth child was born in 1877 (Tenth Census (U.S.) manuscripts, 1880).

45. Thernstrom, *Poverty and Progress*, pp. 84–85.

46. This is only a minimum period of residence because the parents may have spent many years in New York before the birth of the child, especially if it was their first child.

47. A. Stürenburg, *Klein-Deutschland: Bilder aus dem New Yorker Alltagsleben*, p. 185.

CHAPTER THREE

1. Robin Fox, *Kinship and Marriage: An Anthropological Perspective*, pp. 13–16; William J. Goode, *The Family*, pp. 1–6.

2. This sometimes resulted in scandal when it turned out that the old family ties included a wife left behind. New York's German newspapers were periodically enlivened by such discoveries.

3. The practice of marrying only within the group, be it a tribe, an ethnic group, or a nation.

4. See Chapter 1 above and Walker, *Germany and the Emigration*, pp. 46, 50, 74, 87–89.

5. Kawaguchi ("Making of Philadelphia's German-America," pp. 212–17) found an increase in intermarriage for Philadelphia's Germans in this period, but German immigration to Philadelphia was declining and the proportion of potential spouses among the children of earlier immigrants was therefore much greater than in New York—a factor that Kawaguchi neglects even though the data are readily available from the 1880 census.

6. All figures are drawn from the author's census samples. As these samples are drawn from the most heavily German wards, they would lose those who not only married out but also moved out.

7. Doubtless, the endogamy rate for all of New York's Germans would also be somewhat lower than that for Kleindeutschland alone. The Detroit study (Zunz, *Changing Face of Inequality*, pp. 244–48) is the only one to date that gives intermarriage rates for Germans, besides the Kawaguchi study cited above.

8. See Philip Mayer, *Townsman or Tribesman* and "Migrancy and the Study of Africans in Towns," pp. 576–92; Marc Howard Ross and Thomas S. Weisner, "The Rural-Urban Migrant Network in Kenya: Some General Implications," pp. 359–76; and Aidan Southall, ed., *Urban Anthropology: Cross-Cultural Studies of Urbanization*. Particularly significant in relation to our current discussion is the material on the formation of friendships in Ross and Weisner, "Rural-Urban Migrant Network," pp. 369–70.

9. Josef Barton (*Peasants and Strangers*, pp. 58–59) found even stronger regional endogamy rates for Cleveland's Italians, 93–97 percent for heavily represented regions, and rates for Slovaks and Rumanians that he characterized as low, even though they still ran from 73 percent to 89 percent for heavily represented regions. June Granatir Alexander (*The Immigrant Church and Community*, pp. 101–4) found extremely high regional endogamy rates among Pittsburgh's pre-1915 Slovaks. They even managed to maintain a 65 percent endogamy rate on the county-of-origin level. As similar patterns are known to have applied to Eastern European Jews (with Lithuanians, Poles, Galicians, Hungarians, Rumanians, and Germans as rough regional equivalents) and are even hinted at for the Irish (see Groneman Pernicone, "'Bloody Ould Sixth,'" p. 61), we may well suspect that we are dealing with a rather-more-common pattern than has been noted heretofore.

10. In this discussion we are again counting only those marriages where the oldest child was born in New York, so as to minimize the inclusion of marriages formed in Europe.

11. Author's census samples.

12. Prussian "nationality" should be divisible into more meaningful categories—separating the Rhineland-Westphalians from Brandenburg-Prussians from Silesians, etc.—but the census data are limited to state categories and don't provide the discrimination necessary to do this.

13. Only eighty-eight members.

14. This is in accord with the general rule that "a group is less likely to maintain its barriers against outmarriage if it is small, but a group can remain exclusive if it is large" (Goode, *Family*, p. 35).

15. In 1880 Badeners were only 7 percent of the German-born in New York,

so this still works out to 3.4 times the rate that would have resulted from random marriages among the German-born.

16. More complete figures can be found in Stanley Nadel, "Kleindeutschland: New York City's Germans, 1845–1880," appendix D.

17. See Bernhardt, *Sprachkarte;* and Keller, *German Dialects.*

18. Kawaguchi, "Making of Philadelphia's German-America," pp. 212–17; and Faires, "Ethnicity in Evolution," pp. 598–604. Kawaguchi's figures are strongest for the southern German states that she groups together (67–79 percent endogamy from 1860 to 1880). Her other regions are much harder to defend as separate units, allowing some quite short-distance marriages to be counted as exogamous, so it is no surprise that her other regions appear less endogamous. Even so, her data still support my general argument regarding regional endogamy as a widespread marriage pattern.

19. Again see the discussion in Ross and Weisner, "Rural-Urban Migrant Network," pp. 369–70. Also see Chapter 6, below, on the organization of social life and Chapter 9 on German particularism.

20. Even this "unification" left a large portion of Europe's Germans outside its borders (in Austria, Switzerland, etc.) and lasted for less than seventy-five years.

21. Modell, Furstenberg, and Strong ("The Timing of Marriage," pp. 139–40) provide some analysis of the close proximity between marriage and first birth early in the twentieth century. There is no reason to suppose that there was any substantial difference in the relationship between the two in Kleindeutschland a generation or so earlier. Michael W. Flinn (*The European Demographic System, 1500–1820*, p. 127) cites a number of demographic studies of German districts that indicate a mean age at first marriage of 27.5, substantially older than our Kleindeutschland figure. As the German studies focus on rural districts where marriage was often delayed until property was acquired and our figures deal with an urban situation in which employment and income were readily available, there is no problem explaining the discrepancy.

22. W. R. Lee (*Population Growth, Economic Development and Social Change in Bavaria, 1750–1850*, p. 36) reports that men in Bavaria, like women, delayed marriage—in their case to an average of 31.4 years of age.

23. This is suggested by the appearance in the census manuscripts of increasing numbers of women whose older children had different surnames than their husbands and younger children. These same women also appear to be the ones most likely to be older than their husbands.

24. Ages at first birth were given above (p. 59). Average age at last birth varied from a low of 35.3 to a high of 36.8, but there is no apparent pattern to this variation. Flinn (*European Demographic System*, p. 129) gives a figure of 39.6 for Germany in this period, a substantially higher figure.

25. Author's census samples—see Appendix D.

26. Edward A. Wrigley, *Population and History*, p. 183, and *Industrial Growth and Population Change*, p. 133. Actually it is difficult to know the religious affiliation of the immigrants from many parts of Germany. The majority of Badeners were Protestant, for example, but the very large Catholic minority may well have provided the bulk of emigrants. The kingdom of Bavaria was

officially Catholic and Bavarians were generally Catholics, but the Bavarian kingdom's city of Nuremberg (and much of the surrounding region) was mostly Protestant. Furthermore, a large proportion of German Jewish immigrants came from this same kingdom. Thus glib attributions of populations to one religion or another on the basis of their origin in Germany are to be taken with many a grain of salt.

27. Lee (*Population Growth*, p. 36) reports that demographers have generally found that the mean age of last birth for populations where birth control is not practiced runs around forty-to-forty-two years of age. It is also striking that the Kleindeutschland figure would be even lower were there not a pattern of a number of women having had a child in their mid- or late forties after a gap of many years. It is not unlikely that many of these were "surprise" babies born to women who thought that they were beyond childbearing age and who had therefore stopped practicing birth control (or whose husbands had stopped doing so). That contraception methods were already known to German immigrants is suggested by Lee's statement (p. 51) that "control of conception was indeed practiced toward the end of the century . . . even in such a strongly Catholic region as Bavaria." The New York pattern appears to be very different from Zunz's findings in Detroit (*Changing Face of Inequality*, pp. 73–79, 246–53), where German women are reported to have generally continued childbearing through age forty—leading Zunz to conclude that they were not practicing birth control.

28. For pills, see NYSZw 9/27/1853; for medical abortions see NYSZw 2/22/1856 and 2/16/1860. On infanticide, we have the unfortunate example of Frau Weidemeyer of 74 Mulberry Street. After being widowed early in pregnancy, she was arrested early in 1848 for strangling her newborn baby and claiming that it had been stillborn (NYSZw 2/19/1848). It may be indicative of her isolation from the German community, however, that she was not living in Kleindeutschland but in the desperate poverty of the notorious Five Points district.

29. All figures are in Appendix C. Zunz (*Changing Face of Inequality*, pp. 73–79, 246–53) found some relationship between occupational group and family structure in Detroit, but he characterizes it as weak compared to the ethnic link. Nonetheless, his data indicate that the link was stronger and more straightforward among Detroit's Germans than for the population as a whole. In Bavaria, Lee found a clear-cut relationship between lower economic strata and later marriage (*Population Growth*, p. 37), as have many other demographers' studies of other places—though this pattern is generally broken in areas like textile-producing regions where there is an alternative source of income and there is also a positive economic value (i.e., employment) for children.

30. This is particularly likely when notice is taken of a common pattern found in the census manuscripts. Store clerks (the most common white-collar occupation) often shared the residence and surname of the owner and were likely to be near relations. Probably they would either be promoted to partner as they got older or set up in their own shops. The grocery-owning cousin who brought Frederick Bultman to New York from Germany in 1852 offered to set him up in his own shop after he learned the business (Bultman Memoirs). Mercantile expansion

based on kinship links was a very common practice in this period. If promising young men were not to be found in the family, they were often recruited through marriage—providing another avenue of mobility into the ranks of the propertied for those white-collar workers who managed to marry the boss's daughter. Stephen Mostov ("A 'Jerusalem' on the Ohio: The Social and Economic History of Cincinnati's Jewish Community, 1840–1875") provides an extensive analysis of mercantile kinship networks among German Jewish immigrants in the Midwest. See also the anecdotal references throughout Stephen Birmingham's *"Our Crowd": The Great Jewish Families of New York.*

31. This may be an example of the general proposition that "when contraceptives are introduced, the upper social strata are more likely to begin using them than are the lower social strata" (Goode, *Family,* p. 81).

32. Zunz, *Changing Face of Inequality,* pp. 74–79.

33. This generalization may at first appear ethnocentric, as reference to tallies of numbers of societies preferring one family form or another will quickly show (see, for example, George P. Murdock's discussion in his *Social Structure,* p. 2). The numerical predominance of nuclear families, even in many societies where other forms of the family are considered ideal, does justify operating from this premise, however. This is especially the case when we are doing so in a context that is based on observed behavior and not on cultural preferences. For further discussion of the general issue see Goode, *Family,* pp. 46–55.

34. The exact figures for female-headed families were: 1860—Kleindeutschland, 5.3 percent, U.S., 10.1 percent; 1870—Kleindeutschland, 8.2 percent, U.S., 11.1 percent; 1880—Kleindeutschland, 7.4 percent, U.S. 10.1 percent. U.S. figures from Rudy Ray Seward, *The American Family: A Demographic History,* p. 91.

35. Groneman Pernicone, " 'Bloody Ould Sixth,' " p. 74. This is attributed to the severe shortage of Irish men available as potential remarriage partners in a community where women heavily outnumbered men.

36. Seward, *American Family,* p. 109.

37. The most common form of extended family was the nuclear family plus a widowed parent or unmarried sibling. Only a very small percentage of families included more than one married couple, though this form of extended family was considerably more common in 1850 than in later years.

38. Zunz, *Changing Face of Inequality,* p. 70.

39. Groneman Pernicone, " 'Bloody Ould Sixth,' " p. 80.

40. This came out when Carl testified before the U.S. Senate Committee on Education and Labor (*Report of the Committee of the Senate Upon Relations Between Labor and Capital,* p. 421).

41. Stuart B. Kaufman, *The Gompers Papers,* vol. 1, pp. 153–55.

42. In America's social sciences this formulation was established by the Chicago School of sociologists, with W. I. Thomas and F. Znaniecki's *Polish Peasant in Europe and America* and Louis Wirth's *The Ghetto.* Redfield's "The Folk Society" and Handlin's *The Uprooted* were major sources of the intellectual predominance of this idea in the 1950s, while Jane Jacob's *The Death and Life of Great American Cities* led the pro-urban reaction.

43. Seward, *American Family,* p. 109.

44. This would tend to bear out my suggestions about the relationship between the extended family and economic insecurity, but it seems to apply only to the working classes—as we shall see when we consider proprietors and professionals below. None of the theoretical literature on the family seems to account for this pattern, though Michael Anderson (*Family Structure in Nineteenth Century Lancashire*) does suggest an increase in the utility of the extended family under early industrial conditions, and Olivier Zunz points out that most of Detroit's extended families were incomplete and seemed to be responses to crises rather than the fulfillment of an ideal.

45. Mostly, but by no means entirely, shopkeepers and manufacturers.

46. Goode, *Family,* pp. 84–88.

47. See Seward (*American Family,* pp. 216–20) for a discussion of the rules for sorting relationships from these censuses and the problems and uncertainties in doing so.

48. Some of the apparently nonfamily members were certainly distant kin, though there is no indication of this in the census listings. Carl Hauselt, for example, arrived in New York in 1849 and moved in with Theodor Rose, a "distant relation." The census records, however would not give any indication of a relationship in this case (Theodor Lemke, *Geschichte des Deutschtums von New York: von 1848 bis auf die Gegenvart,* pp. 24–25).

CHAPTER FOUR

1. See Ernst, *Immigrant Life,* pp. 12–24; Degler, "Labor in New York," pp. 2–10; Costello, "New York Labor Movement," pp. 13–37.

2. Ernst, *Immigrant Life,* pp. 206–21. The figures on occupations in 1855 are derived from Ernst's tabulations.

3. A complete list of German-dominated trades would be impossible to determine without retabulating over 200,000 census listings giving occupations, as Ernst sometimes tabulated diverse occupations together. For example, Ernst tabulated painters, paperhangers, and varnishers together, but varnishers were furniture makers and mostly Germans, while painters and paperhangers were in the building trades and were mostly Irish or Americans. German trades were also often shared with workers born in other countries (Switzerland, Holland, and even France) who may very well have been ethnic Germans.

4. The real extent of skill involved in each trade was highly variable from trade to trade, time to time, and even from shop to shop. Some trades were still engaged in artisan modes of production while others were truly industrial or in transition. As time passed, it becomes noticeable that many artisan trades were depressed in standards and skills while the standards and skills of skilled factory workers rose. For further discussion of this problem see Michael Katz, "Occupational Classification in History," and Bruce Laurie, Theodore Hershberg, and George Alter, "Immigrants and Industry: The Philadelphia Experience, 1850–1880." On New York's artisan trades in the first half of the nineteenth century see Howard Rock, *Artisans of the New Republic,* and Sean Wilentz, *Chants Democratic.*

5. The complete breakdown for New York City's labor force for German- and Irish-born immigrants from 1855 to 1880 is in Nadel, "Kleindeutschland," appendix G.

6. See Kessner, *Golden Door,* for a study of the Jews and Italians who took their places in the years between 1880 and 1915.

7. See Conzen, *Immigrant Milwaukee,* pp. 64–74; Nora Faires, "Occupational Patterns of German-Americans in Nineteenth-Century Cities"; Kamphoefner, *Westfalians* and "Predisposing Factors in German-American Urbanization"; along with Stanley Nadel, "German-Americans and the American City in the Nineteenth Century," and n. 8, below.

8. By 1870, the leading occupations for those born in Ireland accounted for 43 percent of all working Irish, the two leading occupations for native-born New Yorkers accounted for 17 percent of them, and the two leading occupations for the German-born accounted for only 12.5 percent of the Germans (Costello, "New York Labor Movement," p. 124).

9. That is, of those who were self-employed and engaged in the selling or manufacturing of goods (author's census samples). Further figures on this and the material below will be found in Appendix E. Again, the most similar occupational structure would have been found among the Germans of Philadelphia, but the skilled workers and shopkeepers of most urban German-American settlements seem to have gravitated toward similar trades and businesses that reflected their training and experience in Germany—the making of clothing, furniture, and shoes and the sale of foods and dry goods. See Burstein, "Residential Distribution," p. 11; Greenberg, "Industrialization in Philadelphia," p. 30; Kawaguchi, "Making of Philadelphia's German-America," pp. 158–59, 165; Faires, "Ethnicity in Evolution," pp. 217–19, 228, 248; Glasco, "Ethnicity and Social Structure," pp. 93, 119–20; Dobbert, *Disintegration,* p. 32; Hartmut Keil, "Chicago's German Working Class in 1900"; and Conzen, *Immigrant Milwaukee,* pp. 64–74.

10. See the discussion of the bakers' lot, below.

11. Author's census samples.

12. Jessie Pope, *The Clothing Industry in New York,* pp. 12–19, 24, 28.

13. Author's census samples.

14. Ibid.

15. Ibid.

16. Thernstrom, *Other Bostonians,* pp. 111–44, 251–56; Kessner, *Golden Door,* pp. 120–26; Bodnar, *Immigration and Industrialization,* pp. 132–36.

17. See Nadel, "German-Americans," and Greenberg, "Industrialization in Philadelphia." Griffen and Griffen (*Natives and Newcomers,* pp. 182–84) found a strong tendency for second-generation Germans in Poughkeepsie to stick with declining trades, though there was some movement toward more white-collar work. JoEllen Vineyard (*The Irish on the Urban Frontier,* pp. 322–23) claims that a very high proportion were in unskilled work in Detroit in 1870, while Zunz (*Changing Face of Inequality,* pp. 36–38, 220–24) finds a strong second-generation shift to white-collar occupations a generation later—this could be a function of Detroit's industrialization in those years, but it is more likely an error on the part of one of the two historians (Vineyard's reported 42 percent of *second*-generation

Germans in unskilled work is suspiciously close to Zunz's report that 42.4 percent of *first*-generation Germans worked in unskilled labor in 1880). Keil ("Chicago's German Working Class") found only a small white-collar shift in Chicago in 1880, but he reports a very large shift appearing by 1900 as the effects of industrialization on the crafts became clear—along with the familiar sharp decline in unskilled labor (from 36 percent of the first generation to 22 percent of the second).

18. Hanover was, of course, a major source of Plattdeutsch-speaking immigrants, though Hanoverians were only 6 percent of Kleindeutschland's working population in 1860.

19. The Hanoverian grocers appear to have prospered enough to have moved on to bigger and better businesses. See the discussion of clerical workers below.

20. In 1880, 71 percent of all tailors were of Prussian origin while Prussians constituted only 37 percent of Kleindeutschland's workers.

21. Using Cramer's v as a measure of the strength of the relationship gives us 0.55 in 1860, 0.53 in 1870, and 0.62 in 1880. Alternatively, the asymmetric uncertainty coefficients for each of those years (with occupation as the independent variable) are 0.45, 0.42, and 0.53.

22. Bultman Memoirs.

23. Griesinger, *Lebende Bilder,* p. 36.

24. Wolfgang Helbich, Walter D. Kamphoefner, and Ulrike Sommer, *Briefe aus Amerika: Deutsche Auswanderer schreiben aus der Neuen Welt, 1830–1930* (Munich, 1988), p. 356.

25. Griesinger, *Lebende Bilder,* p. 36.

26. New York *Sun,* 11/16/1863; Rock, *Artisans,* pp. 155, 165, 239–40, 248, 250, 265–68; and Wilentz, *Chants Democratic,* pp. 28, 30, 32, 115, 120–21.

27. U.S. Senate Committee on Education and Labor, *Relations Between Labor and Capital,* testimony of Conrad [*sic*] Carl, pp. 413–21.

28. Ibid., testimony of Charles Miller, pp. 751–52.

29. Carl Wittke, *Utopian Communist,* pp. 279, 310–12.

30. NYSZ, 7/14/1849.

31. U.S. Senate Committee on Education and Labor, *Relations Between Labor and Capital,* testimony of Charles Miller, pp. 746–54.

32. Richard B. Stott, "The Worker in the Metropolis: New York City, 1820–1860," pp. 236–48.

33. Theodore E. Steinway, *People and Pianos,* p. 16.

34. New York *Daily News,* 7/25/1864.

35. New York *Sun,* 4/14/1863.

36. Ibid., 4/7/1868.

37. Ibid., 5/27/1872.

38. New York *Tribune,* 9/9/1845.

39. Rock, *Artisans,* pp. 9–12, 155, 165, 239, 248–50, 258–59, 265–68; Wilentz, *Chants Democratic,* pp. 28–32, 115, 124–27; and Alan Dawley, *Class and Community.*

40. John R. Commons, "American Shoemakers 1648–1895," pp. 72–73.

41. Costello, "New York Labor Movement," pp. 30–33.

42. New York *Tribune*, 5/7/1853; New York *Daily News*, 11/17/1865; Hermann Schlüter, *The Brewing Industry and the Brewery Worker's Movement in America*, pp. 90–94.

43. Gompers, *Seventy Years*, pp. 33–34.

44. Ibid., p. 43.

45. Ibid., pp. 44–45.

46. Quoted in Elizabeth A. Ingerman, "Personal Experiences of an Old New York Cabinetmaker," pp. 575–80.

47. Stott, "Worker in the Metropolis," p. 117.

48. Ibid., pp. 203–8.

49. Ingerman, "Personal Experiences," p. 580; and Steven J. Ross, *Workers on the Edge*, pp. 102–4.

50. Singer, "Labor-Management Relations at Steinway and Sons," p. 12.

51. Horace Greeley, *The Great Industries in the United States, 1871–1872*, pp. 324–28.

52. *Asher & Adams' Pictorial Album of American Industry, 1876*, pp. 62, 80, 112, 154.

53. Joseph D. Weeks, *Report on the Statistics of Wages in Manufacturing Industries*, p. 292.

54. All these figures come from the author's Kleindeutschland census samples, as do unfootnoted figures below.

55. New York *Tribune*, 6/8/1853.

56. Ibid., 3/22/1864; William Sanger, *The History of Prostitution*, p. 524.

57. Coroner's Inquisitions on the bodies of Cecelia, Wanda, and Edward Stein, Sept. 5, 1855; NYSZ, 9/7/1855.

58. New York *Tribune*, 9/16/1846, 11/6/1845; Griesinger, *Lebende Bilder*, pp. 88–93.

59. Helen Sumner, *History of Women in Industry in the United States*, pp. 177–83; Griesinger, *Lebende Bilder*, p. 90; Christine Stansell, *City of Women: Sex and Class in New York, 1789–1860*, pp. 155–68.

60. Part of the decline may be attributable to a partial abandonment of Kleindeutschland by the upper German elite in the 1870s, but most of the decline was due to a real reluctance by German girls to enter service if they had alternatives available. In all years, some domestic servants of German origin would have been missed by our sample because they worked in American homes outside the German district, but their numbers would have remained small as long as English-speaking Irish girls and women were available.

61. New York *Tribune*, 3/7/1845.

62. Their ability to do this, if not their preference, stands in apparent contrast to the Irish women of the Sixth Ward (see Groneman Pernicone, " 'Bloody Ould Sixth,' " chap. 5) and the women of Kleindeutschland's early years.

63. Griesinger, *Lebende Bilder*, pp. 172–78, and Mathew H. Smith, *Sunshine and Shadow in New York*, pp. 216–17.

64. New York *Tribune*, 11/11/1863.

65. Sanger, *Prostitution*, p. 524.

66. Griesinger, *Lebende Bilder*, pp. 75–76.

67. Ibid., and New York *Tribune*, 11/11/1863.

68. New York Association for the Improvement of the Condition of the Poor, *Annual Report, 1861*, pp. 23–24. For consideration of child labor in New York during this period by historians, see: Commons, *History of Labour*, vol. 2, pp. 81–84, 258–60; Costello, "New York Labor Movement," p. 72; Degler, "Labor in New York," pp. 121–23; Ernst, *Immigrant Life*, pp. 59, 65–66, 77, 86, 140; Groneman Pernicone, " 'Bloody Ould Sixth,' " pp. 143–44. For a more thorough consideration of the place of child labor in New York near the end of the century, see Martin Dann, "Little Citizens: Working-Class and Immigrant Childhood in New York, 1880–1915."

69. New York *Times*, 1/13/1855.

70. Charles Loring Brace, "Sketch of the Formation of the Newsboys' Lodging-House," and "Little Laborers of New York." Brace says that the majority of the Lodging House boys of 1867 had been born in the United States (though some of these may have been the children of immigrants), while 3,000 had been born in Ireland and 380 in Germany.

71. Author's census samples.

72. Zunz, *Changing Face of Inequality*, pp. 233–40. Unfortunately Zunz doesn't give a clear breakdown by age on his child-labor figures so they are not truly comparable. His figures on girls are virtually useless for comparative purposes because he gives figures only for the combined category of all girls from 12 to 20.

73. It is impossible, unfortunately, to estimate the proportion of girls working in trades that allowed homework who actually did work at home.

74. The following data come from a surviving record book of the society's contacts from September of 1854 to January of 1856.

75. Though we would expect them to be underrepresented to some extent because the language barrier would surely have kept some needy German children from turning to the Children's Aid Society for help.

76. Griesinger, *Lebende Bilder*, pp. 20–26, and Eric E. Hirschler, *Jews from Germany in the United States*, pp. 36–38, 59–60.

77. The Seligman brothers, for example, started as peddlers, moved up to rural storekeeping and then returned to open a store in Kleindeutschland in 1847. When a couple of the brothers opened a branch store in San Francisco during the gold rush, they laid the foundations for the Seligman banking house (Hirschler, *Jews from Germany*, pp. 61–62).

78. Lemke, *Geschichte*, p. 71.

79. In 1870, New York City produced nearly 25 percent of the nation's men's clothing and almost 30 percent of the women's clothing, while the 1880 figures were 29 percent and 59 percent respectively (Ninth Census, *Statistics of the Population*, vol. 3, pp. 394–98, 702; Tenth Census, *Compendium*, vol. 2, pp. 934–35, 1072–73; James O'Neal, *A History of the Amalgamated Ladies' Garment Cutters' Local Number 10*, p. 7; and Pope, *Clothing Industry*, pp. 12–19, 24, 28).

80. See Bultman Memoirs and Griesinger, *Lebende Bilder*, pp. 65–72.

81. Griesinger, *Lebende Bilder*, pp. 56–60.

82. Eugen Lievre's Shakespeare Hotel was a center for German republicans, radicals, and communists in the 1850s, while Justus Schwab's saloon served a similar function in the 1870s and 1880s. The latter place was the scene of a fight between a young trade unionist, Samuel Gompers, and the famous German anarchist, Johann Most (Gompers, *Seventy Years*, pp. 100–101).

83. *Katholik Kirchenzeitung*, 7/30/1857 and 9/23/1858.

84. *Criminal Zeitung und Belletristisches Journal* (hereafter CZBJ), 12/21/1855.

85. New York *World*, 7/25/1860, and NYSZ, 7/26/1860.

86. Eighth Census (U.S.), *Manufacturers*, pp. 379–85.

87. Schlüter, *Brewing Industry*, pp. 62–75.

88. Ibid., pp. 67–68.

89. George Ehret, richest of the brewer princes, is credited with making the Arion Singing Society Hall possible. See Lemke, *Geschichte*, for biographies of many members of the rising German-American elite of New York City, with George Ehret's on pp. 150–52.

90. Ibid., pp. 85–90, 138–40, 147–49.

91. Ibid.

92. He was, nonetheless, included in Lemke's book (ibid., p. 106).

93. Ibid., pp. 98–100.

94. Ronald C. Newton, *German Buenos Aires, 1900–1933*, pp. xi–31. Of course German Buenos Aires was tiny by comparison with German New York, numbering fewer than 4,000 in 1880 and only about 30,000 in 1914.

95. The Germania Life Insurance Company was very successful, selling insurance first to German-Americans and then to Germans, establishing a very profitable German branch in 1868. When the United States appeared likely to go to war against Germany in 1917, it was deemed advisable to change the company name, and it is now the Guardian Life Insurance Company of America. See Anita Rapone, *The Guardian Life Insurance Company, 1860–1920*.

96. Lemke, *Geschichte*, pp. 34–52; Greeley, *Great Industries*, pp. 324–28.

97. Lapham, "German-Americans," pp. 142–52. Poppenhusen later got involved in the railroad business and went bankrupt in 1877.

98. One example would be the famous furniture maker John Henry (Johann Heinrich) Belter, who came to New York in the 1840s to open a small furniture-making shop. He invented a process for making curved rosewood furniture and opened a large factory using the process in 1858 (Virginia Bohlin, "Better Pieces, Better Prices").

99. Wittke, *Utopian Communist*, pp. 280–81.

100. See Frederic Cople Jaher, *The Urban Establishment*, pp. 159–315.

101. Herbert Asbury, *The Gangs of New York*, and George W. Walling, *Recollections of a New York Chief of Police*.

102. NYSZw, 4/22/1848.

103. Asbury, *Gangs of New York*, p. 234.

104. The police campaign consisted of attacking the gangsters on sight and beating them unconscious, a technique developed by "Clubber" Williams in 1871 (ibid., pp. 233, 235).

105. The earliest Jewish gangs, like Monk Eastman's and the Dopey Benney

Gang, grew out of the very same Tenth Ward tenements that the Germans had abandoned as Kleindeutschland began its transformation into the Lower East Side. Even the Dutch Mob was at least partly Jewish, as indicated by the nickname of its leader—"Sheeny" Mike Kurtz.

106. A full catalogue of the runners' tricks can be found in the *Report of the Select Committee Appointed to Investigate Frauds Upon Emigrant Passengers* (New York State Assembly Document No. 250, 1847), and Friedrich Kapp, *Immigration and the Commissioners of Emigration of the State of New York*, pp. 63–86. Particular attention to the German runners is paid by Christoph Vetter, *Zwei Jahre in New York*, pp. 32–41, and Griesinger, *Lebende Bilder*, pp. 122–28.

107. The runners were banned from the facility (Kapp, *Immigration and the Commissioners of Emigration*, pp. 84–86).

108. New York *Tribune*, 10/8/1856.

109. See, for example, NYSZ, 11/23/1858.

110. Walling, *Recollections*, p. 255; and Asbury, *Gangs of New York*, p. 215.

111. New York *Tribune*, 7/26/1854, and Asbury, *Gangs of New York*, p. 212. The names of the German fences suggest that they were Jewish—as was their better-known colleague "Marm" Mandelbaum (see below), who was said to have been a generous contributor to her synagogue (Walling, *Recollections*, pp. 280–91). It was only a short step from the traditional Jewish roles as pawnbrokers and dealers in secondhand merchandise to that of receivers of stolen goods. That step was taken many times, both in America and in Europe. In Europe the Jewish fence was incorporated into literature, as in Charles Dickens's *Oliver Twist*. At least one item in the vocabulary of nineteenth-century thieves' cant in London and New York, the word *gonoph* (meaning thief), came from Hebrew via Yiddish (*Oxford English Dictionary*, p. 1173). It has been suggested by one student of the nineteenth-century London underworld that there was an international network for the disposal of stolen goods that was organized around a focus among the Dutch Jews. He reports that one London fence claimed that he could dispose of the crown jewels through that network if only he could find someone to steal them.

112. She retired to Montreal (Walling, *Recollections*, pp. 280–91; Asbury, *Gangs of New York*, pp. 214–18).

113. New York *Sun*, 7/17/1873.

114. Walling, *Recollections*, p. 87; Asbury, *Gangs of New York*, p. 216.

115. Asbury, *Gangs of New York*, pp. 175–77.

116. Sanger, *Prostitution*, pp. 460, 675; NYSZ, 1/26/1856 and 11/11/1858.

117. Sanger, *Prostitution*, pp. 559–63.

118. This theme will be developed more fully and references given in Chapters 7 and 8.

119. Gompers, *Seventy Years*, pp. 43–53, 60–62, 69–88; and Kaufman, *Samuel Gompers*.

120. See Chapter 8.

CHAPTER FIVE

1. Yet another reminder of the folly committed by so many scholars who assumed that they could use a German's state or region of birth as a surrogate for his or her religion. This is brought home most clearly by Nora Faires's analysis of German congregations in Pittsburg ("Ethnicity in Evolution," pp. 256–57), where she found that 22 percent of the members of a Lutheran congregation had come from Bavaria.

2. Cunz, *Maryland Germans*, p. 357.

3. NYSZ, 10/25/1860.

4. NYSZ, 5/14/1856.

5. The *Katholische Volkszeitung*, which was widely read in New York, marked the quadricentennial of Luther's birth (1883) with more than sixty articles attacking Luther and Protestantism in general (Cunz, *Maryland Germans*, p. 356).

6. NYSZ, 10/25/1860; Ernst A. Reiter, *Schematismus der Katholischen deutschen Geistlichkeit in den Vereinigten Staaten Nord-Amerika's*, p. 97; Dolan, *Immigrant Church*, pp. 22, 84–85, 182. On the proportion of Catholics in other German-American communities, see Conzen, *Immigrant Milwaukee*, p. 252, and Zunz, *Changing Face of Inequality*, p. 253. We have to note here that these figures, especially Conzen's (based on a contemporary estimate and not on hard data), may not be very reliable.

7. *St. Nicholas Church in Second Street*, p. 25.

8. Coleman Barry, *The Catholic Church and German Americans*, p. 10.

9. Dolan, *Immigrant Church*, p. 71.

10. Barry, *Catholic Church*.

11. Dolan, *Immigrant Church*, pp. 72–73; Lapham, "German-Americans," pp. 57–67.

12. Sydney Ahlstrom, *A Religious History of the American People*, pp. 531–38, 555, 567.

13. Dolan, *Immigrant Church*, pp. 90–92; NYSZ, 12/19/1846, 10/7/1854. For a detailed study of a trusteeship crisis and an exposition of the European roots of trusteeship for some German-Americans, see David Gerber's "Modernity in the Service of Tradition."

14. Raffeiner had moved to Brooklyn after giving up on St. Nicholas (Lapham, "German-Americans," pp. 55–59).

15. Dolan, *Immigrant Church*, p. 82.

16. John L. Obendorfer, C.SS.R., *Portrait of a Mother, Church of the Most Holy Redeemer.*

17. A dubious story reported by Dolan (*Immigrant Church*, p. 155), it nonetheless conveys the spirit of the occasion.

18. Ibid., pp. 153–58.

19. Ibid., pp. 76–77.

20. Ibid., pp. 77, 80–81; *Katholische Kirchenzeitung*, 9/7 and 17/1857, 10/1/1857, 9/2/1858.

21. From the Catholic New York *Sion* according to NYSZ, 3/23 and 7/6/1850.

22. The Ludwig Mission Society and King Ludwig himself had made generous

contributions to Johann Raffeiner's work and the Austrian Leopoldine society was also active in promoting German-American Catholicism. See Lapham, "German-Americans," p. 56, and Barry, *Catholic Church.*

23. NYSZ, 4/28/1852.

24. Wittke, *Against the Current,* p. 5.

25. NYSZ, 8/2/1850.

26. Dolan, *Immigrant Church,* p. 83.

27. *Pionier,* 5/11/1856; NYSZ, 5/14/1856.

28. NYSZ, 10/25/1860. New York really had a German-born population of 119,000 that year and the total German-American population was over 200,000. See table 1.

29. Given the commitment often required of members of Protestant congregations, it is possible that there were thousands more who considered themselves pious Protestants. Nonetheless, they would still have been a small minority. See table 1 and Lapham, "German-Americans," pp. 257–59. Another source, the *Jahrbücher der Deutschen in Amerika, 1873,* credits the Lutheran Synod of New York City and vicinity with 19,104 communicants, a comparable figure.

30. Lapham, "German-Americans," pp. 258–59.

31. Faires, "Ethnicity in Evolution," pp. 297–310, 479–503.

32. Rosenwaike, *Population History,* p. 26.

33. Lapham, "German-Americans," pp. 120–29; NYSZ, 1/3/1846.

34. NYSZ, 5/14/1856.

35. Lapham, "German-Americans," pp. 125–29.

36. Ahlstrom, *Religious History,* pp. 253, 522–26.

37. *Deutsche Schnellpost,* 3/18/1848; NYSZ, 3/3/1853, 3/23/1855.

38. NYSZ, 2/23/1855.

39. NYSZ, 10/28/1848.

40. Lapham, "German-Americans," pp. 95–120. Lapham focuses major portions of his study on the German-Americans of the city of Brooklyn and the towns of Astoria and College Point in Queens County. He thus misses most of the German-Americans of New York City.

41. William H. Luecke, "A Half Century of Testimony of Staunch Lutheranism in New York City," pp. 3–4.

42. See Albert Post, *Popular Free Thought in America, 1825–1850;* Carl Wittke, *Against the Current;* NYSZ, 9/5/1846, 2/29/1850, 7/22 and 10/28/1853, and 9/27/1854; CZBJ 3/17 and 11/10/1854; *Pionier,* 2/8, 3/28, and 4/4/1858; D. T. Valentine's *Manual of the Corporation of the City of New York* for 1845, 1846, and 1847 under Churches.

43. There were two German factions in the Democratic party, a German liberal one associated with Merkle and the *Staats-Zeitung* and a German-Catholic faction led by Joseph Lux—both were associated with Tammany Hall (NYSZ 10/9/1850, 11/1/1860, and 9/15/1853).

44. *Valentine's Manual,* 1845; NYSZ, 9/5/1846, 6/10/1848, and 10/6/1854; *Jahrbücher der Deutschen in Amerika, 1873,* p. 127, Deutscher Ordens der Harugari, *Verhandlungen der Vereinigten Staaten Gross-Loge der Deutschen Ordens der Harugari* (1870–1903), bound reports at New York Public Library.

45. NYSZ, 6/10/1848, 2/29 and 3/23/1850, and 4/28/1852.

46. CZBJ, 3/17/1854; *Pionier,* 4/23/1858; Sigel obituary in New York Public Library Scholer collection.

47. F. A. Sorge, "Erinnerungen eines Achtundvierzigers," *Die Neue Zeit* [New York], pp. 150ff.; Bernstein, *First International;* Philip Foner, "Friedrich Sorge, Father of American Socialism."

48. Bernstein, *First International,* pp. 63, 118, 195, 247.

49. Wittke, *Against the Current,* pp. 206–8, 236; Sorge, *Labor Movement,* pp. 144, 343; Eickhoff, *Neuen Heimath,* pp. 89–118.

50. Stow Persons, *Free Religion: An American Faith,* pp. 70–71; Ethical Culture Society, *Twenty Years of the Ethical Movement in New York and Other Cities;* Rischin, *Promised City,* pp. 196–205; Benny Kraut, *From Reform Judaism to Ethical Culture: The Religious Evolution of Felix Adler.*

51. Griesinger, *Land und Leute,* pp. 572–73.

52. See, for example, the biographical sketch of Isidor Strauss in Lemke (*Geschichte,* pp. 112–16) or the story of the theft of $3,600 worth of diamonds from Jakob Cohn by his uncle (NYSZ, 3/31/1859). The latter was an ideal opportunity for some sort of anti-Semitic allusion so it is all the more striking that there is no reference at all to their Jewishness, but this was the norm for the German press in New York.

53. These figures are actually adjusted totals based on estimates of all Jews in the city—using Grinstein's estimate that about one-half of the city's Jews were German. My belief that these estimates are too low stems from a subjective sense that Jewish names appeared too frequently in my census samples for their population to have been so small. See Stanley Nadel, "Jewish Race and German Soul in Nineteenth Century America"; NYSZ, 10/25/1860; Hyman Grinstein, *The Rise of the Jewish Community of New York, 1654–1860,* pp. 23, 469–71, 528–29, and table 13 above.

54. Grinstein, *Rise of the Jewish Community,* pp. 203–4, 351, 386–87.

55. Ibid., pp. 49–50, 90–91, 170, 353–400; NYSZ, 1/3/1846.

56. Grinstein, *Rise of the Jewish Community,* p. 368; Ahlstrom, *Religious History,* pp. 575–82; Hirshler, *Jews from Germany,* pp. 45–55.

57. Grinstein, *Rise of the Jewish Community,* pp. 353–71.

58. Kraut, *From Reform Judaism to Ethical Culture.*

59. Hirshler, *Jews from Germany,* p. 51. It is curious that the list of great Germans does not include any of those of Jewish origin who might have been included, such as Heinrich Heine, Ludwig Börne, Moses and Felix Mendelssohn, or Giacomo Meyerbeer.

60. Though they did cooperate in joining philanthropic endeavors, as in providing burial services for unattached poor German Jews and in supporting the formation of a Jewish orphanage. See Grinstein, *Rise of the Jewish Community,* pp. 171, 173, 201, 370, 401–2.

61. In the end they even invented a new name for the easterners whose names so often ended with "ki"—they called them "kikes" (Rischin, *Promised City,* p. 98).

62. Grinstein, *Rise of the Jewish Community,* pp. 109–14, 202–5.

63. Ibid., p. 205.

64. Hirschler, *Jews from Germany,* p. 59; Glanz, *Jews in Relation;* NYSZ, 11/2/1855. The leaders of Kleindeutschland were generally quite vocal in their attacks on anti-Semitism—see NYSZ, 2/17 and 6/30/1855, 8/11 and 12/9/1858, and 2/23/1859. It still seems unlikely that the level of anti-Semitism could have been as low as it appears, but it does appear to have been very low. Perhaps this may be partially attributable to the fact that Jewish emancipation (a major concern of early nineteenth-century German anti-Semitism) was not an issue in America, while nearly all of New York's Germans (before the 1880s) had left Germany before the first stirrings of German political anti-Semitism arose in the wake of the Panic of 1873. For more on this issue see Nadel, "Jewish Race and German Soul." On the German situation see Jacob Katz, *From Prejudice to Destruction,* pp. 147–222, 245–73.

65. New York Turn-Verein, *Seventy-fifth Jubilee of the New York Turn-Verein 1850–1925,* pp. 10–31; Eickhoff, *Neuen Heimath,* pp. 101, 125–27; Heinrich Metzner, *Jahrbücher der Deutsch-Amerikanischen Turnerei,* pp. 35–37.

66. He arrived in New York in November, 1853, after being a defendant in the Cologne Communist trial of the preceding year. He was active in Kleindeutschland's radical circles in the 1850s and retained contact with the radicals in later years. See Spengler, *Deutsche Element;* Karl Obermann, *Joseph Weydemeyer,* pp. 292, 322, 323, 329–30, 342; Rhoda Traux, *The Doctors Jacobi;* Morris Schappes, "Two Humanists: Doctors Jacobi." Among other associations, Jacobi was a member of the singing society New Yorker Sängerrunde (*Geschichte der New Yorker Sängerrunde, 1848–1888*).

67. Wittke, *Refugees of Revolution,* pp. 87–88, 224, 288; Leuchs, *Early German Theater,* pp. 65, 96; Hirshler, *Jews from Germany,* pp. 60–71; New York *Tribune,* 8/15/1850, 6/13 and 6/28/1865; Costello, "New York Labor Movement," p. 212; NYSZ, 8/17/1866; Schappes, "Political Origins"; NYSZ, 8/17/1866; Kaufman, *Samuel Gompers;* Rischin, *Promised City,* pp. 174–77; Bernstein, *First International,* pp. 247, 260, 276, 284, 298; Morris U. Schappes, *A Pictorial History of the Jews in the United States,* pp. 111–12. As for unions, there was even a Purim Lodge of the Knights of St. Christopher (shoemakers), New York *Sun,* 5/3/1870.

68. Hessen-Darmstädter Volks-Fest Verein, *Biographisches Handbuch.*

69. NYSZ, 5/13/1848; *Deutsche Schnellpost,* 5/6/1848.

70. Bernhard Meyborg, *Geschichte der Plattdütschen Volksfest-Vereen von New York,* p. 99; and Männergesang Vereins Eichenkranz, *Geschichte der Männergesang Vereins Eichenkranz aus Erinnerung an des 25 jahrige Jubiläum* (New York, 1894), p. 63.

71. Kloss, *Um die Einigung,* and Kloss, "German-American Language Maintenance Efforts."

72. Eduard Pelz, NEW-YORK *und seine Umgebungen,* pp. 47–48.

73. See Chapter 9.

CHAPTER SIX

1. Griesinger, *Lebende Bilder*, pp. 56–57; and *Land und Leute*, pp. 563–64. For later years see Lohr, "New York Deutschtum," p. 12.

2. Griesinger, *Lebende Bilder*, pp. 73–79.

3. Georg Techla, *Drei Jahre in New York*, pp. 100–101.

4. The grand Turnhalle of 1871 can still be seen at 66–68 East Fourth Street and 15–17 East Third Street, as can the considerably less grand Germania Assembly Rooms nearby, at 291–293 Bowery, and the elaborate Schützen Halle at 12 St. Marks Pl.

5. G. Foster, *New York by Gaslight*, pp. 88–89. See also CZBJ, 12/22/1857, and Smith, *Sunshine and Shadow*, pp. 216–17, 228. Griesinger (*Land und Leute*, pp. 572–73) gives a similar description of the Volkstheater, but is much less complimentary about the performances.

6. Leuchs, *Early German Theatre*, p. 239. Anyone interested in the plays and personalities can turn to Leuchs's work for exhaustive detail. Unfortunately he was not interested in the social context of the theater and ignored both the contents and the audience of the plays.

7. Stürenburg, *Klein-Deutschland*, pp. 63–64.

8. NYSZ, 9/5 and 9/12/1846.

9. NYSZ, 5/25/1850.

10. NYSZ, 7/1/1858.

11. Meyborg, *Geschichte des Plattdütschen Volksfest-Vereen*, pp. 11–12.

12. New York *Tribune*, 7/20/1861.

13. For examples see: NYSZ, 9/5 and 9/12/1846; 5/25 and 9/12/1850, 9/9/1853, 5/26/1854, 5/13, 5/16, and 6/20/1856, 7/1 and 9/2/1858; 7/7, 7/14, and 8/28/1859, 6/14 and 8/30/1860; CZBJ, 5/26/1854, 6/29/1855; *Pionier*, 8/1/1858; New York *Sun*, 7/30/1863, 9/12 and 9/15/1864, and 6/8/1869.

14. *Pionier*, 9/6/1857, quoted from the New York *Herald*.

15. NYSZ, 1/29/1856.

16. NYSZ, 5/14/1856.

17. NYSZ, 2/14/1856.

18. Gompers, *Seventy Years*, pp. 28–31.

19. NYSZ, 1/26/1842, 4/28/1858; New York *Tribune*, 5/8 and 6/10/1850; Schlüter, *Anfänge der Deutschen Arbeiterbewegung*, pp. 128–30; James B. Kennedy, *Beneficiary Features of American Trade Unions*, p. 72.

20. Schlüter, *Anfänge der Deutschen Arbeiterbewegung*, p. 128; NYSZ, 1/26/1842, 4/28/1858. The meeting notices in the *Staats-Zeitung* daily edition contain thousands of *Unterstützungsvereine* listings throughout these years.

21. See NYSZ, 4/21/1848, 7/13/1853, 7/16, 8/1, and 12/27/1859 for some of the earliest regional associations. The proliferation is evident in the constituency listing of the Plattdeutschen Volksfest-Verein (Meyborg, *Geschichte des Plattdütschen Volksfest-Vereen*).

22. Meyborg, *Geschichte des Plattdütschen Volksfest-Vereen;* about two-thirds of the older *Unterstützungsvereine* that took part in the Plattdeutschen Volksfest Verein were in this range.

23. This also helped keep the treasurer honest by keeping the temptation to steal down to a manageable level and insuring a high social cost for any theft.

24. *Jahrbücher der Deutschen in Amerika, 1873,* p. 127.

25. German Masons' Lodge 54, *Annual Report* for 1876. For more on the Masons and the relationship between the order and developing notions of middle-class culture and Americanism, see Lynn Dumenil, *Freemasonry and American Culture, 1880–1930.*

26. Although the Druids were a British order, the American branch was heavily German. About two-thirds of the New York State members and all of its New York City local "groves" were German-speaking in the 1870s (United Ancient Order of Druids—Grand Grove New York, *Proceedings*).

27. Named after "Hermann the Conqueror," legendary founder of the German "Volk" (*Jahrbücher der Deutschen in Amerika, 1873,* p. 131).

28. Ibid., pp. 127–35; NYSZ, 1/3/1846, 5/13/1848; Grinstein, *Rise of the Jewish Community,* pp. 109–14, 202–5.

29. Deutscher Ordens der Harugari, *Verhandlungen der Vereinigten Staaten Gross-Loge des Deutschen Ordens der Harugari* (1870), p. 6. We may note in this connection that the activities of the Harugari and the other workers' orders, the Hermannssöhne and the Söhne der Freiheit were regularly reported on in the labor paper, *Arbeiter Union,* in the late 1860s. See for example *Arbeiter Union,* 3/6/1869, p. 6; 3/20/1869, p. 6; 3/27/1869, pp. 5–6).

30. Deutscher Ordens der Harugari, *Verhandlungen der Vereinigten Staaten Gross-Loge des Deutschen Ordens der Harugari* (1879). Including all lodges on the New Jersey side of the Hudson.

31. Ibid. (1908).

32. NYSZ, 5/13/1848.

33. NYSZ, 1/3, 6/18, and 6/24/1852. There were, of course, organizations devoted solely to such activities, but the fraternal orders greatly expanded their base of support.

34. NYSZ, 1/18, 1/22, 2/26, and 4/22/1840; *Deutsche Schnellpost,* 12/16 and 12/23/1840, 12/23/1843, 2/17/1844.

35. NYSZ, 8/1/1851, 9/29/1859. For nativist attacks see below. On the Irish militia companies, see Ernst, *Immigrant Life,* pp. 127–29.

36. Ernst, *Immigrant Life,* p. 129.

37. Jacob Pickard typescript biography of Sigel at the New York Public Library, p. 208.

38. NYSZ, 2/25, 4/26, and 5/5/1856, 7/16, 8/1, 8/9, 9/10, and 10/17/1859.

39. NYSZ, 7/2/1859.

40. NYSZ, 6/30/1856, 7/2/1859.

41. New York *Sun,* 7/30/1869, and Meyborg, *Geschichte des Plattdütschen Volksfest-Vereen,* pp. 15–18.

42. Meyborg, *Geschichte des Plattdütschen Volksfest-Vereen.*

43. The Museum of the City of New York and that of the New-York Historical Society both maintain large collections of prints and equipment relating to the nineteenth-century fire companies.

44. *Annual Report,* Chief of the Fire Department, 2/18/1858; Board of Aldermen, Documents, XXV, no. 6 (1858), pp. 100–103.

45. NYSZ, 3/1, 3/22, and 9/30/1837, and *Deutsche Schnellpost,* 10/19/1844.

46. NYSZ, 4/22 and 4/29/1848.

47. NYSZ, 5/13/1848.

48. Wittke, *Refugees of Revolution,* pp. 290–95. There was a political demonstration of another sort in 1870, when the newly formed New Yorker Männerchor gave a benefit performance to raise money for the relief of Germany's wounded soldiers and the widows and orphans created by the Franco-Prussian War (New Yorker Männerchor, *Geschichte.*)

49. NYSZ, 6/1 and 6/21/1851, 4/17 and 6/26/1852.

50. NYSZ, 7/19/1860.

51. Deutscher Liederkranz in New York, *Jahresbericht,* p. 3.

52. Ibid.

53. Ibid., pp. 6–7.

54. Allegedly over the poor quality of food served at Liederkranz events—the official version is attributed to the minutes of Arion founder Carl Triacca (Liederkranz Gesangverein, *History of the Liederkranz of the City of New York, 1847–1947, and of the Arion, New York,* p. 8).

55. The New York *Sun, The Sun's Guide to New York,* (New York, 1892), pp. 88–89.

56. Liederkranz Gesangverein, *History,* p. 14.

57. Damrosch later founded the New York Symphony Society and the New York Oratorio Society, becoming a major figure in the development of classical music in the United States (Arion Gesangverein *Arion, New York von 1854 bis 1904,* p. 20).

58. Ibid., pp. 27–28; Liederkranz, *History,* p. 15.

59. Arion Gesangverein, *Jahres Bericht-Männer Gesang Verein Arion.* On the other hand, it also hosted a national brewers conference called in 1888 to plan a national anti-union campaign (Schlüter, *Brewing Industry,* p. 149).

60. Beethoven Männer-Chor, "Gedenk-Blatt an die Doppel Feier des 125 Jährigen Geburtstags Ludwig van Beethoven's, 25 Jährigen Bestehens der Beethoven Männer-Chor-Halle in New York," pp. 29–30.

61. Further reference to the Beethoven Männerchor as the idea of a member of the church choir "Cäcilia" (St. Cecilia) also suggests that the Männerchor may have been a largely Catholic organization.

62. Beethoven Männer-Chor, "Gedenk-Blatt."

63. New Yorker Sängerrunde, *Geschichte.*

64. Gesang Verein Schiller-Bund, "Gesang Verein Schiller-Bund, 1850–1900, Goldenes Jubiläum," p. 9; Mainzer Carneval-Verein in New York, *Der Mainzer Carneval-Verein von 1859 bis 1884,* p. 21.

65. For more on the singing societies and their affairs see: NYSZ, 2/12 and 11/24/1848, 1/5 and 9/21/1850, 1/18/1851, 1/6/1852, 2/11/1853, 2/16 and 6/30/1856, and 7/26/1860; CZBJ, 5/26/1854, 1/25 and 6/29/1855; *Pionier,* 12/14/1856; New York *Tribune,* 7/28/1861; New York *Sun,* 1/31/1870. There

is also the fine collection of *Gesangvereine* histories, reports, and records at the Lincoln Center branch of the New York Public Library.

66. The Vereinigte Deutsche Brüder, the Teutonia Club, and the New York Schützen-Corps were not explicitly regional, but they all participated in the formation of the Plattdeutschen Volksfest-Verein (Meyborg, *Geschichte des Plattdütschen Volksfest-Vereen,* pp. 1–5). Lapham ("German-Americans," p. 263) found similar exclusivity in the Fourth German Reformed Church of Manhattan.

67. See "Germans in the U.S., Bound Pamphlets, not catalogued," vols. 3, 5, and 8; Meyborg, *Geschichte des Plattdütschen Volksfest-Vereen,* pp. 1–15.

68. They probably existed elsewhere as well, at least in large centers like Baltimore and St. Louis (and possibly in smaller ones like Pittsburgh, Detroit, and Buffalo). Guido Dobbert (*Disintegration,* pp. 61–63, 148–51) went so far as to say that in Cincinnati "Their local regional societies . . . were, next to the churches, the most durable organizations." For Philadelphia see Kawaguchi ("Making of Philadelphia's German-America," p. 307–8) and for Chicago see Hartmut Keil, "German Immigrant Workers in Nineteenth-Century America: Working-Class Culture and Everyday Life in an Urban Industrial Setting," p. 201.

69. Canstatter Volksfestverein, "58th Canstatter Volksfest Program."

70. Ibid., p. 21.

71. Meyborg, *Geschichte des Plattdütschen Volksfest-Vereen,* pp. 1–5.

72. "Germans in the U.S., Bound Pamphlets not Catalogued," vol. 3.

73. A poem by Gustav Holthusen on the presentation of a banner by the women's auxiliary of the Plattdeutschen Volksfest-Verein (Meyborg, *Geschichte des Plattdütschen Volksfest-Vereen,* pp. 10–11).

74. From the anonymous "Salute to the Homeland," Hessen-Darmstädter Volks-Fest Verein, *Biographisches Handbuch,* p. 8. Also note the poem on p. 7.

75. From the "Song of the Bavarian-Americans," by Edmund Fuerholzer in Bayerisches Volks Fest Verein von New York, *Fest Zeitung.*

76. Sorge, *Labor Movement,* p. 76; Schlüter, *Anfänge der Deutschen Arbeiterbewegung,* pp. 23–25. On the league, see Wittke, *Utopian Communist,* pp. 20–22, 29, 34, 39, 48, 101, 108, 111, 115–16, 122, 126, 189; and Werner Kowalski, *Vorgeschichte und Enstehung des Bundes der Gerechten,* pp. 57–81. It may also be noted that the Social Reform Association provided a model for the better-known German Workers' Educational Union established in London in 1847.

77. NYSZ, 1/10, 1/17, 4/4, and 4/11/1846.

78. Sorge, *Labor Movement,* p. 77; Schlüter, *Anfänge der Deutschen Arbeiterbewegung,* pp. 28–40; and Wittke, *Utopian Communist,* pp. 116–19.

79. Schlüter, *Anfänge der Deutschen Arbeiterbewegung,* p. 24.

80. Ibid., pp. 40–41.

81. Ibid., pp. 44–45.

82. Ibid., pp. 45–47.

83. Ibid., pp. 47–48. Though Schlüter does mention that the association continued under that name into the 1870s and that branches survived under other names past the turn of the century. See also Sorge, *Labor Movement,* p. 77. Even Wittke (*Utopian Communist,* pp. 120–21, 124) adds little beyond the fact that they gave Weitling and other refugees financial support through the early 1850s.

84. Schlüter, *Anfänge der Deutschen Arbeiterbewegung,* pp. 131, 137; and Sorge, *Labor Movement,* p. 97.

85. NYSZ, 1/29/1856, 4/29/1858.

86. New York *Sun,* 10/5/1864, 8/12 and 11/26/1868; Costello, "New York Labor Movement," pp. 317–23, on the labor revival of 1868.

87. Heinrich C. A. Metzner, *Geschichte des Turner-Bundes,* pp. 1–20.

88. The story was written by Wilhelm Schlüter, later editor of the New Yorker *Demokrat* (NYSZ, 10/17/1846).

89. NYSZ, 11/18/1848.

90. Schlüter, *Anfänge der Deutschen Arbeiterbewegung,* pp. 199–200; Metzner, *Geschichte des Turner-Bundes,* pp. 21–23.

91. Metzner, *Geschichte des Turner-Bundes,* and Turnverein records in the New York Public Library Scholer Collection.

92. NYSZ, 5/28, 5/30, 6/4, 6/13, and 6/20/1851.

93. New York Turn-Verein, "Seventy-Fifth Jubilee," p. 14. This prominence helped the Turners to maintain a steady supply of militant and enthusiastic young recruits over the years.

94. NYSZ, 8/23/1851.

95. NYSZ, 2/17/1859, and New York Turn-Verein, "Seventy-Fifth Jubilee," p. 16.

96. New York *Tribune,* 2/24/1854.

97. At first the *Staats-Zeitung* simply took an anti-free-soil position and favored colonization, the resettling of freed slaves in Africa (4/1/1852, 7/6/1853), but it denied that it supported slavery (5/16 and 6/6/1855). When some southern Turners split the national organization over its pro-abolition stand, the *Staats-Zeitung* tried to promote a split in New York too (11/22/1855). By 1856, however, the *Staats-Zeitung* was referring to its opponents' "Niggerblätter" (Nigger Papers) (8/26/1856) and to "black Republican Nigger love" (9/26/1856).

98. Former general Franz Sigel, for example, was appointed assessor at the Internal Revenue office in New York in the 1870s (Pickard typescript [Scholer Collection, New York Public Library], p. 221A); and Dr. Scholer of the Turnverein, who was also a Republican party activist, was a New York County coroner.

99. NYSZ, 5/9, 5/23, and 6/27/1861.

100. New York Turn-Verein, "Seventy-Fifth Jubilee," pp. 20–21.

101. New York *Sun,* 11/3 and 11/16/1863, 6/15/1869.

102. Gompers, *Seventy Years,* pp. 43–44. Kuhn reappears as president of a German cigar makers' association in 1876 (New York *Times,* 1/19/1876).

103. Along with the Freethinkers, with whom they shared many members (New York *Sun,* 1/31/1874). See also Herbert G. Gutman, "The Tompkins Square 'Riot' in New York City on January 13, 1874: A Re-Examination of Its Causes and Its Aftermath."

CHAPTER SEVEN

1. Schlüter, *Anfänge der Deutschen Arbeiterbewegung,* pp. 19–28.
2. NYSZ, 1/10/1846.
3. NYSZ, 1/17, 2/14, 4/4, 4/7, and 4/11/1846.
4. NYSZ, 1/10/1846.
5. NYSZ, 8/23/1846.
6. Schlüter, *Anfänge der Deutschen Arbeiterbewegung,* pp. 49–56; Wittke, *Utopian Communist,* pp. 120–23.
7. NYSZ, 3/2/1850; Schlüter, *Anfänge der Deutschen Arbeiterbewegung,* p. 78.
8. Wittke, *Utopian Communist,* pp. 132–33.
9. Schlüter, *Anfänge der Deutschen Arbeiterbewegung,* p. 89.
10. Sorge, *Labor Movement,* pp. 89–91; Schlüter, *Anfänge der Deutschen Arbeiterbewegung,* pp. 71–79; Wittke, *Utopian Communist,* pp. 220–25; *Republik der Arbeiter,* Jan. 1850.
11. Schlüter, *Anfänge der Deutschen Arbeiterbewegung,* p. 102.
12. NYSZ, 1/26/1850, 2/9/1850.
13. NYSZ, 3/16/1850.
14. Ibid.
15. NYSZ, 4/27, 5/11, and 5/18/1850; New York *Tribune,* 4/9, 4/20, 4/23, 4/24, and 7/26/1850; New York *Sun,* 3/25 and 5/4/1850; New York *Herald,* 3/11, 3/13, and 4/12/1850; New York *Evening Post,* 4/17 and 4/18/1850; Schlüter, *Anfänge der Deutschen Arbeiterbewegung,* pp. 79–80.
16. Schlüter, *Anfänge der Deutschen Arbeiterbewegung,* pp. 79–80.
17. NYSZ, 5/7, 5/31, and 6/8/1850; Wittke, *Utopian Communist,* p. 190; New York *Tribune,* 4/24, 7/3, 7/6/1850; Schlüter, *Anfänge der Deutschen Arbeiterbewegung,* p. 130; Sorge, *Labor Movement,* pp. 91–92.
18. New York *Tribune,* 4/24 and 8/15/1850; Schlüter, *Anfänge der Deutschen Arbeiterbewegung,* p. 181.
19. Sorge, *Labor Movement,* p. 90.
20. NYSZ, 3/2, 7/27, 8/2, 8/10, 8/17, and 8/24/1850; New York *Herald,* 7/23 and 7/25/1850; New York *Tribune,* 7/25, 8/6, 8/7, and 12/16/1850.
21. NYSZ, 8/24/1850.
22. Wittke, *Utopian Communist,* pp. 188–219; Schlüter, *Anfänge der Deutschen Arbeiterbewegung,* pp. 79–127; Sorge, *Labor Movement,* pp. 89–94.
23. New York *Herald,* 11/20/1852; New York *Sun,* 12/3/1852, 2/22/1854.
24. NYSZ, 4/15/1853; New York *Times,* 11/10/1853.
25. Schlüter, *Anfänge der Deutschen Arbeiterbewegung,* pp. 88–93.
26. *Turn-Zeitung,* vol. 1, pp. 10, 18–19, 114–15.
27. Franz Mehring, "Neue Beitrage Zur Biographie von Karl Marx und Friedrich Engels."
28. Obermann, *Joseph Weydemeyer,* p. 270.
29. NYSZ, 3/4/1853; Wittke, *Utopian Communist,* p. 213.
30. NYSZ, 3/3, 4/1, 4/8, and 5/6/1853; Schlüter, *Anfänge der Deutschen Arbeiterbewegung,* pp. 132–34; Obermann, *Joseph Weydemeyer,* pp. 297–303.

31. NYSZ, 3/18/1853.

32. Obermann, *Joseph Weydemeyer,* p. 298; Wittke, *Utopian Communist,* p. 215.

33. Schlüter, *Anfänge der Deutschen Arbeiterbewegung,* p. 138.

34. *Turn-Zeitung,* vol. 1, pp. 220–21 (6/1/1853); *Reform,* 10/12/1853.

35. Schlüter, *Anfänge der Deutschen Arbeiterbewegung,* pp. 135–39; Obermann, *Joseph Weydemeyer,* pp. 298–300.

36. Obermann, *Joseph Weydemeyer,* p. 316.

37. Ibid., pp. 318–40; Schlüter, *Anfänge der Deutschen Arbeiterbewegung,* pp. 135–56.

38. NYSZ, 12/21/1854, 1/12/1855.

39. New York *Tribune,* 1/9/1855.

40. Schlüter, *Anfänge der Deutschen Arbeiterbewegung,* p. 156.

41. NYSZ, 10/22 and 10/29/1852.

42. NYSZ, 8/17, 8/23, and 8/26/1853.

43. NYSZ, 9/16/1853.

44. NYSZ, 11/3/53.

45. NYSZ, 2/24/1854.

46. NYSZ, 3/10/1854.

47. NYSZ, 7/22 and 7/23/1853.

48. NYSZ, 3/30/1855; CZBJ, 11/3/1854; Edward Spann, *The New Metropolis,* pp. 368–75; Gustavus Myers, *The History of Tammany Hall,* pp. 174–80.

49. Spann, *New Metropolis,* pp. 386–93; Asbury, *Gangs of New York,* pp. 105–11.

50. Spann, *New Metropolis,* pp. 393–94; Asbury, *Gangs of New York,* pp. 111–17.

51. New York *Tribune,* 7/13/1857.

52. Ibid., 7/14/1857.

53. Ibid.

54. Ibid., 7/15/1857.

55. Ibid., 7/14/1857.

56. Ibid., 7/23/1857.

57. There is a striking similarity here to riots of the 1960s and 1970s that involved nervous white policemen from the suburbs patrolling black urban ghettos with American flags flying from their cars and their hands on their guns—or similar National Guardsmen ordered to "pacify" college campuses. Note, too, that these conclusions are based on the reports of a Republican newspaper, the New York *Tribune.*

58. See Bruce C. Levine, " 'In the Spirit of 1848': German-Americans and the Fight over Slavery's Expansion."

59. We may note that Dr. Wilhelm's successor as coroner was the chairman of the German Democratic Central Club, Dr. Schirmer. Later on Dr. Hermann of the Seventeenth Ward German Democratic Committee was coroner. It would appear that this office had become a customary patronage position for the German Democrats (NYSZ, 9/27/1860; New York *Times,* 9/7/1871.

60. New York *Tribune,* 7/15/1857.

61. Ibid.
62. Ibid., 8/22/1856.
63. Ibid., 10/8/1856; NYSZ, 10/10/1856.
64. NYSZ, 10/9/1856.
65. NYSZ, 11/7/1856.
66. Spann, *New Metropolis*, pp. 378–400.
67. NYSZ, 11/8/1860.

CHAPTER EIGHT

1. See excerpts from the club's statutes in Obermann, *Joseph Weydemeyer*, p. 345; and Schlüter, *Anfänge der Deutschen Arbeiterbewegung*, pp. 161–62.
2. New York *Times*, 11/3/1857; New York *Herald*, 11/3 and 11/6/1857; New York *Tribune*, 11/6/1857.
3. Schlüter, *Anfänge der Deutschen Arbeiterbewegung*, pp. 165–74; Obermann, *Joseph Weydemeyer*, pp. 344–57.
4. NYSZ, 4/26 and 5/5/1858.
5. NYSZ, 3/7, 4/21, 8/3, 11/10, and 11/26/1859; New York *Sun*, 3/11, 3/22, 3/25, 4/2, and 4/29/1859; New York *Tribune*, 9/28/1859, 4/3 and 4/30/1860; Schlüter, *Anfänge der Deutschen Arbeiterbewegung*, pp. 176–77.
6. Costello, "New York Labor Movement," p. 173; New York *Sun*, 5/21, 6/4, 10/28, 10/30, 11/8, 11/18, and 11/19/1862; New York *Herald*, 12/8/1863.
7. New York *Sun*, 11/5, 11/13, and 11/19/1862.
8. Ibid., 7/30, 8/3, and 8/15/1863.
9. Ibid., 3/9, 7/13, 7/30, 8/3, 10/3, 10/5, 10/16, 10/28, 11/16, 11/18, 11/19, and 12/21/1863; New York *Tribune*, 6/27/1863.
10. New York *Sun*, 7/30, 8/3 and 8/15/1863.
11. Ibid., 10/5/1864.
12. Ibid., 6/5 and 6/11/1869.
13. Obermann, *Joseph Weydemeyer*, p. 347.
14. Costello, "New York Labor Movement," p. 173, appendix II.
15. Sorge, *Labor Movement*, p. 107; Costello, "New York Labor Movement," pp. 173–74.
16. New York *Sun*, 3/23, 3/25, 3/27, 4/20, 4/27, 7/30, 8/3, 8/11, 8/15, 8/29, 9/26, 10/2, 10/3, and 10/5/1863, 3/3, 3/15, 4/11, 4/27, 4/30, 10/6, 10/27, and 10/29/1864; New York *Herald*, 3/24, 3/25, 3/26, 3/30, and 4/3/1863; New York *Daily News*, 2/5, 2/8, 2/26, 2/31, 3/1, 3/8, 3/22, 3/23, 3/30, 4/4, 4/11, 4/12, 5/2, 10/4, and 10/5/1864.
17. New York *Daily News*, 7/9 and 10/8/1864.
18. Hermann Schlüter, *Die Internationale in Amerika*, p. 95; Costello, "New York Labor Movement," p. 182.
19. John R. Commons, ed., *A Documentary History of American Industrial Society*, vol. 9, pp. 69–71.
20. New York *Herald*, 2/6, 2/14, and 2/18/1868; New York *Tribune*, 2/12/1868.

21. New York *Herald,* 1/23/1868.

22. New York *Sun,* 5/4, 5/12–15, 5/20–22, and 5/27/1868; New York *Herald,* 5/11/1868; *Workingman's Advocate,* 5/23 and 6/20/1868.

23. New York *Herald,* 7/25/1870; Costello, "New York Labor Movement," pp. 319–34.

24. Kelloggism was a response to the deflationary economy that characterized much of the nineteenth century. The rapidly increasing productivity of factories and farms tended to drive down prices for commodities but not to affect the nominal value of debts. The relative value of debts, in terms of what had to be produced to pay them off, was therefore rising. This, it was believed, gave the moneylenders or "capitalists" an unearned dividend. Kellogg argued that this dividend was transferring wealth from the beleaguered producers into the pockets of the "capitalists," and that the process could be reversed by driving interest rates down to near zero. This was to be accomplished by abolishing private bank notes in favor of federal treasury notes that would be loaned out from a national safety fund at very low interest rates. The cheap credit provided by this "true American, or people's money system" would then promote economic growth and also ensure a redistribution of wealth back from "non-producing capital" to "labor" (Edward Kellogg, *A New Monetary System*). See also *Workingman's Advocate,* 12/7/1867, and Chester McArthur Destler, *American Radicalism, 1865–1901,* pp. 50–77.

25. *Arbeiter Union,* 10/31/1868 et seq.

26. Ibid., 5/1/1869.

27. Ibid., 5/8/1869.

28. New York *Sun,* 6/8 and 6/9/1869.

29. Sorge, *Briefe,* pp. 4–5; Bernstein, *First International,* pp. 37–39; Schlüter, *Internationale,* pp. 80–90.

30. Costello, "New York Labor Movement," pp. 329–31, 516–17.

31. Schlüter, *Internationale,* pp. 421–23; Bernstein, *First International,* pp. 162–63; Gompers, *Seventy Years,* pp. 48–49, 57, 60, 82–84.

32. *Arbeiter Union,* 7/30 and 8/12/1870; New York *World,* 11/20/1870, 1/7/1871; *Workingman's Advocate,* 12/3/1870, 1/14 and 1/28/1871; Schlüter, *Internationale,* pp. 115–25; Bernstein, *First International,* pp. 43–49.

33. Schlüter, *Internationale,* pp. 121–22.

34. Costello, "New York Labor Movement," pp. 357–60; New York *Sun,* 5/22 and 5/27–30/1872; New York *Times,* 5/24, 5/28, and 5/30/1872; NYSZ, 5/14–18, 5/20, 5/22, 5/24, 5/27, 5/28, 5/30, and 5/31/1872.

35. New York *Sun,* 5/25/1872.

36. New York *Herald,* 5/25 and 5/26/1872.

37. New York *Sun,* 5/30/1872; Costello, "New York Labor Movement," p. 536.

38. Costello, "New York Labor Movement," pp. 171–72; New York *Sun,* 7/17, 7/30, 8/5, and 10/7/1868; NYSZ, 5/16 and 5/18/1872. German immigrants of the 1860s may have been happy to work a ten-hour day because workers in Germany were still agitating and striking to reduce the workday to ten hours (Michael Neufeld, "The Dialectic of Craft and Class: The Nuremberg Skilled Metalworkers and their Unions, 1869–1905," p. 6). After longer resi-

dence in New York they may have assimilated the desire for a further cut in working hours. They were active in the eight-hour movement only a few years later.

39. New York *Sun*, 5/28/1872; NYSZ, 5/28/1872; New York *Times*, 5/28/1872.

40. Singer, "Labor Management Relations at Steinway and Sons," pp. 69–70.

41. Ibid., p. 70; New York *Times*, 5/30/1872; New York *Sun*, 6/15/1872; NYSZ, 5/30, 5/31, and 6/1/1872.

42. New York *Sun*, 6/6/1872; NYSZ, 6/6/1872; New York *Times*, 6/7/1872; Singer, "Labor Management Relations at Steinway and Sons," pp. 70–71.

43. NYSZ, 5/30, 6/1, 6/3, 6/4, 6/7, 6/9–11, and 6/13–17/1872; New York *World*, 6/11/1872; Singer, "Labor Management Relations at Steinway and Sons," p. 72.

44. New York *Times*, 6/8/1872.

45. New York *Sun*, 6/11/1872.

46. New York *Times*, 6/11/1872; New York *Tribune*, 6/11/1872.

47. NYSZ, 6/16/1872.

48. New York *Times*, 6/13, 6/15, 6/16, and 6/17/1872.

49. NYSZ, 6/16/1872; New York *Times*, 6/16/1872.

50. NYSZ, 6/16/1872; New York *Sun*, 6/16/1872.

51. New York *Herald*, 6/18/1872; New York *Sun*, 6/18/1872; NYSZ, 6/18/1872; New York *Times*, 6/18/1872.

52. New York *Times*, 6/18/1872.

53. NYSZ, 6/19/1872; New York *Sun*, 6/19/1872.

54. NYSZ, 6/17–21, 6/25/1872.

55. NYSZ, 6/20/1872; New York *Times*, 6/21/1872.

56. NYSZ, 6/24 and 6/25/1872; New York *Times*, 6/24 and 6/25/1872; New York *Sun*, 6/17, 6/25, 6/26, 7/2, 7/3, and 7/8/1872; New York *Herald*, 7/1–4/1872.

57. New York *Herald*, 7/23/1872; Gompers, *Seventy Years*, pp. 43–44.

58. New York *Tribune*, 7/11/1872; New York *Herald*, 7/2/1872.

59. Bureau of Statistics of Labor, Massachusetts, *Fourth Annual Report* (1873), pp. 255–59.

60. Costello, "New York Labor Movement," pp. 129–44, 186–91, 194–96, 262–65.

61. Both John W. Pratt ("Boss Tweed's Public Welfare Program") and Seymour J. Mandelbaum (*Boss Tweed's New York*, p. 70) note the unwillingness of the political machine to oppose strikes.

62. Oswald Ottendorfer Memorial Committee, "Oswald Ottendorfer, Zur Erinnerung an Oswald Ottendorfer, 1900" and "In Memoriam. Oswald Ottendorfer"; Anna Ottendorfer Memorial Committee "Zur Erinnerung an Anna Ottendorfer, 1884," Ottendorfer branch of the New York Public Library.

63. New York *Times*, 12/28/1864; NYSZ, 11/1/1860.

64. Board of Alderman (New York City,) *Proceedings*, vol. 81, pp. 25–26; New York *Times*, 11/28/1861; Myers, *History of Tammany Hall*, p. 196.

65. Oswald Ottendorfer Memorial Committee, "In Memoriam. Oswald Ottendorfer," p. 14.

66. New York *Times*, 11/28/1861.

67. Ibid., 11/28/1861. Norman Dain, "The Social Composition of the Leadership of Tammany Hall in New York City, 1855 to 1865," pp. 135–36.

68. Faust, *German Element*, vol. 2, p. 126.

69. NYSZ, 5/9, 5/23, and 6/27/1861; Irving Katz, *August Belmont*, pp. 111–12.

70. Oswald Ottendorfer Memorial Committee, "In Memoriam. Oswald Ottendorfer"; Mandelbaum, *Boss Tweed's New York*, p. 22.

71. Myers, *History of Tammany Hall*, pp. 205–52.

72. Ibid., pp. 206–8.

73. Irving Katz, *August Belmont*, pp. 89–149.

74. Ibid., p. 139.

75. Mandelbaum, *Boss Tweed's New York*, pp. 76–79, 82; Myers, *History of Tammany Hall*, pp. 235–42.

76. Irving Katz, *August Belmont*, pp. 188–93.

77. Leo Hershkowitz, *Tweed's New York: Another Look*, pp. 172–83; Steiger, *Dreiundfunfzig Jahre Buchhändler*, p. 171.

78. New York *Times*, 10/28/1871.

79. Ibid., 9/15/1871; NYSZ, 9/5/1871.

80. NYSZ, 9/5/1871.

81. Oswald Ottendorfer Memorial Committee, "Zur Erinnerung Oswald Ottendorfer," p. 15; "In Memoriam. Oswald Ottendorfer," p. 16.

82. Mandelbaum, *Boss Tweed's New York*, pp. 80–97; David Hammack, *Power and Society: Greater New York at the Turn of the Century*, pp. 130–32.

83. Howard B. Furer, "The Public Career of William Frederick Havemeyer," p. 277.

84. Mandelbaum, *Boss Tweed's New York*, pp. 105–8.

85. Ibid., p. 108.

86. New York *Times*, 10/14 and 10/21/1874; New York *Tribune*, 10/10 and 10/12/1874; Mandelbaum, *Boss Tweed's New York*, p. 112; Myers, *History of Tammany Hall*, pp. 255–57; Hammack, *Power and Society*, pp. 132–33.

87. Hammack, *Power and Society;* Myers, *History of Tammany Hall*, pp. 250–53.

88. New York *Times*, 11/3/1874.

89. Mandelbaum, *Boss Tweed's New York*, pp. 169–72; *Report of the Commission to Devise a Plan for the Government of Cities in the State of New York, Presented to the Legislature, March 6th, 1877.*

90. Deutscher Ordens der Harugari, *Verhandlungen der Vereinigten Staaten Gross-Loge des Deutschen Ordens der Harugari* (1872, 1874, and 1878); United Ancient Order of Druids—Grand Grove, State of New York, *Proceedings*, 1873–80.

91. Bernstein, *First International*, pp. 220–35; Gutman, "Tompkins Square 'Riot.'"

92. Gompers, *Seventy Years*, p. 96.

93. Ibid., p. 97; Bernstein, *First International*, pp. 238–39.

94. Bernstein, *First International*, pp. 237–38.
95. Ibid., pp. 245–98.

CHAPTER NINE

1. Krebs, *Atlas der Deutschen Lebensraumes in Mitteleuropa* and *Landeskunde von Deutschland;* Darby and Fullard, *New Cambridge Modern History Atlas*, pp. 140–42, 147; Henderson, *Rise of German Industrial Power*, pp. 31–32; Barraclough, *Origins of Modern Germany*, pp. 406–12.
2. Dickinson, *Regions of Germany* and *Germany: A General and Regional Geography*, pp. 306–66; Lüdtke and Mackensen, *Deutscher Kulturatlas;* Keller, *German Dialects;* Bernhardt, *Sprachkarte.*
3. Meyborg, *Geschichte des Plattdütschen Volksfest-Vereen*, pp. 2–3, 15–18, and Chapter 6 above.
4. Rosenwaike (*Population History*, p. 83) gives the figure of 23 percent.

Selected Bibliography

Archival Collections and Private Papers

Bultman Memoirs (family). Copy in author's possession.
Children's Aid Society of New York Record Books. Children's Aid Society, New York.
Coroners' Inquisitions, 1854–57, New York City Municipal Archives.
Diecks-Schissler Papers, New York Public Library.
Scholer Collection, New York Public Library.
Sorge Collection, New York Public Library.

Census Manuscripts

Seventh Census of the United States, 1850. New York County, 10th, 11th, 13th, and 17th Wards.
Census of the State of New York, 1855. New York County, 10th, 11th, 13th, and 17th Wards.
Eighth Census of the United States, 1860. New York County, 10th, 11th, 13th, and 17th Wards.
Ninth Census of the United States, 1870. New York County, 10th, 11th, 13th, and 17th Wards.
Tenth Census of the United States, 1880. New York County, 10th, 11th, 13th, and 17th Wards.

Government Documents and Reports

NEW YORK CITY

Board of Aldermen. Documents, XXV, No. 6, 1858.
——. *Proceedings*, vol. 81, 1861.
Chief of the Fire Department. *Annual Reports*, 1855–58.
Valentine, David T., compiler. *Manual of the Corporation of the City of New York*, 1845–48.

NEW YORK STATE

Assembly Documents

Report of the Select Committee Appointed to Investigate Frauds Upon Emigrant Passengers, 1847, No. 250. Albany, 1847.
Report of the Select Committee to Investigate the Board of Emigration, 1852, No. 34. Albany, 1852.
Report of the Select Committee on Tenement Houses in New York and Brooklyn, 1856, No. 199. Albany, 1856.

Report of the Select Committee to Examine into the Conditions of Tenement Houses, 1857, No. 205. Albany, 1857.

Report of the Commission to Devise a Plan for the Government of Cities in the State of New York, Presented to the Legislature, March 6th, 1877. Albany, 1877.

Report of the Tenement House Committee of 1894. Albany, 1894.

Secretary of State

Census of the State of New York for 1845. Albany, 1847.

Census of the State of New York for 1855. Albany, 1857.

Census of the State of New York for 1865. Albany, 1867.

Census of the State of New York for 1875. Albany, 1877.

MASSACHUSETTS

Bureau of Statistics of Labor, *Fourth Annual Report.* Boston, 1873.

UNITED STATES

Seventh Census of the United States. Washington, 1851.

Eighth Census of the United States. Washington, 1866.

Ninth Census of the United States. Washington, 1871.

Compendium of the Tenth Census of the United States. Washington, 1881.

U.S. Senate Committee on Education and Labor, *Report of the Committee of the Senate Upon Relations Between Labor and Capital.* Vol. 1. Washington, 1885.

Private Agency Reports

Arion Gesangverein. *Jahres Bericht-Männer Gesang Verein Arion.* New York, 1880–90.

Citizens Association of New York. *Report of the Council of Hygiene and Public Health.* New York, 1865.

Citizens Association of New York. *Report Upon the Sanitary Condition of the City of New York.* New York, 1865.

Deutsche Gesellschaft der Stadt New York. *Annual Reports.* New York, 1845–80.

Deutscher Liederkranz in New York. *Jahresbericht.* New York: E. Steiger, 1869.

Deutscher Ordens der Harugari. *Verhandlungen der Vereinigten Staaten Gross-Loge des Deutschen Ordens der Harugari.* New York, 1870–1908.

German Masons' Lodge 54. *Annual Report.* New York, 1876.

New York Association for the Improvement of the Condition of the Poor. *Annual Reports.* New York, 1845–90.

United Ancient Order of Druids—Grand Grove New York. *Proceedings.* New York, 1870–87.

Newspapers

ENGLISH

National Workman, 1866.
New York *Daily News*, 1863–65.
New York *Evening Post*, 1850–59.
New York *Herald*, 1850–80.
New York *Journal of Commerce*, 1857.
New York *Sun*, 1850–80.
New York *Times*, 1853–80.
New York *Tribune*, 1845–84.
New York *World*, 1850–80
Workingman's Advocate, 1870–71.

GERMAN

Arbeiter, 1858.
Arbeiter Stimme, 1874–78.
Arbeiter Union, 1868–70.
Arbeiter Zeitung, 1873–74.
Criminal Zeitung und Belletristiches Journal, 1852–80.
Deutsche Schnellpost, 1848–51.
Katholische Kirchenzeitung, 1857–58.
New Yorker *Demokrat*, 1853–65.
New Yorker *Staats-Zeitung*, 1845–80 (daily only after 1853).
Pionier, 1856–59.
Reform, 1853–54
Republik der Arbeiter, 1850–55.
Soziale Republik, 1858–60.
Turn-Zeitung, 1851–54.
Volkstribun, 1846.

Published Contemporary Works

Anna Ottendorfer Memorial Committee. "Zur Erinnerung an Anna Ottendorfer, 1884." New York: n.p., 1884.

Asher & Adams Pictorial Album of American Industry, 1876. New York: Asher & Adams, 1876.

Baxter, J. H. *Statistics of the Provost-Marshal-General's Bureau.* Vol. 1. Washington: Government Printing Office, 1875.

Bayerisches Volks Fest Verein von New York. *Fest Zeitung.* New York, n.d.

Bebel, Ferdinand August. *Aus meinem Leben.* Rpt. Berlin: Dietz Verlag, 1961.

Beethoven Männer-Chor. "Gedenk-Blatt an die Doppel Feier des 125 Jahrigen Geburtstags Ludwig van Beethoven's, 25 Jahrigen Bestehens der Beethoven Männer-Chor-Halle in New York." New York: Beethoven Männer-Chor, 1895.

Brace, Charles Loring. *The Dangerous Classes of New York.* New York: Wynkoop & Hallenbeck, 1872.

——. "Little Laborers of New York." *Harper's Magazine.* 47 (Aug. 1873).
——. "Sketch of the Formation of the Newsboys' Lodging-House, No. 128 Fulton Street." N.p., n.d.
Canstatter Volksfest Verein. "58th Canstatter Volksfest Program." New York: n.p., 1920.
Cooper, James Fenimore. *Correspondence.* New Haven: Yale University Press, 1922.
Deutscher Ordens der Harugari. *1847–1895, Funfzig Jubiläum.* New York: O. Neuberg, 1897.
Dooley, Patrick J. Fifty Years in Yorkville, 1866–1916. New York: Parish House, 1917.
Dulon, Rudolf. *Aus Amerika über Schule.* Leipzig: C. F. Winter, 1866.
Eickhoff, Anton. *In der Neuen Heimath.* New York: Deutsche Gesellschaft der Stadt New York, 1884.
Ethical Culture Society. *Twenty Years of the Ethical Movement in New York and Other Cities, 1876–1896.* Philadelphia: Weston, 1896.
Fairfield, Francis G. *The Clubs of New York.* New York: Henry Hinton, 1873.
Forman, Allen. "Some Adopted Americans." *American Magazine,* 9 (Nov. 1888).
Foster, G. *New York by Gaslight.* New York: Dewitt Davenport, 1850.
Frei, Johann. *Drei Monat in New York.* Zurich: Frei Verlag, 1869.
Fröbel, Julius. *Ein Lebenslauf.* Stuttgart: J. G. Cotta, 1890.
"Germans in the U.S., Bound Pamphlets Not Catalogued." Vols. 3, 5, and 8. New York Public Library.
Gesang Verein Schiller-Bund. "Gesang Verein Schiller-Bund, 1850–1900, Goldenes Jubiläum." New York, 1900.
Gompers, Samuel. *Seventy Years of Life and Labor.* New York: E. P. Dutton and Company, 1925.
Greeley, Horace, et al. *The Great Industries in the United States, 1871–1872.* Hartford: J. B. Burr Hyde, 1872.
Griesinger, Theodor. *Lebende Bilder aus Amerika.* Stuttgart: Winitzschke, 1858.
——. *Land und Leute in Amerika.* Stuttgart: A. Kröner, 1863.
Griscom, John H. *The Sanitary Condition of the Laboring Population of New York.* New York: n.p., 1845.
——. *The Uses and Abuses of Air.* New York: J. S. Redfield, 1848.
Gutzkow, Karl. *Pariser Briefe.* Leipzig: F. A. Brockhaus, 1842.
Hessen-Darmstädter Volks-Fest Verein. *Biographisches Handbuch der Hessen-Darmstädter Element Vereinigten Staaten.* New York: n.p., n.d.
Jahrbücher der Deutschen in Amerika, 1873. New York: E. Steiger, 1873.
Kapp, Friedrich. *Immigration and the Commissioners of Emigration in the State of New York.* New York: Nations Press, 1870.
——. *Die Deutschen im State New York.* New York: E. Steiger & Co, 1884.
——. *Briefe: 1843–1884.* Frankfurt am Main: Insel Verlag, 1969.
Kellogg, Edward. *A New Monetary System.* New York: Putnam, 1861.
Lemke, Theodor. *Geschichte des Deutschtums von New York: von 1848 bis auf die Gegenvart.* New York: T. Lemke, 1891.
Lening, Gustav. *Die Nachtseiten von New York.* New York: Friedr. Gerhard, 1873.

Lohr, Otto. "Das New York Deutschtum der Vergangenheit." In Otto Spengler, *Das Deutsche Element der Stadt New York*. New York: E. Steiger Co., 1913.

Mainzer Carneval-Verein in New York. *Der Mainzer Carneval-Verein von 1859 bis 1884*. New York: n.p., 1884.

——. *1859–1909, Einst und Jetzt*. New York: n.p., 1909–10.

Männergesang Vereins Eichenkranz. *Geschichte der Männergesang Vereins Eichenkranz aus Erinnerung an des 25 jahrige Jubiläum*. New York: n.p., 1894.

Manson, George. "The Foreign Element in New York City: The Germans." *Harper's Weekly*, 32 (Aug. 1888).

Metzner, Heinrich C. A. *Geschichte des Turner-Bundes*. Indianapolis: Zukunft, 1874.

——. *Jahrbücher der Deutsch-Amerikanischen Turnerei*. New York: Heinrich Metzner, 1892–94.

Meyborg, Bernhard. *Geschichte des Plattdütschen Volksfest–Vereen von New York*. New York: Plattdütsche Post, 1892.

Mosenthal, Hermann. *Geschichte des Vereins Deutscher Liederkranz in New York*. New York: F. A. Ringler Co., 1897.

New York *Sun*. *The Sun's Guide to New York*. New York, 1892.

New Yorker Männerchor. *Geschichte der New Yorker Männerchor, 1870–1895*. New York: H. Bortsch, 1895.

New Yorker Sängerrunde. *Geschichte der New Yorker Sängerrunde, 1848–1888*. New York: n.p., 1888.

New York Turn-Verein. *Seventy-fifth Jubilee of the New York Turn-Verein, 1850–1925*. New York: n.p., 1925.

Oswald Ottendorfer Memorial Committee. "Oswald Ottendorfer, Zur Erinnerung an Oswald Ottendorfer, 1900." New York: n.p., 1900.

——. "In Memoriam. Oswald Ottendorfer." New York: n.p., 1900.

Pelz, Eduard. NEW-YORK *und seine Umgebungen*. Hamburg: n.p., 1867.

Reiter, Ernst A. *Schematismus der Katholischen deutschen Geistlichkeit in den Vereinigten Staaten Nord-Amerika's*. New York: F. Pustet, 1869.

Rittig, Johann. *Federzeichnungen aus dem Amerikanischen Stadtleben*. New York: E. Steiger & Co., 1884.

Ruge, Arnold. *Zwei Jahre in Paris: Studien und Erinnerungen*. Leipzig: Verlagsbureau, 1846.

Sanger, William. *The History of Prostitution*. New York: Harper & Row, 1859.

Schurz, Carl. *Lebenserinnerungen*. Berlin: Georg Reimer, 1906.

Smith, Mathew H. *Sunshine and Shadow in New York*. Hartford: J. B. Burr & Co., 1868.

Sorge, Friedrich A. *The Labor Movement in the United States*. Edited by P. Foner and B. Chamberlin. Westport, Conn.: Greenwood Press, 1977.

——. "Erinnerungen eines Achtundvierzigers." *Die Neue Zeit* (New York), 17, pt. 2 (1899).

Spengler, Otto. *Das Deutsche Element der Stadt New York*. New York: E. Steiger Co., 1913.

Statistics of the Jews of the United States. Philadelphia, 1880.

Steiger, Ernst. *Dreiundfunfzig Jahre Buchhändler in Deutschland und Amerika.* New York: E. Steiger, 1901.

Struve, Gustav. *Wegweiser für Auswanderer.* Bamberg: Suchner, 1866.

Stürenburg, A. *Klein-Deutschland: Bilder aus dem New Yorker Alltagsleben.* New York: E. Steiger Co., 1886

Techla, Georg. *Drei Jahre in New York.* Zwickau: Verein zur Verbreitung Volksschriften, 1862.

Vetter, Christoph. *Zwei Jahre in New York.* Hof, Bavaria: n.p., 1849.

Walling, George W. *Recollections of a New York Chief of Police.* New York: Caxton Book Concern, Ltd., 1887.

Weeks, Joseph D. *Report on the Statistics of Wages in Manufacturing Industries.* Washington: Government Printing Office, 1886.

Weinstein, Gregory. *The Ardent Eighties.* New York: International Press, 1928.

Zeydel, Edwin Hermann. "The German Theater in New York City with Special Regard to the Years 1878–1914." *Deutsch-Amerikanische Geschichtsblätter,* 15 (1915), 255–309.

Secondary Sources

Abbott, Edith. *Women in Industry: A Study in American Economic History.* New York: D. Appleton Co., 1910.

Ahlstrom, Sydney. *A Religious History of the American People.* New Haven: Yale University Press, 1972.

Albion, Robert G. *Rise of the Port of New York, 1815–1860.* New York: C. Scribner's Sons, 1939.

Alexander, June Granatir. *The Immigrant Church and Community: Pittsburgh's Slovak Catholics and Lutherans, 1880–1915.* Pittsburgh: University of Pittsburgh Press, 1987.

Amos, Harriet E. *Cotton City: Urban Development in Antebellum Mobile.* University: University of Alabama Press, 1985.

Anderson, Michael. *Family Structure in Nineteenth Century Lancashire.* New York: Cambridge University Press, 1971.

——. "Household Structure and Industrial Revolution: Mid-Nineteenth Century Preston in Comparative Perspective." In *Household and Family in Past Time,* edited by Peter Laslett, 215–35. Cambridge: Cambridge University Press, 1972.

Anderson, Perry. *Passages from Antiquity to Feudalism.* London: New Left Books, 1974.

Arion Gesangverein. *Arion, New York von 1854 bis 1904.* New York: Arion, 1904.

Asbury, Herbert. *The Gangs of New York.* New York: Alfred A. Knopf, 1928.

Baker, Thomas S. *Lenau and Young Germany in America.* Philadelphia: P. C. Stockhausen, 1897.

Barraclough, Geoffrey. *The Origins of Modern Germany.* New York: G. P. Putnam's Sons, 1963.

——, ed. *Eastern and Western Europe during the Middle Ages.* London: Thames and Hudson, 1970.

Barry, Coleman. *The Catholic Church and German Americans.* Washington: Catholic University of America, 1953.

Barth, Fredrik, ed. *Ethnic Groups and Boundaries.* Boston: Little, Brown, 1969.

Barton, Josef. *Peasants and Strangers: Italians, Rumanians and Slovaks in an American City, 1890–1950.* Cambridge: Harvard University Press, 1975.

Beck, Walter. *Lutheran Elementary Schools in the United States.* St. Louis: Concordia, 1965.

Bell, Daniel. *Marxian Socialism in the United States.* Princeton: Princeton University Press, 1967.

Benson, James. "Irish and German Families and the Economic Development of Midwestern Cities, 1860–1895: St. Paul, Minnesota as a Case Study." Ph.D. dissertation, University of Minnesota, 1980.

Bergquist, James. "German Communities in American Cities: An Interpretation of the Nineteenth-Century Experience." *Journal of American Ethnic History,* 4 (Fall 1984), 19–30.

Bernard, Richard M. *The Melting Pot and the Altar.* Minneapolis: University of Minnesota Press, 1980.

Bernhardt, Karl. *Sprachkarte von Deutschland.* Kassel: n.p., 1849.

Bernstein, Samuel. *The First International in America.* New York: August M. Kelly, bookseller, 1965.

Birmingham, Stephen. *"Our Crowd": The Great Jewish Families of New York.* New York: Harper & Row, 1967.

Bloch, Marc. *Feudal Society.* Chicago: University of Chicago Press, 1961.

Bodnar, John. *Immigration and Industrialization: Ethnicity in an American Mill Town, 1870–1940.* Pittsburgh: University of Pittsburgh Press, 1977.

——. *The Transplanted: A History of Immigrants in Urban America.* Bloomington: Indiana University Press, 1985.

Bohlin, Virginia. "Better Pieces, Better Prices." *Boston Globe,* Mar. 9, 1980.

Bopp, P. Hartwig. *Die Entwicklung des deutschen Handwerksgesellentums im 19. Jahrhundert.* Paderborn: F. Schöningh, 1932.

Braudel, Fernand. *The Mediterranean and the Mediterranean World in the Age of Philip II.* 2 vols. New York: Harper & Row, 1972.

Bretting, Agnes. *Soziale Problem deutscher Einwanderer in New York City, 1800–1860.* Wiesbaden: F. Steiner Verlag, 1981.

Bridges, Amy. *A City in the Republic.* New York: Cambridge University Press, 1984.

Bruncken, Ernest. *German Political Refugees in the United States.* Chicago: Deutscher Amerikanische Historischen Gesellschaft von Illinois, 1904.

Buhle, Mari Jo. *Women and American Socialism, 1870–1920.* Urbana: University of Illinois Press, 1981.

Burstein, Alan. "Residential Distribution and Mobility of Irish and German Immigrants in Philadelphia, 1850–1880." Ph.D. dissertation, University of Pennsylvania, 1975.

——. "Immigrants and Residential Mobility: The Irish and Germans in Philadelphia, 1850–1880." In *Philadelphia,* edited by Theodore Hershberg, 174–203. New York: Oxford University Press, 1981.

Čapek, Thomas, *The Čechs (Bohemians) in America.* New York: Houghton Mifflin, 1920.

——. *The Čech (Bohemian) Community of New York.* New York: America's Making, 1921.

Chudakoff, Howard P. *Mobile Americans: Residential and Social Mobility in Omaha, 1880–1920.* New York: Oxford University Press, 1972.

——. "A New Look at Ethnic Neighborhoods: Residential Dispersion and the Concept of Visibility in a Medium-Sized American City." *Journal of American History,* 60 (1973), 76–93.

Cohen, Abner, ed. *Urban Ethnicity.* London: Tavistock Pub., 1974.

Cohen, Naomi W. *Encounter with Emancipation: The German Jews in the United States, 1830–1914.* Philadelphia: Jewish Publication Society of America, 1984.

Cohen, Ronald. "Ethnicity: Problem and Focus in Anthropology." *Annual Reviews in Anthropology, 1978,* 379–93.

Cole, Donald B. *Immigrant City: Lawrence, Massachusetts, 1845–1921.* Chapel Hill: University of North Carolina Press, 1963.

Commons, John R. "American Shoemakers, 1648–1895." *Quarterly Journal of Economics,* 24 (Nov. 1909), 23–84.

——, ed. *A Documentary History of American Industrial Society.* Vol. 9. Cleveland: A. H. Clark Co., 1911.

Commons, John R., et al. *History of Labour in the United States.* 4 vols. New York: Macmillan Co., 1918–35.

Conzen, Kathleen N. *Immigrant Milwaukee, 1836–1860: Accommodation and Community in a Frontier City.* Cambridge: Harvard University Press, 1976.

——. "Immigrants, Immigrant Neighborhoods, and Ethnic Identity: Historical Issues." *Journal of American History,* 66 (1979), 603–15.

——. "German-Americans and the Invention of Ethnicity." In *America and the Germans,* edited by Frank Trommler and Joseph McVeigh, vol. 1, 131–47. Philadelphia: University of Pennsylvania Press, 1985.

Costello, Lawrence. "The New York Labor Movement, 1861–1873." Ph.D. dissertation, Columbia University, 1967.

Cronau, Rudolf. *Drei Jahrhunderte Deutsche Lebens in Amerika.* Berlin: D. Reimer, 1909.

Cunz, Dieter. *The Maryland Germans.* Princeton: Princeton University Press, 1948.

Dain, Norman. "The Social Composition of the Leadership of Tammany Hall in New York City, 1855 to 1865." Columbia University M.A. thesis, 1951.

Dann, Martin. "Little Citizens: Working-Class and Immigrant Childhood in New York, 1880–1915." Ph.D. dissertation, City University of New York, 1978.

Darby, H. C., and Harold Fullard, eds. *The New Cambridge Modern History Atlas.* Cambridge: Cambridge University Press, 1978.

David, Henry. *The History of the Haymarket Affair.* New York: Collier Books, 1963.

Dawley, Alan. *Class and Community: The Industrial Revolution in Lynn.* Cambridge: Harvard University Press, 1976.

Degler, Carl. "Labor in the Economy and Politics of New York City, 1850–1860." Ph.D. dissertation, Columbia University, 1952.

Demos, John. *Past, Present, and Personal: The Family and the Life Course in American History.* New York: Oxford University Press, 1986.

Demos, John, and Sarane Spence Boocock, eds. *Turning Points: Historical and Sociological Essays on the Family.* Chicago: University of Chicago Press, 1978.

Despres, Leo. "Toward a Theory of Ethnic Phenomena." In *Ethnicity and Resource Competition in Plural Societies,* edited by Leo Despres, 187–207. The Hague: Mouton, 1975.

Destler, Chester McArthur. *American Radicalism, 1865–1901.* Chicago: Quadrangle Paperbacks, 1966.

Dickinson, Robert E. *The Regions of Germany.* London: K. Paul, Trench, Trubner Co., Ltd., 1945.

——. *Germany: A General and Regional Geography.* New York: Dutton, 1953.

Dobbert, Guido. *The Disintegration of an Immigrant Community: The Cincinnati Germans, 1870–1920.* New York: Arno Press, 1980.

Doerries, Reinhard R. *Iren und Deutsche in der Neuen Welt.* Wiesbaden: Steiner, 1986.

Dolan, Jay P. *The Immigrant Church.* Baltimore: Johns Hopkins University Press, 1975.

Dollar, Charles M., and Richard J. Jensen. *Historian's Guide to Statistics: Quantitative Analysis and Historical Research.* New York: Holt, Rinehart and Winston, 1971.

Dominick, Raymond H., III. *Wilhelm Liebknecht.* Chapel Hill: University of North Carolina Press, 1982.

Douglass, Paul F. *The Story of German Methodism: Biography of an Immigrant Soul.* New York: Methodist Book Concern, 1939.

Duis, Perry R. *The Saloon: Public Drinking in Chicago and Boston, 1880–1920.* Urbana: University of Illinois Press, 1983.

Dumenil, Lynn. *Freemasonry and American Culture, 1880–1930.* Princeton: Princeton University Press, 1984.

Durkheim, Emile. *The Division of Labor in Society.* New York: Free Press, 1964.

Eliot, T. S. *Notes toward the Definition of Culture.* New York: Faber and Faber, 1949.

Ely, Richard T. *The Labor Movement in America.* New York: T. Y. Crowell Co., 1886.

Engels, Friedrich. *The German Revolutions.* Chicago: University of Chicago Press, 1967.

Ernst, Robert. *Immigrant Life in New York City, 1825–1863.* New York: Kings Crown Press, 1949.

European Historical Statistics, 1750–1970. New York: Columbia University Press, 1975.

Evans-Pritchard, Edward E. *The Nuer.* Oxford: Clarendon Press, 1940.

Faires, Nora. "Ethnicity in Evolution: The German Community in Pittsburgh and

Allegheny City, Pennsylvania, 1845–1885." Ph.D. dissertation, University of Pittsburgh, 1981.

——. "Occupational Patterns of German-Americans in Nineteenth-Century Cities." In *German Workers in Industrial Chicago, 1850–1910,* edited by Hartmut Keil and John B. Jentz, 37–51. DeKalb: Northern Illinois University Press, 1983.

Faust, Albert B. *The German Element in the United States.* 2 vols. Boston: Houghton, Mifflin Co., 1909.

Fishman, Joshua, ed. *Language Loyalty in the United States.* The Hague: Mouton, 1966.

Flinn, Michael W. *The European Demographic System, 1500–1820.* Baltimore: Johns Hopkins University Press, 1981.

Foner, Philip S. *History of the Labor Movement in the United States.* Vol. 2. New York: International Publishers, 1955.

——. "Friedrich Sorge, Father of American Socialism." Introduction to *The Labor Movement in the United States,* by Friedrich Sorge, 3–41. Westport, Conn.: Greenwood Press, 1977.

Fox, Robin. *Kinship and Marriage: An Anthropological Perspective.* Baltimore: Penguin Books, 1967.

Frankenberg, R. J. *Village on the Border: A Social Study of Religion, Politics and Football in a North Wales Community.* London: Cohn Wert, 1957.

Frisch, Michael H. *Town into City: Springfield, Massachusetts and the Meaning of Community.* Cambridge: Harvard University Press, 1972.

Furer, Howard B. "The Public Career of William Frederick Havemeyer." Ph.D. dissertation, New York University, 1903.

Gabaccia, Donna. *From Italy to Elizabeth Street.* Albany: SUNY Press 1983.

Gans, Herbert J. *The Urban Villagers: Group and Class in the Life of Italian-Americans.* New York: Free Press of Glencoe, 1962.

Gerber, David. "Modernity in the Service of Tradition: Catholic Lay Trustees at Buffalo's St. Louis Church and the Transformation of European Communal Traditions, 1829–1855." *Journal of Social History,* 15 (1982), 655–84.

Gjerde, Jon. *From Peasants to Farmers: The Migration from Balestrand, Norway, to the Upper Middle West.* New York: Cambridge University Press, 1985.

Glanz, Rudolph. *Jews in Relation to the Cultural Milieu of the Germans in America up to the 1880s.* New York: YIVO, 1947.

Glasco, Lawrence. "Ethnicity and Social Structure: Irish, Germans and Native-Born of Buffalo, New York, 1850–1860." Ph.D. dissertation, SUNY Buffalo, 1973.

Glazer, Nathan, and Daniel P. Moynihan. *Beyond the Melting Pot.* Cambridge: MIT Press, 1963.

——, eds. *Ethnicity: Theory and Experience.* Cambridge: Harvard University Press, 1975.

Gleason, Philip. *The Conservative Reformers: German-American Catholics and the Social Order.* Notre Dame: University of Notre Dame Press, 1968.

Gluckman, Max. *Custom and Conflict in Africa.* Oxford: Blackwell, 1955.

Golab, Caroline. *Immigrant Destinations.* Philadelphia: Temple University Press, 1977.

Goode, William J. *The Family.* Englewood Cliffs, N.J.: Prentice-Hall, 1964.

Gordon, Milton. *Assimilation in American Life.* New York: Oxford University Press, 1964.

Greeley, Andrew M. *Ethnicity in the United States: A Preliminary Reconnaissance.* New York: John Wiley and Sons, 1974.

Greenberg, Stephanie. "Industrialization in Philadelphia: The Relationship between Industrial Location and Residential Patterns, 1880–1930." Ph.D. dissertation, Temple University, 1977.

——. "Industrial Location and Ethnic Residential Patterns." In *Philadelphia,* edited by Theodore Hershberg, 204–31. New York: Oxford University Press, 1981.

Griessinger, Andrew. *Das symbolische Kapital der Ehre.* Frankfurt: Ullstein, 1981.

Griffen, Clyde. "Occupational Mobility in Nineteenth-Century America: Problems and Possibilities." *Journal of Social History,* 5 (1972), 310–30.

——. "Community Studies and the Investigation of Nineteenth-Century Social Relations." *Social Science History,* 10 (1986), 315–38.

Griffen, Clyde, and Sally Griffen. *Natives and Newcomers.* Cambridge: Harvard University Press, 1978.

Grinstein, Hyman B. *The Rise of the Jewish Community of New York, 1654–1860.* Philadelphia: Jewish Publication Society of America, 1945.

Groneman Pernicone, Carol. "The 'Bloody Ould Sixth.'" Ph.D. dissertation, University of Rochester, 1973.

Gutman, Herbert G. "The Tompkins Square 'Riot' in New York City on January 13, 1874: A Re-Examination of Its Causes and Its Aftermath." *Labor History,* 6 (1965), 44–62.

——. "Class, Status and Community Power in Nineteenth Century American Industrial Cities—Paterson, New Jersey: A Case Study." In *The Age of Industrialism in America,* edited by Frederick C. Jaher, 263–87. New York: Free Press, 1968.

Hamerow, Theodore S. *Restoration, Revolution, Reaction: Economics and Politics in Germany, 1815–1871.* Princeton: Princeton University Press, 1958.

Hammack, David C. *Power and Society: Greater New York at the Turn of the Century.* New York: Russell Sage Foundation, 1982.

Handlin, Oscar. *Boston's Immigrants: A Study in Acculturation.* Cambridge: Harvard University Press, 1941.

——. *The Uprooted.* Boston: Little, Brown and Company, 1951.

Hansen, Marcus Lee. *The Atlantic Migration.* Cambridge: Harvard University Press, 1940.

Hawgood, John. *The Tragedy of German-America.* New York: Putnam, 1940.

Hayward, John F. "English Swords, 1600–1650." In *Arms and Armour Annual,* edited by Robert Held. Vol. 1 (1973), 158–61.

Hechter, Michael. "The Political Economy of Ethnic Change." *American Journal of Sociology,* 79 (1974), 1151–78.

Helbich, Wolfgang, Walter D. Kamphoefner, and Ulrike Sommer. *Briefe aus*

Amerika: Deutsche Auswanderer schreiben aus der Neuen Welt, 1830–1930. Munich: C. H. Beck, 1988.

Henderson, W. O. *The Rise of German Industrial Power, 1834–1914.* Berkeley: University of California Press, 1975.

Hershberg, Theodore, ed. *Philadelphia.* New York: Oxford University Press, 1981.

Hershberg, Theodore, and Robert Dockhorn. "Occupational Classification." *Historical Methods Newsletter,* 9, nos. 2–3 (1976), 59–98.

Hershkowitz, Leo. *Tweed's New York: Another Look.* Garden City, N.Y.: Anchor Press/Doubleday, 1978.

Higham, John. *Send These to Me: Jews and Other Immigrants in Urban America.* New York: Atheneum, 1975.

——, ed. *Ethnic Leadership in America.* Baltimore: Johns Hopkins University Press, 1978.

Hilquit, Morris. *History of Socialism in the United States.* New York: Dover Press, 1971.

Hirsch, Susan. *Roots of the American Working Class: The Industrialization of Crafts in Newark, 1800–1860.* Philadelphia: University of Pennsylvania Press, 1978.

Hirschler, Eric E., ed. *Jews from Germany in the United States.* New York: Farrar, Straus and Cudahy, 1955.

Horowitz, Donald L. "Ethnic Identity." In *Ethnicity: Theory and Experience,* edited by Nathan Glazer and Daniel P. Moynihan, 111–40. Cambridge: Harvard University Press, 1975.

Howe, Irving, and Kenneth Libo. *World of Our Fathers.* New York: Harcourt Brace Jovanovich, 1976.

Hraba, Joseph. *American Ethnicity.* Itasca, Ill.: F. E. Peacock Publishers Inc., 1979.

Huebner, Theodor. *The Germans in America.* Philadelphia: Chilton Co., 1962.

Hutchinson, E. P. *Immigrants and Their Children, 1850–1950.* New York: John Wiley and Sons, 1956.

Hvidt, Kristian. *Flight to America: The Social Background of 300,000 Danish Emigrants.* New York: Academic Press, 1975.

Ingerman, Elizabeth A. "Personal Experiences of a New York Cabinetmaker." *Antiques,* Nov. 1963, 575–80.

Jaher, Frederic Cople. *The Urban Establishment: Upper Strata in Boston, New York, Charleston, Chicago, and Los Angeles.* Urbana: University of Illinois Press, 1982.

Jordan, Terry G. *German Seed in Texas Soil.* Austin: University of Texas Press, 1966.

Kamphoefner, Walter D. *The Westfalians: From Germany to Missouri.* Princeton: Princeton University Press, 1987.

——. "Predisposing Factors in German-American Urbanization." Paper presented at the 1982 meeting of the Organization of American Historians.

Katz, Irving. *August Belmont.* New York: Columbia University Press, 1968.

Katz, Jacob. *From Prejudice to Destruction: Anti-Semitism, 1700–1933.* Cambridge: Harvard University Press, 1980.

Katz, Michael. *The People of Hamilton, Canada West: Family and Class in a Mid-Nineteenth Century City.* Cambridge: Harvard University Press, 1975.

———. "Occupational Classification in History." *Journal of Interdisciplinary History,* 3 (1972), 63–89.

Kaufman, Stuart B. *Samuel Gompers and the Origins of the American Federation of Labor, 1848–1896.* Westport, Conn.: Greenwood Press, 1973.

———, et al., eds. *The Gompers Papers.* Vol. 1. Urbana: University of Illinois Press, 1986.

Kawaguchi, Lesley Ann. "The Making of Philadelphia's German-America: Ethnic Group and Community Development, 1830–1883." Ph.D. dissertation, UCLA, 1983.

Keil, Hartmut. "The German Immigrant Working Class of Chicago, 1875–1890: Workers, Labor Leaders and the Labor Movement." In *American Labor and Immigration History, 1877–1920s: Recent European Research,* edited by Dirk Hoerder, 156–75. Urbana: University of Illinois Press, 1983.

———. "Chicago's German Working Class in 1900." In *German Workers in Industrial Chicago, 1850–1910,* edited by Hartmut Keil and John B. Jentz, 19–36. DeKalb: Northern Illinois University Press, 1983.

———. "German Immigrant Workers in Nineteenth-Century America: Working-Class Culture and Everyday Life in an Urban Industrial Setting." In *America and the Germans,* edited by Frank Trommler and Joseph McVeigh, vol. 1, pp. 189–206. Philadelphia: University of Pennsylvania Press, 1985.

Keller, Rudolf E. *German Dialects: Phonology and Morphology with Selected Texts.* Manchester: Manchester University Press, 1961.

Kennedy, James B. *Beneficiary Features of American Trade Unions.* Baltimore: Johns Hopkins Press, 1908.

Kessner, Thomas. *The Golden Door: Italian and Jewish Immigrant Mobility in New York City, 1880–1915.* New York: Oxford University Press, 1977.

Keyes, Charles F., ed. *Ethnic Adaptation and Identity.* Philadelphia: ISHI, 1979.

Kirk, Gordon W., and Carolyn T. Kirk. "Migration, Mobility and the Transformation of the Occupational Structure of an Immigrant Community: Holland Michigan, 1850–1880." *Journal of Social History,* 7 (1974), 142–64.

Kloss, Heinz. *Um die Einigung des Deutschamerikanertums: die Geschichte einer unvollendeten Volksgruppe.* Berlin: Volk und Reich Verlag, 1937.

———. "German-American Language Maintenance Efforts." In *Language Loyalty in the United States,* edited by Joshua Fishman, 206–52. The Hague: Mouton, 1966.

Knights, Peter. *The Plain People of Boston, 1830–1860.* New York: Oxford University Press, 1971.

Knodel, John E. *The Decline of Fertility in Germany, 1871–1939.* Princeton: Princeton University Press, 1974.

Köllmann, Wolfgang, and Peter Marschalck. "German Emigration to the United States," translated by Thomas C. Childers. *Perspectives in American History,* 7 (1973), 499–554.

Kowalski, Werner. *Vorgeschichte und Enstehung des Bundes der Gerechten.* Berlin: Rütten und Loening, 1962.

Kraut, Benny. *From Reform Judaism to Ethical Culture: The Religious Evolution of Felix Adler.* Cincinnati: Hebrew Union College Press, 1979.

Krebs, Norbert. *Atlas der Deutschen Lebensraumes in Mitteleuropa.* Leipzig: Bibliographisches institut ag., 1937–39.

——, ed. *Landeskunde von Deutschland.* Leipzig: B. G. Teubner, 1931–35.

Lapham, James S. "The German-Americans of New York City, 1860–1890." Ph.D. dissertation, St. John's University, 1977.

Laslett, John H. *Labor and the Left.* New York: Basic Books, 1970.

Laurie, Bruce, Theodore Hershberg, and George Alter. "Immigrants and Industry: The Philadelphia Experience." *Journal of Social History,* 9 (1975), 219–67.

Lee, W. R. *Population Growth, Economic Development and Social Change in Bavaria, 1750–1850.* New York: Arno Press, 1977.

Leuchs, Frederick A. H. *Early German Theater in New York, 1840–1872.* New York: Columbia University Press, 1928.

Levine, Bruce C. " 'In the Spirit of 1848': German-Americans and the Fight over Slavery's Expansion." Ph.D. dissertation, University of Rochester, 1980.

Lieberman, Richard. "Social Change and Political Behavior: The East Village of New York City, 1880–1905." Ph.D. dissertation, New York University, 1976.

Liederkranz Gesangverein. *History of the Liederkranz of the City of New York, 1847–1947, and of the Arion, New York.* New York: Liederkranz, 1948.

Luebke, Frederick C. *Immigrants and Politics: The Germans of Nebraska, 1880–1900.* Lincoln: University of Nebraska Press, 1969.

——. *Bonds of Loyalty: German Americans and World War I.* DeKalb: Northern Illinois University Press, 1974.

Luecke, William H. "A Half Century of Testimony of Staunch Lutheranism in New York City." *Concordia Historical Institute Quarterly,* 32 (1959), 3–23.

Lüdtke, Gerhard, and Lutz Mackensen. *Deutscher Kulturatlas.* 5 vols. Berlin and Leipzig: W. de Gruyter & Co., 1931–39.

McNeil, William H. *The Rise of the West.* Chicago: University of Chicago Press, 1963.

McNeil, William H., and Ruth S. Adams. *Human Migration: Patterns and Policies.* Bloomington: Indiana University Press, 1978.

Mandel, Bernard. *Samuel Gompers.* Yellow Springs, Ohio: Antioch Press, 1963.

Mandelbaum, Seymour J. *Boss Tweed's New York.* New York: John Wiley and Sons, 1965.

Marschalck, Peter. *Deutsche Überseewanderung im 19. Jahrhundert.* Stuttgart: Klett, 1973.

Mayer, Philip. *Townsman or Tribesman.* Cape Town: Oxford University Press, 1961.

——. "Migrancy and the Study of Africans in Towns." *American Anthropologist,* 64 (1962), 576–92.

Mehring, Franz. "Neue Beitrage Zur Biographie von Karl Marx und Friedrich Engels." *Die Neue Zeit,* 25 (1907), 99.

Modell, John, Frank Furstenberg, and Douglas Strong. "The Timing of Marriage." In *Turning Points: Historical and Sociological Essays on the Family,* edited by John Demos and Sarane Spence Boocock, 120–50. Chicago: University of Chicago Press, 1978.

Modell, John, and Tamara K. Haraven. "Urbanization and the Malleable Household: An Examination of Boarding and Lodging in American Families." *Journal of Marriage and the Family,* 35 (1973), 467–79.
Moltmann, Günter, ed. *Deutsche Amerikaauswanderung im 19. Jahrhundert.* Stuttgart: Metzler, 1976.
Montgomery, David. *Beyond Equality: Labor and the Radical Republicans, 1862–1872.* New York: Alfred A. Knopf, 1967.
Morris, Richard B. *Encyclopedia of American History.* New York: Columbia University Press, 1953.
Mostov, Stephen. "A 'Jerusalem' on the Ohio: The Social and Economic History of Cincinnati's Jewish Community, 1840–1875." Ph.D. dissertation, Brandeis University, 1981.
Murdock, George P. *Social Structure.* New York: Macmillan Co., 1949.
Myers, Gustavus. *The History of Tammany Hall.* 1901; rpt. New York: Dover Publications, 1971.
Nadel, Stanley. "Kleindeutschland: New York City's Germans, 1845–1880." Ph.D. dissertation, Columbia University, 1981.
——. "German-Americans and the American City in the Nineteenth Century." Paper presented at the 1982 meeting of the Organization of American Historians.
——. "Jewish Race and German Soul in Nineteenth Century America," *American Jewish History,* 77 (Sept. 1987), 6–26.
——. "From the Barricades of Paris to the Sidewalks of New York: German Artisans and the European Roots of American Labor Radicalism." *Labor History,* 30 (Winter 1989), 47–75.
Nelli, Humbert. *The Italians in Chicago, 1880–1930.* New York: Oxford University Press, 1970.
Neufeld, Michael J. *The Skilled Metalworkers of Nuremberg: Craft and Class in the Industrial Revolution.* New Brunswick: Rutgers University Press, 1989.
——. "The Dialectic of Craft and Class: The Nuremberg Skilled Metalworkers and Their Unions, 1869–1905." Typescript.
Newton, Ronald C. *German Buenos Aires, 1900–1933.* Austin: University of Texas Press, 1977.
Obendorfer, John L. *Portrait of a Mother: Church of the Most Holy Redeemer.* New York: n.p., n.d.
Obermann, Karl. *Joseph Weydemeyer: ein Lebensbild, 1818–1866.* Berlin: Dietz Verlag, 1968.
Olson, Audrey L. "St. Louis' Germans, 1850–1920." Ph.D. dissertation, University of Kansas, 1970.
O'Neal, James. *A History of the Amalgamated Ladies' Garment Cutters' Local Number 10.* New York: Local 10, 1927.
Perlman, Selig. "Upheaval and Reorganization." In *History of Labour in the United States,* by John R. Commons et al., vol. 2, 203–402. New York: Macmillan Co., 1918–35.
Persons, Stow. *Free Religion: An American Faith.* New Haven: Yale University Press, 1947.

Phillips, Jenny. "Conflict and Identity among Armenian Americans." Paper delivered at the annual meeting of the American Anthropological Association in 1976.

Pickard, Jacob. "Franz Sigel." Typescript, NYPL Scholer Collection.

Pleasants, Samuel. *Fernando Wood of New York.* New York: Columbia University Press, 1948.

Pletsch, Carl. " 'The Socialist Nation of the German Democratic Republic' or the Asymmetry in Nation and Ideology between the Two Germanies." *Comparative Studies in Society and History,* 21 (1979), 323–45.

Pochman, Henry A. *German Culture in America, 1600–1900.* Madison: University of Wisconsin Press, 1957.

Pope, Jessie. *The Clothing Industry in New York.* Columbia: University of Missouri Press, 1905.

Post, Albert. *Popular Free Thought in America, 1825–1850.* New York: Columbia University Press, 1943.

Posten, M. M. "Economic Relations between Eastern and Western Europe." In *Eastern and Western Europe during the Middle Ages,* edited by Geoffrey Barraclough, 125–76. London: Thames and Hudson, 1970.

Pratt, John W. "Boss Tweed's Public Welfare Program." *New-York Historical Society Quarterly,* Oct. 1961, 396–411.

Previté-Orton, C. W. *The Shorter Cambridge Medieval History.* 2 vols. Cambridge: Cambridge University Press, 1953.

Rapone, Anita. *The Guardian Life Insurance Company, 1860–1920.* New York: New York University Press, 1987.

Redfield, Robert. "The Folk Society." *American Journal of Sociology,* 52 (1947): 293–308.

Rischin, Moses. *The Promised City.* New York: Harper & Row, 1970.

Rock, Howard B. *Artisans of the New Republic.* New York: New York University Press, 1979.

Rosenwaike, Ira. *The Population History of New York City.* Syracuse: Syracuse University Press, 1972.

Ross, Marc Howard, and Thomas S. Weisner. "The Rural-Urban Migrant Network in Kenya: Some General Implications." *American Ethnologist,* 4 (1977), 359–76.

Ross, Steven J. *Workers on the Edge.* New York: Columbia University Press, 1985.

Rothan, Emmet H. *The German Catholic Immigrant in the United States, 1830–1860.* Washington: Catholic University of America Press, 1946.

Rygg, A. N. *Norwegians in New York, 1825–1895.* Brooklyn: Norwegian News, 1946.

St. Nicholas Church in Second Street: History of the Pioneer German Catholics in New York. New York: n.p., 1932.

Sanders, Ronald. *The Downtown Jews.* New York: Harper & Row, 1969.

Sartorius von Waltershausen, A. *Der Moderne Socialismus in den Vereinigten Staaten von Amerika.* Berlin: H. Bahr, 1890.

Saxton, Alexander. *The Indispensable Enemy: A Study of the Anti-Chinese Movement in California.* Berkeley: University of California Press, 1971.

Schappes, Morris U. *A Pictorial History of the Jews in the United States.* New York: Marzani & Munsell, 1965.

——. *A Documentaty History of the Jews in the United States, 1654–1875.* New York: Schocken Books, 1971.

——. "Two Humanists: Doctors Jacobi." *Jewish Life,* Sept. 1952, 22–25.

——. "The Political Origins of the United Hebrew Trades, 1880." *Journal of Ethnic Studies,* 5 (1977), 13–41.

Scherzer, Kenneth A. "The Unbounded Community: Neighborhood Life and Social Structure in New York City, 1830–1875." Ph.D. dissertation, Harvard University, 1982.

Schlüter, Hermann. *Die Anfänge der Deutschen Arbeiterbewegung in Amerika.* Stuttgart: J. H. W. Dietz, 1907.

——. *The Brewing Industry and the Brewery Worker's Movement in America.* Cincinnati: International Union of United Brewery Workers of America, 1910.

——. *Die Internationale in Amerika.* Chicago: Deutsche sprachgruppe der Sozialist partei der V. S., 1918.

——. *Lincoln, Labor and Slavery.* Rpt. New York: Russell Russell, 1965.

Schnore, Leo. "Community." In *Sociology: An Introduction,* edited by Neil Smelser, 84–99. New York: John Wiley and Sons, 1967.

Schraepler, Ernst. *Handwerkerbünde und Arbeitervereine, 1830–1853.* Berlin: Walter de Gruyter, 1972.

Sennett, Richard, and Jonathan Cobb. *The Hidden Injuries of Class.* New York: Alfred A. Knopf, 1973.

Seward, Rudy Ray. *The American Family: A Demographic History.* Beverly Hills: Sage Publications, 1978.

Shaw, Douglas V. *The Making of an Immigrant City.* New York: Arno Press, 1976.

Sheehan, James J. "What Is German History?" *Journal of Modern History,* 53 (1981), 1–23.

Shorter, Edward. *The Historian and the Computer: A Practical Guide.* New York: W. W. Norton Co., 1975.

Simon, Andrea. "The Sacred Sect and the Secular Church: Symbols of Ethnicity in Astoria's Greek Community." Ph.D. dissertation, City University of New York, 1977.

Singer, Aaron. "Labor-Management Relations at Steinway and Sons, 1853–1896." Ph.D. dissertation, Columbia University, 1977.

Smith, Timothy L. "New Approaches to the History of Immigration in Twentieth-Century America." *American Historical Review,* 71 (1966), 1265–79.

Sollors, Werner. *Beyond Ethnicity: Consent and Descent in American Culture.* New York: Oxford University Press, 1986.

Southall, Aidan, ed. *Urban Anthropology: Cross-Cultural Studies of Urbanization.* New York: Oxford University Press, 1973.

Spann, Edward K. *The New Metropolis: New York City, 1840–1857.* New York: Columbia University Press, 1981.

Srebnick, Amy. "True Womanhood and Hard Times: Women and Early New York Industrialization, 1840–1860." Ph.D. dissertation, SUNY Stony Brook, 1979.

Stansell, Christine. *City of Women: Sex and Class in New York, 1789–1860.* Urbana: University of Illinois Press, 1987.

Steinway, Theodore E. *People and Pianos.* New York: Steinway & Sons, 1953.

Stokes, Isaac N. *Iconography of Manhattan Island.* New York: R. H. Dodd, 1915–28.

Stott, Richard. "The Worker in the Metropolis: New York City, 1820–1860." Ph.D. dissertation, Cornell University, 1983.

Sumner, Helen. *History of Women in Industry in the United States.* Washington: Government Printing Office, 1910.

Swieringa, Robert, and Harry Stout. "Dutch Emigration in the Nineteenth Century, 1820–1877: A Quantitative Overview." *Indiana Social Studies Quarterly,* 28 (1975), 7–34.

——. "Socio-economic Patterns of Migration from the Netherlands in the Nineteenth Century." In *Research in Economic History,* edited by Paul Uselding, vol. 1, 298–333. Greenwich, Conn.: JAI Press, 1976.

Taylor, A. J. P. *The Habsburg Monarchy, 1809–1918.* Chicago: University of Chicago Press, 1948.

——. *Bismarck: The Man and the Statesman.* New York: Random House, 1967.

Taylor, George R. *The Transportation Revolution, 1815–1860.* New York: Holt, Rinehart and Winston, 1962.

Thernstrom, Stephan. *Poverty and Progress.* Cambridge: Harvard University Press, 1964.

——. *The Other Bostonians.* Cambridge: Harvard University Press, 1973.

Thernstrom, Stephan, and Richard Sennett, eds. *Nineteenth Century Cities: Essays in the New Urban History.* New Haven: Yale University Press, 1969.

Thomas, William I., and Florian Znaniecki. *The Polish Peasant in Europe and America.* 2 vols. Rpt. New York: Octagon, 1974.

Toury, Jacob. "Jewish Manual Labor and Emigration." In *Leo Baeck Yearbook, 1971,* 45–62. New York: Leo Baeck Institute, 1971.

Townsend, Andrew. *The Germans of Chicago.* Chicago: University of Chicago Press, 1932.

Traux, Rhoda. *The Doctors Jacobi.* Boston: Little, Brown, 1952.

Trefousse, Hans. *Carl Schurtz: A Biography.* Knoxville: University of Tennessee Press, 1982.

Trommler, Frank, and Joseph McVeigh, eds. *America and the Germans.* 2 vols. Philadelphia: University of Pennsylvania Press, 1985.

van den Berghe, Pierre. *Race and Ethnicity.* New York: Basic Books, 1970.

Vincent, Joan. "The Structure of Ethnicity." *Human Organization,* 33 (1974), 375–89.

Vineyard, JoEllen. *The Irish on the Urban Frontier.* New York: Arno Press, 1976.

Walker, Mack. *Germany and the Emigration, 1816–1885.* Cambridge: Harvard University Press, 1964.

——. *German Home Towns: Community, State and General Estate, 1648–1871.* Ithaca: Cornell University Press, 1971.

Ward, David. *Cities and Immigrants: A Geography of Change in Nineteenth-Century America.* New York: Oxford University Press, 1971.

——. "The Emergence of Central Immigrant Ghettoes in American Cites: 1840–1920." *Annals of the Association of American Geographers,* 58 (1968), 343–59.

Warner, Sam Bass, Jr. "If All the World Were Philadelphia: A Scaffolding for Urban History." *American Historical Review,* 74 (1968), 26–43.

Warner, W. Lloyd, and Leo Srole. *The Social Systems of American Ethnic Groups.* New Haven: Yale University Press, 1945.

Warren, Roland. *The Community in America.* New York: Rand McNalley Co., 1972.

——. "Towards a Reformulation of Community Theory." *Human Organization.* 15 (1966), 3–21.

Wheeldon, P. D. "The Operation of Voluntary Associations and Personal Networks in the Political Processes of an Inter-Ethnic Community." In *Social Networks in Urban Situations,* edited by J. Clyde Mitchell, 128–80. Manchester: Manchester University Press, 1969.

White, Joseph. "Religion and Community: Cincinnati Germans, 1814–1870." Ph.D. dissertation, Notre Dame University, 1980.

Wilcox, Walter F., ed. *International Migrations.* Vol. 1: *Statistics.* New York: National Bureau of Economic Research, 1929.

Wilentz, Sean. *Chants Democratic: New York City and the Rise of the American Working Class, 1788–1850.* New York: Oxford University Press, 1984.

Wirth, Louis. *The Ghetto.* Chicago: University of Chicago Press, 1928.

Wittke, Carl. *We Who Built America: The Saga of the Immigrant.* New York: Prentice Hall, 1939.

——. *Against the Current: The Life of Karl Heinzen.* Chicago: University of Chicago Press, 1945.

——. *The Utopian Communist.* Baton Rouge: Louisiana State University Press, 1950.

——. *Refugees of Revolution.* Philadelphia: University of Pennsylvania Press, 1952.

——. *The German Language Press in America.* Lexington: University Press of Kentucky, 1957.

Wrigley, Edward A. *Industrial Growth and Population Change.* Cambridge: Cambridge University Press, 1961.

——. *Population and History.* New York: McGraw-Hill, 1969.

Yox, Andrew. "Decline of the German-American Community in Buffalo." Ph.D. dissertation, University of Chicago, 1983.

——. "Bonds of Community: Buffalo's German Element, 1853–1871." *New York History,* 66 (Apr. 1985), 141–63.

Zucker, Adolf. *The Forty-Eighters.* New York: Columbia University Press, 1950.

Zunz, Olivier. *The Changing Face of Inequality.* Chicago: University of Chicago Press, 1982.

Index

A Note on the Author

Stanley Nadel received his Ph.D. in history from Columbia University in 1981. A gypsy scholar for nine years, he has taught at SUNY Potsdam, St. Lawrence University, the University of Illinois, and Pennsylvania State University. He is currently teaching history at Austin Peay State University. His previous publications include "Reds Versus Pinks: A Civil War in the International Ladies Garment Workers Union"; "Jewish Race and German Soul in Nineteenth-Century America"; "From the Barricades of Paris to the Sidewalks of New York: German Artisans and the European Roots of American Labor Radicalism"; and "The Forty-Eighters and the Politics of Class in New York City." Professor Nadel is now working on a history of suicide in the United States.